*The Familiar Letter as a Literary Genre
in the Age of Pushkin*

The Familiar Letter as a Literary Genre in the Age of Pushkin

William Mills Todd III

NORTHWESTERN UNIVERSITY PRESS / EVANSTON, ILLINOIS

Northwestern University Press
Evanston, Illinois 60208-4210

Printed in the United States of America

ISBN 0-8101-1711-8

Library of Congress Cataloging-in-Publication Data

Todd, William Mills, 1944–
        The familiar letter as a literary genre in the age of Pushkin /
William Mills Todd III.
                p.   cm. — (Studies in Russian literature and theory)
        Originally published: Princeton, N.J. : Princeton University
Press, c 1976.
        Includes bibliographical references and index.
        ISBN 0-8101-1711-8 (paper : alk. paper)
        1. Russian letters—History and criticism. 2. Pushkin, Aleksandr Sergeevich,
1799–1837. 3. Literary form. 4. Arzamas (Literary circle) I. Title. II. Series.
PG3099.L4T6 1999
891.76'309—dc21   99-29221
                                                                                                CIP

For Eva and Karen

Contents

Transliteration

Not wishing to distract the general reader with diacritic marks that only a specialist could understand (a specialist would hardly need them), I follow several recent books in using the system found in D. S. Mirsky's *History of Russian Literature*. I have, however, made these exceptions:

e (initial)	ye
ё	e
щ	shch
э	e
кс	ks
ье	ye
ью	yu
ья	ya
-ий, -ый	i

Acknowledgments

No less than any other piece of scholarly writing, this book owes much to the generosity of sponsors, the hospitality of libraries, and the kind attention of its author's colleagues. Let no one think my gratitude less than profound because many before me have acknowledged such assistance in these or similar words. Conventions become hollow, after all, only when they no longer relate to individual experience, and for me writing this book has been a happily social occasion.

This project has been supported by the Russian Institute at Columbia, by the Center for Russian and Eastern European Studies at Stanford, and by general funds of these two universities. A Fulbright-Hays Fellowship and a grant from the International Research and Exchanges Board provided an academic year (1970–71) at Leningrad University.

It would have been impossible for me to study the familiar letter as a literary genre without holding many of those letters in my hands. I am most grateful to the Central State Archive of Literature and Art (TsGALI) in Moscow and to the Academy of Sciences' Institute of Russian Literature (Pushkinski Dom) in Leningrad for giving me this opportunity. The scholarly hospitality, knowledge, and efficiency of the *Pushkinisty* at the latter institution saved me hours of precious research time.

I would like to thank the following publishers for permission to quote copyright materials: E. P. Dutton, for A. S. Pushkin, *Eugene Onegin: A Novel in Verse,* translated by Walter Arndt (1963); Larousse & Co., for Guez de Balzac and Vincent Voiture, *Oeuvres choisies,* edited by Gabriel Raibaud (1936); Penguin Books, for Cicero's *Selected Works,* translated by Michael Grant (1960); Random House, Modern Library, for Nicholai Gogol, *Dead Souls,* translated by B. G. Guerney (© 1965); Stanford University Press, for E. J. Brown, *Stankevitch and His Moscow Circle, 1830–1840* (1966); University of Wisconsin Press, for *The Letters of Alexander Pushkin,* translated by J. Thomas Shaw (© 1967 by the Regents of the University of Wisconsin).

Many friends and colleagues have given this study their advice and criticism. In the early stages of my research Robert Belknap and L. Ya. Ginzburg shared theoretical insights; M. I. Gillelson and Antonia Glasse lent me their intimate knowledge of the Alexandrine period; V. A. Manuilov smoothed my transition into Soviet academic life. At later stages Joseph Bauke, James M. Coulter, Milton Ehre, William Harkins, John Malmstad, and Richard Sheldon read the manuscript and offered invaluable, carefully considered suggestions for its revision. Edward J. Brown has provided, through his own work and in criticism of mine, necessary lessons in critical excernment. Mrs. Nora B. Beeson and Mrs. Arthur Sherwood have guided the manuscript into the press with constant encouragement to its anxious author. Ms. Connie Martin made many excellent editorial changes in the final version.

Eva Andenaes Todd patiently corrected my English and served as the educated general reader for whom one struggles to write. The dedication says the rest.

Because his guidance cannot be attributed to any single moment in the planning, writing, and rewriting of this study, I have saved my heartfelt thanks to Robert Maguire for last. Had the heavy demands of his own writing or the conventional boundaries of advisorship and friendship limited his frequent contributions of encouragement and constructive criticism, I cannot imagine how this book would have been written.

*The Familiar Letter as a Literary Genre
in the Age of Pushkin*

Introduction

At a particular time in Russia, familiar letters were related to
literature by more than etymology; the period was a brief but
turbulent one—from approximately 1808 to 1825. It coincided with the prehistory, rise, and fall of Arzamas, a circle of
young writers and public servants who met informally in Moscow and Petersburg and later formed a playful literary society
not unlike the Temple in France or the Scriblerians in England.
A variety of social and intellectual connections held the group
together—a Neoclassical approach to literary criticism, an
Epicurean interpretation of the Enlightenment, a serious commitment to establishing a European level of culture in Russia.
At this time Russia could not support a literary profession, and
the Arzamasians were amateurs, deriving their income from
their estates and government service. The group merits our attention, nevertheless, because its members were the most
accomplished Russian poets, critics, and essayists of their time,
as well as Russia's most enthusiastic practitioners of familiar
correspondence.[1]

Within these confines it is possible to treat the familiar
letter as a literary genre whose structure differs significantly
from the structures of other genres of the period, yet is
related to them as one member of a group. Some may consider the familiar letter too free, too individual a form of
expression to permit general characterization. However, a

[1] Appendix I lists the members of Arzamas and briefly describes the
education, social background, career, and literary interests of each.
Readers unfamiliar with the period may wish to refer to this list before
continuing. Detailed discussion of the group's aesthetics and milieu
appears in Chapter II.
I shall generally refer to Russia's "national poet," Aleksandr Pushkin, by his surname alone, reserving initials for his less distinguished
uncle, V. L. Pushkin.

conscientious genre study will more precisely articulate these freedoms than an *a priori* rejection of the enterprise. Even the most resolute twentieth-century opponent of genre studies, Benedetto Croce, conceded that "such distinctions, as empirical classes, can aid memory and learning."[2] Thus encouraged, I attempt to characterize this elusive genre because the excellence of the letters of Pushkin and his fellow Arzamasians invites scrutiny. At the same time, the study should contribute to our understanding of Arzamas, the cultural situation of its time, and the differences between its most important members. But the focus of the study will be on the letters as literary structures. The English-speaking reader can find biographies of Pushkin in any good bookstore. French Positivist scholarship has in recent years given us useful studies of the literary milieu of the early nineteenth century.[3] The time has come to confront the works of the Arzamasians directly, showing how they select and shape ideas and historical reality.

This analysis of familiar letters, however, cannot be merely formal. The modern reader—for whom letter writing is often a tiresome obligation, who finds the novel the most suitable genre for investigating human experience, and whose sense of literary decorum may be slowly escaping from Victorian norms—cannot fail to ask how familiar letter writing could attract talented writers, how a genre of such brevity could prove adequate for recording human experience, and how such a ribald, paratactic style could have an aesthetic function. Such questions occur most quickly to specialists in Russian literature, which lacks the centuries-old epistolary heritage of Latin, French, or English literature. These are legitimate literary questions, involving the relationship of form and theme. Without recourse to social and intellectual illumination, however, one cannot find satisfactory

[2] Benedetto Croce, *Aesthetic as Science of Expression and General Linguistic,* trans. Douglas Ainslie, 2nd ed. (London, 1922), p. 72.

[3] See especially the works by M. Ehrhard (1938) and A. Meynieux (1966) cited in the bibliography. M. I. Gillelson's works on Vyazemski (1969) and Arzamas (1974) take a similar approach.

Full bibliographical information on works mentioned in this foreword appears in the bibliography.

answers. Literature is language in its aesthetic function, but every age redefines "aesthetic function," as Yuri Tynyanov and Roman Jakobson have taught us.[4] Letters, always a means of social interaction, can become "literature" in an age dominated by aristocratic amateurs, respect for the details of everyday life, and a cultural situation in which polite society itself becomes a work of art. When Arzamas was active as a group, literary structure and the structures of polite social intercourse were open to influence by each other. Before this time and after it letters lacked the same literary importance.

The familiar letter, like other genres, has changed and evolved in the course of Western literary history and has captured the attention of literary legislators. It is well known that history and theory present the chicken-egg problem of genre studies: how does one know the genre without knowing the record of its manifestations; how does one know the genre's history without knowing what to look for in the first place?[5] In practice, nevertheless, awareness of how tradition and theoretical prescription interact sets features of individual re-creations of the genre in sharper relief. I shall outline the evolution of European familiar correspondence and examine formularies, the teaching of literary theoreticians, and the Arzamasians' statements about letter writing, using them as a context for discussing the familiar letters of Arzamas. But I shall concentrate on this one group, hoping that the methods and analytic scheme developed here will prove more useful for the further study of familiar letters than the meagre, impressionistic sketch of the entire evolution that a single volume could offer.

To describe the elusive familiar letter we need an analytic

[4] R. Jakobson, "The Dominant," and Yu. Tynyanov, "On Literary Evolution," in L. Matejka and K. Pomorska, eds., *Readings in Russian Poetics: Formalist and Structuralist Views* (Cambridge, Mass., 1971), pp. 69 and 85.

[5] Further discussions of the problem appear in Karl Viëtor, "Probleme der literarischen Gattungsgeschichte," *Deutsche Vierteljahrschrift für Literaturwissenschaft und Geistesgeschichte* 9 (1931), 425–47, and in René Wellek, "Genre Theory, the Lyric, and *Erlebnis*," *Discriminations: Further Concepts of Criticism* (New Haven, 1970), pp. 225–52.

scheme that allows more possibilities for comparison with other genres than does the tersest definition of a literary genre: a form, distinct from other forms, whose materials and devices are arranged so as to satisfy the typological expectations of its readers.[6] The Arzamasians, as we shall see, distinguished a genre by its dominant feeling, and they analyzed letters in terms of style, persona, and content. These all help guide our description of familiar letters and do not contradict the basic definition of a genre. A dominant feeling is, after all, created by the selection and juxtaposition of such materials as will by association convey that feeling to the reader; the poet's separation from his beloved in an elegy, for example, inspires the necessary and anticipated feeling of melancholy.

However, recent discussions of genre suggest that the Arzamasians' categories do not encompass all the aspects of a genre. Northrop Frye uses the "radical of presentation" to distinguish the four genres, which others have called "types" (Wellek and Warren), "universals" (Guillén),[7] or *"Grundhaltungen"* (Viëtor)—the drama is acted, the epic recited, the lyric sung or chanted for the audience, and fiction presented through the medium of the printed page.[8] Frye's "radical of presentation" will help us come to grips with the complex problems of the

---

[6] In essence this agrees with the definition of genre in René Wellek and Austin Warren, *Theory of Literature,* 3rd ed. (New York: Harcourt, Brace & World, Harvest Books, 1956), p. 231.

[7] Claudio Guillén, "On the Uses of Literary Genre," *Literature as System: Essays Toward the Theory of Literary History* (Princeton, 1971), pp. 114–21.

[8] Northrop Frye, *Anatomy of Criticism* (Princeton, 1957), pp. 246–47. Frye's discussion does much to rescue the concept of genre as a useful critical tool. He sees the poet's intention to work in a certain genre as the sort of intention critics can discuss without violating the "intentional fallacy" (86, 246), and he also brings the audience back into the picture by saying that genre is "determined by the conditions established between the poet and his public" (247). There is some inconsistency, inevitable in such a complex book, in the use of the term "genre." At times Frye, indulging his weakness for the number *four,* limits "genre" to his extension of the Aristotelian division: drama, epic, lyric, fiction. At other times he applies the term to the wide range of historical literary kinds recognized as genres in the age of Neoclassicism and by most modern students of genre.

6

familiar letter's intended audience (immediate and ultimate) and with the principles of selecting content.

Chapters on the principles of selecting and arranging content and on the parts of the letter complete my analytic scheme. Of course, other early nineteenth-century genres have some features in common with letters. Both the comic poem and the letter, for example, feature lowly details of everyday life. But the combination of associative or paratactic organization with lowly detail distinguishes the letter from the comic poem, whose plot unfolds in temporal sequence. Thus a genre is differentiated from other genres by the sum of its materials and devices, not necessarily by individual ones or by a single *sine qua non.*

Dissecting the familiar letter in such fashion may seem a cut-and-dried, excessively abstract procedure. It is, however, a necessary one for discussing the more than ten thousand Arzamasian letters that have come down to us and for coherently comparing aspects of the letters with similar aspects of other genres. In the ensuing chapters, examples and close readings will "reassemble" letters as whole literary works and show the relationships of their various devices. I have preferred this exemplary method to a statistical one out of respect for both literary history and mathematics. "Majority rules" in a democracy, not necessarily in the republic of letters. In statistical analysis a percentage is meaningless without standards of significant deviation or statistical relevance. Such problems have been worked out for versification, but not for larger literary units. In terms of literary "impact" a single instance can overwhelm hundreds of others and so occupy the minds of contemporaries and successors that, in itself, it constitutes tradition. The epistolary manuals that I cite and the statements of the Arzamasians help to reveal conventional expectations and to demonstrate the existence of the genre. The examples of Arzamasian letters that I use are, unless otherwise indicated, typical in their themes and devices. The reader can test the validity of a generalization by ascertaining whether it applies to letters discussed in other chapters.

The English term "familiar," derived from the Latin *familiaris,* adequately translates the Russian *druzheskoye* (literally "friendly," "familiar"), which has been in use since the eighteenth century. Each distinguishes the casual, seemingly unorganized type of letter, which was recognized as literature and was more or less intended to find its way into print, from letters of biographical importance that were not considered literature in their time, such as official correspondence or correspondence too personal or trivial to be placed before the public. The following letter from Pushkin to his fellow Arzamasian Vyazemski reveals many of the features of the familiar letter that this study will examine in greater detail: a self-depreciating persona who is concerned with literature and friendship, who describes people in literary terms, who plays with words (the double meaning of *istoricheski*—"historical" and "scandalous"), who composes a letter in chains of associations, and who does not shun mild scabrousness. That Vyazemski included a message to Pushkin in a letter to Turgenev shows that their letters circulated within the group; this and Pushkin's account of the literary situation describe the sort of milieu in which such genres as the familiar letter could gain respectability.

I read my Preobrazhenski friend [the poet Katenin] the several lines you wrote for me in your letter to Turgenev, and I congratulated him upon the happy evacuation of his Homeric feasts. He replied that the shit is yours, not his. It is desirable that the affair stop here—he seems to fear your satiric club; your first four lines about him in the epistle to Dmitriyev are fine; the rest, necessary for explaining his personality, are weak and cold. Friendship for him aside, Katenin is worth something better and more malicious. He was born too late—with his character and way of thinking he belongs entirely to the eighteenth century. The same authorial arrogance, the same literary gossiping and intrigues as in the heralded age of philosophy. At that time the quarrel of Fréron and Voltaire occupied Europe, but now no one would be interested in

8

it; say what you will, our age is not an age of poets—that seems nothing to regret, but, still, it's a pity. The circle of poets gets narrower by the hour—soon we will be forced for want of listeners to read our verses aloud to each other. And that's not a bad thing. In the meantime, send me your own verses. They're captivating and enlivening— "The First Snow" is charming; "Dejection," even more so. Have you read the latest works of Zhukovski, who rests in peace? Have you heard his "Voice from the Other World"? [a translation of Schiller's "Thekla, eine Geiste-stimme"]—and what do you think of it? Petersburg is stifling for a poet. I thirst for foreign lands; perhaps the southern air will enliven my soul. I finished my poem ["Ruslan and Lyudmila"]. And only the last (that is, the concluding) line brought me real satisfaction. You will read fragments of it in the journals and will receive it once it's printed. It bores me so that I can't bring myself to copy it piecemeal for you. My letter is boring because ever since I have become a historical figure for the gossiping women of St. Petersburg, I grow stupider and older—not by the week but by the hour. Farewell. Answer me, please—I am very glad that I've taken up corresponding.[9]

This letter contained nothing to conceal from posterity, and Vyazemski himself published it in 1874. The following letter

[9] A. S. Pushkin, *Polnoye sobraniye sochineni,* 17 vols. (Moscow-Leningrad, 1937–59), XIII, 14–15. Written not later than 21 April 1820. Subsequent references to this edition will appear in the text. Translations are my own with three exceptions that are generally respected by students of Russian literature: Walter Arndt's translation of Pushkin's *Eugene Onegin,* Bernard Guilbert Guerney's version of Gogol's *Dead Souls,* and J. Thomas Shaw's well annotated, generally accurate translation of Pushkin's letters. In most cases, however, I provide my own version of Pushkin's letters so that the differences in style between the Arzamasians will not be distorted by differences in translators' approaches. In these cases I have carefully consulted Shaw's edition and the reviews of it by Ralph E. Matlaw and Walter Arndt. In translating the letters of the Arzamasians I have endeavored to preserve their occasional redundancy, ambiguity, and faulty syntax—such forms of *neglegentia epistolarum* lend the letter much of its illusion of intimacy.

to Pushkin's brother-in-law, which appeared only in 1970, is clearly personal and features none of the literary markings of the letter to Vyazemski. Like many of Pushkin's business or personal letters, it was written in French.

I received your letter just as I was getting ready to write you in order to talk with you about my difficulties in connection with the impending confinement of Natasha [Pushkin's wife] and about the money that will be extremely necessary to me. And so, our requests have collided. Meanwhile, I have succeeded in doing something. Prince Vladimir Sergeyevich Golitsyn is now here, and I spoke with him about you and your affair. He seemed disposed to show favor toward you and said that at the end of the month he would be in Moscow, where you will be able to negotiate with him. If you arrange that loan, please lend me for six months 6,000 rubles, which I need very badly and do not know where to get; and since it is all the same to Prince Golitsyn whether he lends 35 or 40,000 or even more, this is just that source from which you will be so good as to draw, if possible. I cannot do this myself because I cannot give him any other guarantee than my word, and I do not wish to risk a refusal.

Since you are the head of the family into which I have had the honor of entering and are for us a real and good brother, I take the liberty of boring you by talking about my affairs. My family is growing, my occupations force me to live in Petersburg, expenses take their course, and, since I did not think it possible to discharge them in the first year of my marriage, my debts have also increased. I know that at the present time you can do nothing for us, having a greatly disordered fortune, debts, and a family on your hands. But if Natalya Ivanovna [Pushkin's mother-in-law] would be so good as to do something for Natasha, however little, that would be a great help to us. You understand that, knowing about her constantly straightened circumstances, I would never have resolved to tax her with requests, but extreme need and even duty force me to do so since, naturally, this is not for me, but only for Natasha and our children, whose future I am considering. I am not rich, and my present affairs do not permit me to occupy myself with literary work, which gave me the means to live. If I die, my wife will be in the streets and my children in poverty. All of this is grievous and brings me to despondency.[10]

This material is useful for the biographer, but the story that it related was far too personal and shameful—by the standards of that time—for circulation. This type of writing is altogether different from that of the familiar letter.

The nature of this distinction will become clearer as the study progresses, although it would be naive to deny that borderline cases arise between personal, business, and familiar correspondence. The following letter falls into all three categories: it is a personal request for the repayment of a debt, couched in a style-conscious parody of a business document:

In 1811 my uncle Vasili Lvovich, in accordance with his favorable inclination toward me and all my family, during a trip from Moscow to Saint Petersburg, borrowed from me 100 rubles in paper money which had been given to me for pocket money by my late grandmother Varvara Vasilievna Chicherina and my late aunt Anna Lvovna. The witness of this loan was a certain Ignati; but Vasili Lvovich himself, in the nobility of his heart, will not deny the same. Since more than ten years have already passed without any exaction or presentation for the same, and since I have already lost my legal right to exact the repayment of the aforementioned 100 rubles (with interest for 14 years, which makes more than 200 rubles), I humbly beg his High Nobility, Dear Sir, my uncle, to pay me these 200 rubles according to Christian duty—I name

[10] A. S. Pushkin, "Redchayshaya nakhodka: neizvestnoye pismo Pushkina," *Literaturnaya gazeta,* 9 December 1970, p. 6.

as my plenipotentiary to receive this same money Prince Peter Andreyevich Vyazemski, a well-known man of letters.

> Collegiate Secretary
> Aleksandr son of Sergey Pushkin
> (XIII, 210–11; 14–15 August 1825)[11]

Stylistic exuberance and parody, and the fact that Pushkin could include this letter in a letter to Vyazemski, mark it as an Arzamasian familiar letter. The letter is amusing and of literary interest to a greater audience than the immediate recipient. At the same time the markers of the familiar letter mask personal problems (Pushkin's poverty, the thoughtlessness of his uncle) and enable Pushkin to make a personal request without humiliating either himself or his uncle by direct mention of his problems. Thus the familiar plays a strategic role in the personal, and the personal provides a point of departure for the familiar. I shall consider such borderline cases familiar letters if it can be demonstrated that they have a significant number of features in common with letters that are obviously familiar.[12] The need for such critical decisions arises because writers do not merely copy the schema a genre sets before them but make a personal relationship to it a part of their creative fusion of material and form, adapting, rejecting, or changing the schema that they share with the experienced reader. The somewhat blurred generalization that includes such borderline cases would distress the Cartesian mind but is consistent with twentieth-century genre theory, which seeks to account for the richness of genres, not to prescribe rigid limits and rules for them.[13]

[11] *The Letters of Alexander Pushkin,* trans. J. Thomas Shaw (1963; reprint, Madison, Wis., 1967), p. 246.

[12] This criterion derives from Ludwig Wittgenstein's suggestions for treating "concepts with blurred edges" in game theory, *Philosophical Investigations,* trans. G. E. M. Anscombe, 3rd ed. (New York, 1968). It has recently been applied to literary concepts by Robert C. Elliot, "The Definition of Satire," *Yearbook of Comparative and General Literature* XI (1962), 22–23, and by Claudio Guillén, *Literature as System,* p. 131.

[13] Wellek and Warren, *Theory of Literature,* pp. 234–35.

Some of Russia's finest critics have studied letters (see "Works on Russian Letter Writing" in the bibliography. Ivan Sokolski (1795) and N. I. Grech (1819–21) wrote prescriptive manuals, valuable today for determining the conventional background against which the great letter writers performed.[14] A few of these writers, such as Pushkin (1836) and Vyazemski (1867), left light appreciations of letter writing, useful for demonstrating the literary importance of letters to the public of their time.

Letters had primarily biographical importance to the Russian scholars of the nineteenth century, who published many letters of scant literary interest, such as business letters and brief notes. Problems of literary form had little place in their studies. Although V. A. Sipovski (1902) noted Pushkin's ability to characterize his recipients, he neither expanded upon this observation nor tried to apply it to other letter writers. The same general failing occurs in both prerevolutionary and Soviet studies of Pushkin's letters.[15] The most valuable contribution of the early scholars remains their collections of letters, which captured in careful annotations the intimate associations and references of the genre.

The first studies of Russian letters as literature appeared during the 1920s as a result of the Formalists' interest in "uncanonized" and "laboratory" genres. The enthusiasm of the late 1920s for "documentary" literature (memoirs, diaries, letters) spurred further editions and discussions of letters. Nevertheless, these studies are generally brief and tentative. G. O. Vinokur's article (1929) indicates the similarities between Pushkin's letters and his other works without analyzing the differences. A. Z. Lezhnev (1937) shows that Pushkin's letters have more figures and tropes than his other prose. L. P. Grossman (1928) mentions Pushkin's knowledge of French

---

[14] A translation of Grech's treatise appears in Appendix II.

[15] Useful summaries of previous studies of Pushkin's letters are provided in B. L. Modzalevski, "Predisloviye," in A. S. Pushkin, *Pisma*, vol. I (Moscow-Leningrad, 1926), pp. iii–xlviii; and Ya. L. Levkovich, "Pisma," *Pushkin: Itogi i problemy izucheniya* (Moscow-Leningrad, 1966), pp. 529–34.

letter writing, sees the cynicism of *Les Liaisons dangereuses* in Pushkin's letters, and lists some of their devices, but never really defines "epistolary style." B. V. Kazanski (1937) offers a fascinating analysis of Pushkin's drafts for a letter describing a quarrel with his parents (to Zhukovski, 31 October 1824).

These and subsequent studies by I. S. Ilyinskaya (1946), N. L. Stepanov (1926), I. M. Semenko (1962), V. A. Malakhovski (1937, 1938), and G. M. Fridlender (1967) employ a common scientific analogy for epistolary creation: letters are a "laboratory" for the writer's linguistic and literary "experiments." Like many analogies this one is as misleading as it is helpful. Though letters can playfully explore the possibilities of a language, during the Neoclassical period of Russian literature their playfulness was more an end in itself than a means of developing something outside themselves. The "laboratory" view of letters refuses to acknowledge that familiar letters, with their humor and observation of particular phenomena, could be a part of the genre system of Russian Neoclassicism, which Soviet critics persist in characterizing as rational, abstract, and overly solemn.[16]

Among the Formalists, Yu. N. Tynyanov and his students, especially N. L. Stepanov, have left us the most stimulating studies of letters. Although Tynyanov never devoted a separate article to them, letters provide the central illustration for his theory of literary relevance, in which subliterary writing (personal letters, salon word games) can achieve literary status at the same time that established genres become disreputable as literature (for example, odes on events at court).[17] Tynyanov believed that genres are always changing and that they cannot

[16] Andrey Sinyavski, whose orthodox Soviet criticism provided a front for his underground writing, presents such a view of Neoclassicism in his famous essay "On Socialist Realism" (1960). Ye. N. Kupreyanova has recently argued against such critical clichés as "dogmatic" and "rationalistic" and has showed the role of Empiricism and common sense in eighteenth-century thought; see "K voprosu o klassitsizme," *XVIII vek: Sbornik chetverty* (Moscow-Leningrad, 1959), pp. 5–44.

[17] Yu. N. Tynyanov, "Literaturni fakt," *Arkhaisty i novatory* (Leningrad, 1929), pp. 20–24.

14

be given static definitions that adequately account for them.[18] Thus, he outlined some changes in letter-writing styles without providing examples or much description of the genre.

Tynyanov was a stimulating teacher whose every sentence seemed to contain the subject for a possible essay. His lectures inspired N. L. Stepanov's article on familiar letters of the early nineteenth century (1926). Examining a wider range of letters than I shall, Stepanov rejected the idea of a single epistolary genre and proposed classifying letters by purpose, the literary orientation of the writer, subject, or style (business, narrative, sermon, note). His list of epistolary devices is similar to Tynyanov's but better documented. Like Tynyanov, Stepanov treats literary change as an autonomous process, independent of social, psychological, intellectual, or historical currents; he accepts analogies with nonliterary speech (oratorical, conversational) alone as relevant to literary study and ignores the parallels between literature and other cultural areas. But whereas Tynyanov suggests that literary works can be "oriented" toward nonliterary speech (odes on the teaching of rhetorical manuals, for example), Stepanov attempts to show that Arzamasian letters "consist" to a large extent of "conversational" speech. As we shall see, the idea that familiar correspondence is conversational in nature has been a cliché since Greek and Roman antiquity; Cicero and Demetrius used it, as did the Humanists for their Latin letters. This cliché and his oversimplification of Tynyanov's theory led Stepanov to contradict his own empirical observation that familiar letters could be rather "ornamental" in style.

A tendency to force chronological patterns at the expense of portraying the period's complexity also lessens the value of Stepanov's article. He wrote, for example, that Batyushkov moved from monumental, oratorical prose to letters.[19] In fact, Batyushkov wrote both at the same time. This sort of thinking

[18] *Ibid.*, p. 7.

[19] N. L. Stepanov, "Druzheskoye pismo nachala XIX v.," in *Russkaya proza,* ed. B. Eykhenbaum and Yu. Tynyanov (1926; reprint, The Hague, 1963), p. 72. Tynyanov had suggested a similar development in Karamzin's prose in "Literaturni fakt," p. 21.

15

may have resulted in part from Tynyanov's theory of genre as "direction" (*napravleniye,* i.e., orientation toward a particular type of nonliterary speech), which is in most cases accurate but which cannot account for the variety of literary endeavor expected of a writer at the beginning of the nineteenth century.[20] As we shall see in the second chapter, the age demanded versitility because the representation of reality and the writer's own personality was parcelled out among the members of the genre system.

When Tynyanov and Stepanov were writing about letters both they and Formalism were still very young. As the movement matured, it began to lose its schematic, polemical edges and considered the relationship of ideas and social conditions to literary form. Had Formalism spread beyond the confines of its several subgroups, its members might have filled in ellipses of definition and documentation. Instead, it was tragically crippled by Stalinist attacks. The effect on genre studies, which Formalism encouraged, has been disastrous, as a glance at the indexes of the latest Soviet bibliographies of Russian literature reveals.[21] It would be possible, of course, for imaginative Marxist critics to analyze genres by the sociological method. The familiar letter, for example, is preeminently an aristocrat's genre. But the variety of Marxist criticism prevalent in the Soviet Union evidently hesitates to study such phenomena as genres, which suggest that the writer's most immediate purpose may not be to reflect socioeconomic reality and that conventions figure significantly in the creative process. Recent genre studies either ignore the problem of defining genre or confuse genre with such concepts as mode or technique. A. A. Morozov's otherwise fine article "Parody as a Literary Genre" (1960) illustrates this confusion; parody can hardly

[20] Victor Erlich finds that in general the Formalists implied that a genre was "a cluster of compositional devices." *Russian Formalism: History—Doctrine,* 2nd ed. (The Hague, 1965), pp. 246–47.

[21] K. D. Muratova, ed., *Istoriya russkoy literatury XIX veka: Bibliograficheski ukazatel* (Moscow-Leningrad, 1962); P. N. Berkov, ed., *Istoriya russkoy literatury XVIII veka: Bibliograficheski ukazatel* (Leningrad, 1968).

be a separate genre since it depends on the form of parodied works. The definition of genre in L. I. Timofeyev's popular dictionary of literary terms for school teachers has not changed in post-Stalin editions:

> LITERARY GENRE (from the French *genre*—type, sort)—types of literature are sometimes named in this way (see LITERATURE): *epic; narrative genre* (novel, tale, story, sketch); *lyric genre* (lyric poem, song); *lyro-epic genre* (narrative poem, ballad); *dramatic genre* (tragedy, comedy, drama, vaudeville).
>
> Using this term, we say that a novel is a kind of narrative *genre;* a song is a kind of lyric *genre;* a comedy is a kind of dramatic *genre.*
>
> It is sometimes said that the adventure novel, the historical novel, and the novel of family life are all separate *genres,* or kinds, of novel.
>
> It is more correct to call a *genre* a type of literature.[22]

It is doubtful that this approach could inspire any serious genre studies.[23]

Since the 1930s Soviet studies of letter writing have been limited to stylistic analyses, introductions to collections of letters, and brief articles. Fridlender (1967) indicates the subjectivity of Romantic letters. Semenko (1962) links Pushkin's

[22] L. I. Timofeyev, ed., *Kratki slovar literaturovedcheskikh terminov: Posobiye dlya uchashchikhsya sredney shkoly,* 4th ed., (Moscow, 1963), p. 49. An expanded version of the dictionary, which appeared in 1974, adds little to this understanding of genre besides the statement that form is dictated by "life" and a simpleminded division of "bourgeois" genre studies into those that see genre as unchanging and those that fail to distinguish between "universals" and historical genres. See S. Kalacheva and P. Roshchin, "Zhanr," in L. I. Timofeyev and S. V. Turayev, eds., *Slovar literaturovedcheskikh terminov* (Moscow, 1974), pp. 82–83.

[23] A promising exception to this neglect of genre studies is the work of the Soviet medievalists, currently the most sophisticated Soviet literary scholars. D. S. Likhachev provides a theoretical overview of medieval Russian genres in *Poetika drevnerusskoy literatury,* 2nd ed. (Leningrad, 1971); a number of individual genres are examined in A. M. Panchenko, ed., *Istoriya zhanrov v russkoy literatury X–XVIIvv.: Trudy otdela drevnerusskoy literatury,* vol. 27 (1972).

letters with his generally laconic, objective style and "Realistic manner." N. V. Fridman (1965) also seeks literary Realism in letters. E. A. Maymin (1962) finds Pushkin's letters much less restrained than his fiction and criticism.

Despite their interest in "sous-littérature" (limericks, detective stories, nonsense verse)[24] the Soviet Structuralists have not taken up the study of familiar letters; their leader, Yu. M. Lotman, whose methods have contributed much to my understanding of literary form, has not yet broken with the habit of using familiar letters merely as a source of political opinion.[25]

Despite previous articles, a number of factors justify another study of familiar correspondence: first, the general reluctance on the part of critics to relate such correspondence to the Russian culture of the early nineteenth century and to the interests of Arzamas; second, the lack of an extensive description of it, and uncritical satisfaction with such clichés as "conversational language," "laboratory," and "experiment"; third, the failure to compare the letters of various writers and to establish the uniqueness of letters compared to other genres of the early nineteenth century; and, fourth, the absence of an account of the directions that the familiar letter took after the Arzamasians disbanded.

[24] Thomas G. Winner, introduction to Yu. M. Lotman, *Lektsii po strukturalnoy poetike* (Providence, 1968), p. ix.
[25] Yu. M. Lotman, "P. A. Vyazemski i dvizheniye Dekabristov," *Uchenye zapiski Tartuskogo Gosudarstvennogo Universiteta* 98 (1960), 24–142.

I

The Epistolary Tradition in Europe and Russia

> Our haughty Russian hardly knows
> How to adjust to postal prose.
> *Eugene Onegin*, III, xxvi
> trans. Walter Arndt

Fascination with letter writing attaches the Arzamasians to a venerable European tradition. Familiar correspondence had excited Western readers since the fourteenth century, when Petrarch's rediscovery of Cicero's letters laid a cornerstone for the early Renaissance.

A number of the conventions of familiar letter writing that Cicero helped to establish have survived him by two millennia. He wrote for his immediate recipients, but planned to edit and publish the letters. Cicero made *neglegentia epistolarum* a virtue and defined the style of his letters as "the language of conversation."[1] Their style served in the seventeenth and eighteenth centuries as an antidote to the measured, rhetorical prose of his speeches. Cicero made his accounts of everyday life and events literary by his literary self-consciousness—as with this well-known epistolary taxonomy in a letter to Gaius Scribonius Curio:

> There are many sorts of letter. But there is one unmistakeable sort, which actually caused letter writing to be invented in the first place, namely the sort intended to give people in other places any information which for our or their sakes they ought to know. . . . There are two other sorts of letter which I like very much, one intimate and humorous, the other serious and profound.[2]

[1] Quoted in W. H. Irving, *The Providence of Wit in the English Letter Writers* (Durham, 1955), p. 44.

[2] Cicero, Marcus Tullius, *Selected Works,* trans. Michael Grant (Baltimore, 1960), p. 70.

19

The later Roman epistolarians Seneca and Pliny the Younger tended to follow the "serious and profound" and "intimate and humorous" lines respectively. Each wrote consciously for publication within his lifetime, and Seneca's letters more closely resembled moral essays than familiar letters. Pliny filled out his letters with details his recipient would have known. Such details make them more comprehensible to the general public, but weaken the illusion of personal correspondence that writers of familiar correspondence seek to create.

The epistolarians of Imperial Rome composed letters in a milieu perfectly suited to the cultivation of such a genre. They read or sent their works to circles of friends for criticism and appreciation. Professional copyists served readers who did not belong to this literary elite; proceeds from the sale of the manuscripts went to the copyists, not the authors, whose livelihood depended on careers in public service or on private wealth (theirs or their patrons'). The writers did not scorn posterity or this larger public—they did, after all, let the copyists have their works—but literature was for them largely a means of civilized recreation. The familiar letter neatly fits what Erich Auerbach has called the ideal of literary life under the Empire: "personal association among highly educated individuals belonging to the same social class."[3]

Roman epistolarians, including Cicero, did not work in a theoretical vacuum. They knew the theory and practice of familiar correspondence from Greek formularies and rhetorical manuals.[4] A stylistic treatise, thought to have been written during the first century by Demetrius, reappeared during the Renaissance, and many of its epistolary precepts found their way into Western and Russian manuals, not necessarily because later formulators borrowed from it, but because the broad outlines of the familiar letter were established in classical antiquity

[3] Erich Auerbach, *Literary Language and its Public in Late Latin Antiquity and in the Middle Ages,* trans. Ralph Manheim (New York, 1965), p. 245.

[4] Klaus Thraede, *Grundzüge griechisch-römischer Brieftopik,* Zetemata: Monographien zur klassischen Altertumswissenschaft, no. 48 (Munich, 1970), pp. 3, 27–28.

and re-created in periods sympathetic to the minor forms of classical literature, such as the Renaissance or the Enlightenment. Demetrius, like Cicero, reveals the Ancients' epistolary self-consciousness.[5] Since Demetrius was writing a prescriptive manual and not a casual taxonomy, it is not surprising that he set stricter norms than did Cicero for the familiar letter. Demetrius limits epistolary topics to the "heart's good wishes" and to "simple subjects in simple terms." Philosophy in a letter should only take the form of proverbs, which are "the wishes of a people, the wisdom of the world," not formal reasoning; the letter must not be a treatise with an epistolary heading. Demetrius makes characterization the central aspect of familiar correspondence; a letter should reveal the writer's soul and character. The nature of the "character" revealed varies, of course, with the writer and the historical period, but self-characterization remains vital to the familiar letter and is, perhaps, its greatest source of interest. Demetrius is well aware that this openness is not a matter of unpremeditated, naive "sincerity." He recommends that the letter be a more studied composition than a dialogue and that it avoid the breaks of oral discourse, since a letter is "committed to writing and is (in a way) sent as a gift."

This highly refined epistolary art all but disappears during the Middle Ages. The Fathers of the Church were trained in the rhetorical arts of antiquity, but the literature of the Christian Middle Ages absorbed only the eloquence that could adorn sermons, admonitions, and self-depreciation. Written literature ceased to be the recreation of cultured amateurs, as it had often been in Roman times, and became instead a means of earning salvation. Predictably, the "intimate and humorous" familiar letter with its exposition of everyday detail held little attraction. The epistolary forms that have survived are hardly familiar: official correspondence (based on Roman models),

[5] Demetrius's text and a translation by W. Rhys Roberts appears in *Aristotle, The Poetics: "Longinus," On the Sublime: Demetrius, On Style,* Loeb Classical Library (Cambridge, Mass., 1932), pp. 495–501. The section on epistolography, which I summarize, is found on pp. 438–445.

complaints, requests, pastoral epistles. The various "renaissances"—Ottonian, Carolingian—brought purification of the Latin literary language and cultivation of epideictic, panegyric eloquence, but not a rebirth of familiar letters. C. H. Haskins finds that of all Cicero's works, the familiar letters are the least likely to be collected in monastic libraries. Seneca's letters, because of their moral seriousness, fare better; there is even a forged correspondence between Seneca (who becomes a Christian!) and St. Paul.[6] In the twelfth century, letter-writing revived as a school exercise, a means of teaching Latin, but did not develop into a form of entertainment for a cultured public. Entertaining literature was generally provided in oral form by minstrels, jongleurs, and the clerics who recited courtly epics.[7]

The Humanists, like the Ancients, made letter writing a self-conscious art. The fascinating history of books of model letters is too long to summarize here, but such formularies, absorbed in our time by books of etiquette, captivated some of the best minds in the Renaissance. Erasmus, for example, wrote a manual, *Libellus de Conscribendis Epistolis* (1521). The self-consciousness of the Humanists sprang in part from the newness of the language they used (a reconstruction of classical Latin), from their desire to follow classical models,[8] and from the fun they had in playing with the new form.

Erasmus understood the tensions involved in letter writing: that familiar letters are both a literary form and a spontaneous outpouring from the writer's pen, that they are written both for the immediate recipient and for the public. Erasmus set elaborate oratorical rules for letters in his epistolary manual but subsequently dismissed it in a letter as "a dull book for a dull

---

[6] C. H. Haskins, *The Renaissance of the Twelfth Century* (Cambridge, Mass., 1933), pp. 111–12.

[7] Auerbach, *Literary Language,* p. 291.

[8] Jacob Burckhardt writes that the cult of Cicero reached such extremes that writers took oaths not to use any words that did not occur in his works. See *The Civilization of the Renaissance in Italy,* trans. S. G. C. Middlemore, 2 vols. (New York, Harper & Row, Torchbooks, 1958), I, 257.

fellow" and urged his correspondent to write whatever came to mind without preparation. Erasmus gave the illusion that his correspondence was intended to be private by complaining that others were publishing it, and like Alexander Pope he used this as an excuse to publish more of it himself.[9]

The vernacular had replaced Latin as the language of literature in most of Europe by the seventeenth century, but the theory of Erasmus, the *neglegentia epistolarum* of Cicero, and the moral epistles of Seneca continued to play a large role in the familiar letters of educated Europeans. In France, Guez de Balzac (1596?–1654) enclosed moral treatises in epistolary form and measured periods, as Seneca had done. Within a few decades, however, Boileau and others, returning to the Ciceronian model, faulted Guez de Balzac for affectation and lack of wit. Familiar letter writing had changed to meet the aesthetics of the newly developed literary salons.

The rise of the salons in France, and later of those in Russia, stimulated the taste for a lighter, more pleasant literary language. As had the Humanists, seventeenth-century writers found letters a useful form for exploring the possibilities of the new language. Gallantry, recherché compliments, and bantering replaced Stoic moralizing. Of Vincent Voiture, the most famous representative of this trend, Voltaire wrote "dans sa manie de broder des riens, [il] avait quelquefois beaucoup de délicatesse et d'agrément."[10] One of the better examples of this embroidery of trifles is Voiture's letter to Mlle de Rambouillet with its fancy, hyperbole, personification, and compliments marshaled in defense of the conjunction *car:*

> Mademoiselle, *car* étant d'une si grande considération dans notre langue, j'approuve extrêmement le ressentiment que vous avez du tort qu'on veut lui faire, et je ne

---

[9] *The Epistles of Erasmus: From His Earliest Letters to His Fifty-first Year Arranged in Order of Time,* trans. Francis Morgan Nichols, 3 vols. (1901–18; reprint, New York: Russell and Russell, 1962), I, lxxvi, lxxviii, lxxxviii, and 51.

[10] François-Marie Arouet de Voltaire, *Oeuvres complètes,* ed. Louis Moland (Paris: Garnier, 1877–85), XIX, 273.

puis bien espérer de l'Académie dont vous me parlez, voyant qu'elle se veut établir par une si grande violence. En un temps où la fortune joue des tragédies par tous les endroits de l'Europe, je ne vois rien si digne de pitié que de faire le procès à un mot qui a si utilement servi cette monarchie et qui, dans toutes les brouilleries du royaume, s'est toujours montré bon Français. Pour moi, je ne puis comprendre quelles raisons ils pourront alléguer contre une diction qui marche toujours à la tête de la raison, et qui n'a point d'autre charge que de l'introduire. Je ne sais pour quel intérêt ils tâchent d'ôter à *car* ce qui lui appartient pour le donner à *pour ce que,* ni pourquoi ils veulent dire avec trois mots ce qu'ils peuvent dire avec trois lettres. Ce qui est le plus à craindre, Mademoiselle, c'est qu'après cette injustice, on en entreprendra d'autres. On ne fera point de difficulté d'attaquer *mais,* et je ne sais si *si* demeurera en sûreté. De sorte qu'après nous avoir ôté toutes les paroles qui lient les autres, les beaux esprits nous voudront réduire au langage des anges, ou, si cela ne se peut, ils nous obligeront au moins à ne parler que par signes. Certes, j'avoue qu'il est vrai ce que vous dites, qu'on ne peut mieux connaître par aucun exemple l'incertitude des choses humaines. Qui m'eût dit, il y a quelques années, que j'eusse dû vivre plus longtemps que *car,* j'eusse cru qu'il m'eût promis une vie plus longue que celle des patriarches. Cependant, il se trouve qu'après avoir vécu onze cents ans, plein de force et de crédit, après avoir été employé dans les plus importants traités, et avoir assisté toujours honorablement dans le conseil de nos rois, il tombe tout d'un coup en disgrace et est menacé d'une fin violente. Je n'attends plus que l'heure d'entendre en l'air des voix lamentables, qui diront: *le grand car est mort,* et le trépas du grand *Cam* [Khan] ni du grand *Pan* ne me semblerait pas si important ni si étrange. Je sais que si l'on consulte là-dessus un des plus beaux esprits de notre siècle et que j'aime extrêmement, il dira qu'il faut condamner cette nouveauté, qu'il faut user du *car* de nos pères, aussi bien que de leur terre et de leur soleil, et que l'on ne doit point chasser un mot qui a été dans la bouche de Charlemagne et de saint Louis. Mais c'est vous principalement, Mademoiselle, qui êtes obligée d'en prendre la protection. Puisque la plus grande force et la plus parfaite beauté de notre langue est en la vôtre, vous y devez avoir une souveraine puissance, et faire vivre ou mourir les paroles comme il vous plaît. Aussi crois-je que vous avez déjà sauvé celle-ci du hasard qu'elle courait, et qu'en l'enfermant dans votre lettre, vous l'avez mise comme dans un asile et dans un lieu de gloire, où le temps et l'envie ne la sauraient toucher.[11]

Such letter writing was remarkably well suited to the salons of Paris, and may be compared as well as connected with that which emerged a century later in the salons of St. Petersburg. It expressed the interests of those who met in the salons—literature, style, social news, current events—in a language whose delicacy and playfulness they found attractive. Letters could be easily read or passed around in such circles. The custom of saving and eventually publishing familiar letters insured the immortality of aristocratic amateurs, who could write with varying degrees of spontaneity for their circles and friends, yet leave posterity favorable characterizations of themselves and reach the public they might pretend to scorn. Even Mme de Sévigné, the most spontaneous of the great epistolarians, was aware that her correspondents were gathering and circulating her letters.[12] Alexander Pope contrived to have three collections of his letters published and tailored some of them for the press by such tricks as changing the addressees' names to those of more prestigious figures. The Russian epistolarians also knew that their familiar letters were being collected, but they did not resort to the deceptions of Pope and Erasmus.

[11] Guez de Balzac and Voiture, Vincent *Oeuvres choisies,* ed. Gabriel Raibaud (Paris: Larousse, 1936), pp. 88–89. The service of *car* to the monarchy (line 9) is in the royal formula "car tel est notre bon plaisir." The writer referred to in lines 38–43 is Guez de Balzac; Voiture pokes fun at his solemnity.

[12] Irving, *Providence of Wit,* p. 82.

Epistolary manuals, once a subject of concern to serious authors, did not interest the letter writers of French and (later) Russian salon society. These writers presumably learned the genre and its style by reading past masters and by listening to the conversation of those around them. Literary entrepreneurs now wrote the manuals, or rather plagiarized and translated from older manuals, for the newly literate members of the rising bourgeoisie. From representative titles one can easily surmise the sophistication of their readers: *The Academy of Compliments, The Young Secretary's Guide,* and *The Young Man's Companion* (from which George Washington copied maxims as a boy). A few manuals, such as Samuel Richardson's, formed miniature epistolary novels by joining several model letters to form a correspondence; other manuals provided amusing anecdotes in their letters, but most just set essentially blank forms before their unimaginative public.[13]

Meanwhile, the establishment of regular, inexpensive postal service in Europe during the seventeenth and eighteenth centuries had considerably facilitated the spreading cult of familiar letter writing.[14] Official documents no longer monopolized the courier service, and private correspondence no longer depended on occasional travelers or expensive messengers.

Although the Russian Middle Ages left examples of business, pastoral, and polemical letters, the Russian epistolary tradition properly begins with Lomonosov. His letters were the first by a Russian author to be collected and printed, and the first familiar letters to which other writers referred. Lomonosov also discussed letters theoretically. In his "Introduction to the Use of Church Books in Russian" (1758), Lomonosov treated the lexical levels appropriate to familiar letters, not

[13] For an exhaustive history of these manuals see Katherine Gee Hornbeck, *The Complete Letter Writer in English: 1568–1800,* Smith College Studies in Modern Language, vol. xv, nos. 3–4 (April–July 1934).

[14] Howard Robinson, *The British Post Office: A History* (Princeton, 1948), is an excellent source of information.

other aspects of their form. He prescribed the lowest of his three styles (high, middle, and low) for them, the style consisting of nonvulgar colloquialisms and Russian words used by cultured people.[15] Lomonosov's critics delight in showing the inadequacy of the theory of the three styles and his own violations of it.[16] He had intended the low and middle styles to imitate conversational speech, but they did not come close, to judge by the few examples he gave. Although Lomonosov did not always write his own letters in conversational Russian, his theory was significant for Russian letters; it grafted them onto the European epistolary tradition with its ideal of "talking on paper."[17]

Lomonosov grew up in a White Sea fishing village reading a rhymed psalter, an arithmetic book, and a grammar of Church Slavonic (Russia's medieval liturgical language, later a source of elevated poetic diction). In maturity he worked in an intellectual milieu dominated by the Academy of Sciences and by the system of literary patronage, which proved more conducive to scholarly studies and panegyric odes than to cultivated literary recreation and familiar letters. The Academy supported "significant" scholarly works, and one did not address one's patron in familiar fashion. Literary salons, which encouraged epistolary writing elsewhere, had little place in Russia during the eighteenth century. Under these circumstances it is not surprising that little humor, bantering, or light verse appeared in Lomonosov's letters. When the letters do reflect the personalities and interests of their recipients, it is less for reasons of social

[15] M. V. Lomonosov, "Predisloviye o polze knig tserkovnykh v rossiskom yazyke," *Sochineniya,* 8 vols. (Moscow-Leningrad, 1891–1948), IV, 228.

[16] V. V. Vinogradov, *Ocherki po istorii russkogo literaturnogo yazyka XVIII–XIX vv.,* 2nd ed. (Moscow, 1939), p. 97.

[17] Alexander Pope used this and similar phrases thirty times. See R. Cowler, "Shadow and Substance: A Discussion of Pope's Correspondence," in Howard Anderson, Philip B. Daghlian, and Irvin Ehrenpreis, eds., *The Familiar Letter in the Eighteenth Century* (Lawrence: University of Kansas Press, 1968), p. 38. A. P. Sumarokov's "Epistle I" ("Epistola I," 1748) expressed similar ideas on letter writing. For an English translation see Harold B. Segel, ed., *The Literature of Eighteenth-Century Russia* (New York: Dutton, 1967), I, 225.

etiquette than for communicating the results of research or making a request. Lomonosov's letters to Teplov, a fellow scholar, tend to be blunt and vernacular, yet do not disregard rhetorical orchestration. One to the Archbishop of Archangel is convoluted, self-effacing, and lofty in diction; it hardly conforms to the lexical levels that Lomonosov suggested for letters. Lomonosov wrote to foreign scholars in German or Latin. Letters to his patron, the statesman I. I. Shuvalov, feature classical allusions, progress reports, and sober reminiscences.[18]

The Arzamasians and those who shared their taste for the casual genres found Lomonosov's letters more interesting than his more famous poetical works. The Arzamasians, as we shall see, turned away from the panegyric odes of the eighteenth century and seemed to find a precedent for their new orientation in Lomonosov. Thus, in an essay on Lomonosov, Batyushkov selected from all of Lomonosov's oeuvre only the letters for analysis.[19] Pushkin admired them, and N. I. Grech chose the one to Shuvalov dated 26 July 1753 as a model, commenting that only the language had become outdated.[20] Describing the death of the scientist G.-V. Richmann in a Franklinian experiment with lightning, it is one of the best narratives of the century and is remarkable for its integration of theme, style, and construction. Lomonosov opens without any polite formulae. He alters the usual ending to fit the situation: "Your Excellency's most humble servant, in tears." The first sentences, disturbed and confused manifestations of *neglegentia epistolarum,* are striking in that Lomonosov was normally a lucid, articulate person:

[18] Lomonosov's concern for reaching his audience is shown not only in his epistolary practice but also in his rhetorical manual (*Kratkoye rukovodstvo k krasnorechiyu: Razdeleniye pervoye, sostoyashcheye iz ritoriki,* 1748). Roughly speaking, the rhetorics and the salon aesthetic emphasized appealing to the audience; the first, by following certain rules; the second, by displaying the intersubjective phenomenon of good taste.

[19] K. N. Batyushkov, "O kharaktere Lomonosova" (1816), *Sochineniya,* ed. L. N. Maykov and V. I. Saitov, 3 vols. (St. Petersburg, 1885–87), II, 175–79. Subsequent references to this edition will appear in the text.

[20] Appendix II, p. 208.

That I am writing to Your Excellency consider a miracle; for the dead do not write. I still do not know, or at least I doubt, whether I am alive or dead.

Что я ныне к Вашему превосходительству пишу, за чудо почитайте, для того что мертвые не пишут. Я не знаю еще или по последней мере сомневаюсь, жив я или мертв.

The third sentence introduces the subsequently intertwining parts of the story—the effects of the lightning bolt on Lomonosov and on Richmann: "I see that Professor Richmann was struck down by lightning in those same circumstances that I was in at the same time." The heirs of Richmann (his son) and Lomonosov (secular scholarship) dominate the second half of the letter.

Lomonosov presents few examples of tortuous Baroque syntax in the letter; generally, he composed it with terse sentences describing one or two actions contiguous in time: setting a table, observing the conducting wire as the cabbage soup grows cold, heeding pleas to come in to dinner. At the center of the letter comes a magnificent long sentence encompassing a much greater period of time and assembling all the fathers and heirs:

The proximity of my own death, his pale corpse, our past accord and friendship, the lament of his wife, children, and household were all so painful that I could not give a speech or answer to the multitude who gathered as I looked at that man with whom I had sat for an hour in the Conference and discussed our future public act.

Then Lomonosov the scientist clinically records the results of his colleague's "lamentable experiment":

The first flash from the suspended line had entered his head, where a cherry-red spot was visible on his forehead; the lightning's electrical force had gone out of his feet into the floor. The leg and toes were blue, the boot torn, but not burned . . . and so by a lamentable experiment he proved that the electricity of lightning can be deflected.

A plea to Shuvalov to educate Richmann's son ("who already shows good promise"), to seek a pension for the widow, and to protect the sciences, lest Richmann's "fine death" have been in vain, concludes the letter.[21]

Unlike many of Lomonosov's letters, this one adheres remarkably well to his stylistic prescriptions, although certain pronouns and adverbs of Church Slavonic origin made its language seem antiquated even to readers of the early nineteenth century. Much of the letter's lexicon, determined by the scientific observation of concrete detail (cabbage soup, torn boot) comes from the non-Slavonic level of Russian that Lomonosov reserved for familiar letters. The syntax, featuring concise sentences and comparatively few participles or compound conjunctions, seems conversational especially when viewed in the context of the convoluted prose of that time. In the following sentence Lomonosov replaces the subordinating conjunction "when" with an asyndetic construction more typical of conversational Russian: "I had just been sitting at the table for several minutes, suddenly a servant of the late Richmann opened the door" ("Tolko ya za stolom posidel neskolko minut, vnezapno dver otvoril chelovek pokornogo Rikhmana"). The confused *ex abrupto* opening of the letter and the modification of the usual concluding formula reinforce the illusion of rapid conversational speech that the letter conveys. Though the Arzamasians later developed a greater number of devices for imitating the intonations of conversation,[22] Lomonosov showed by this example that such imitation was possible. He also proved the ability of a letter to describe serious, even tragic, events with the concrete details from everyday life that Neoclassicism otherwise reserved for comedies and satires.

More representative, however, of the period's prose style is the following epistle dedicatory, which prefaces Lomonosov's

[21] Lomonosov, *Sochineniya*, VIII, 129–31.
[22] See below, Chapter VI, pp. 146–50.

rhetorical manual. It features the inversions, convolutions, and Church Slavonic morphology that set literature apart from lesser forms of writing during the first half of the eighteenth century. The long sentences that end in verbs, a distortion of the syntax of spoken Russian, are typical of this latinate style. The effect it produces on a twentieth-century Russian reader is not unlike the effect of John Donne's considerably more brilliant prose on a modern reader of English. I quote the epistle at some length because I will refer again to this style and because it illustrates the attitude of the time toward language— that it should communicate by its ornateness and grandiloquence the imperial aspirations of the patrons of Russian literature:

That the welfare of the human race depends so much on language anyone can adequately perceive. How would it be possible for dispersed nations to gather into a communal life, raise cities, build temples and ships, take arms against an enemy, and accomplish other matters that demand common effort if they did not have the ability to communicate their thoughts to each other? For this reason the Highest Wisdom added to the gift of reason the gift of speech, which could by skill be increased and used with greater benefit, as intelligent people had already observed in ancient times; to this end they put much effort and indefatigable labor to the elevation and adornment of speech through teaching, at which they had great success and by which they performed noble service in society. At the present time, although there is not such a great need for adorned speech, especially in judicial matters, as there was in the times of the ancient Greeks and Romans, nevertheless, the condition of those nations in which the verbal arts are flourishing clearly demonstrates how useful it [adorned speech] is in propounding the Word of God, correcting the morals of mankind, describing the glorious deeds of great heroes, and in many political communications. The language by which the

31

Russian state rules a great part of the world has in its might a natural abundance, beauty, and strength, in which it yields to no European language.

Lomonosov follows with profuse praise for his addressee, Grand Prince Petr Feodorovich, and concludes in phrases that indicate the Russian writer's lowly role in the middle of the eighteenth century:

May the Almighty Hand of the Most High shield and strengthen the most precious health of Your Highness for the multiplication of prosperity in the empire to which you are heir, for the adornment and defense of the entire North, and for the enjoyment of the human race, and may the generation of Peter [the Great] be confirmed on the Russian throne forever, I desire it from true zeal, Your Highness, Grand Prince, most merciful lord! Your Imperial Highness's most humble and zealous bondsman.[23]

[23] M. V. Lomonosov, *Sochineniya* (Moscow-Leningrad, 1961), pp. 275–76. I have translated *rab* of the closing formula as "bondsman" to distinguish it from the closing formula of the letter to Shuvalov, which used the more usual *sluga* ("servant"). The Russian text of the first part of this epistle illustrates the convolutions of this style:

Блаженство рода человеческого коль много от слова зависит, всяк довольно усмотреть может. Собраться рассеянным народом в общежития, созидать грады, строить храмы и корабли, ополчаться против неприятеля и другие нужные, союзных сил требующие дела производить как бы возможно было, если бы они способа не имели сообщать свои мысли друг другу? Того ради всевышняя премудрость к дарованию разума присовокупила человеку и слова дарование, в котором остроумные люди уже в древние времена приметили, что оное искусством увеличено и тем с вящшею пользою употреблено быть может; для того многое старание и неусыпные труды полагали, чтобы слово свое учением возвысить и украсить, в чем они великие успехи имели, и в обществе показывали знатные услуги. В нынешние веки хотя нет толь великого употребления украшенного слова, а особливо в судебных делах, каково было у древних греков и римлян, однако в предложении Божия слова, в исправлении нравов человеческих, в описании славных дел великих героев и во многих политических поведениях коль оное полезно, ясно показывает состояние тех народов, в которых словесные науки процветают. Язык, которым Российская держава великой части света повелевает, по ея

Language and its artisans—like everyone and everything else in Peter's great plan—were the servants of the state.

During the eighteenth century, open and fictional epistolary forms grew popular in Russia, as they did in the West— epistolary novels, travel letters, journalistic correspondence, verse epistles, and several varieties of ironic letters: imaginary correspondence of unenlightened provincials, letters of spirits, and letters that indirectly treated Russian problems by attacking similar situations in other lands.[24] However, the Russian writers who followed Montesquieu, Voltaire, Diderot, Rousseau, Richardson, and Pope in a variety of epistolary forms showed none of the interest of these writers in composing and preserving familiar correspondence.

Many of the letters that did survive, such as those by Derzhavin, eighteenth-century Russia's greatest poet, concern business or service matters. Another poet, V. V. Kapnist, expressed his feelings in letters only on important occasions and then in the stiff, formal prose of his time. His attempts at familiarity do not yield letters of interest to posterity, and lack the humor, playfulness, and ability to convey interesting news in detail that characterize the letters of the Arzamasians.[25] By the time Derzhavin and Kapnist were writing these letters they were turning to lighter forms of poetry than odes. They formed ties of friendship, celebrated friendship in their poetry, and moved in literary circles—a situation similar to that which aided the development of letter writing in the West. By this time the Russian postal system was adequate for personal correspondence between major cities and regional centers.[26] Despite these

---

могуществу имеет природное изобилие, красоту и силу, чем ни единому европейскому языку не уступает.

[24] A more complete survey of such letters is given in my article "Gogol's Epistolary Writing," in *The Dean's Papers, 1969,* ed. Andrew W. Cordier, Columbia Essays in International Affairs, vol. v (New York, 1970), pp. 56–59.

[25] See, for example, his letters to Derzhavin of 20 July 1786 and 10 May 1789 in V. V. Kapnist, *Sobraniye sochineni v dvukh tomakh* (Moscow-Leningrad, 1960), II, 287–88 and 347–48.

[26] Information on the rapid growth of the Russian postal system appears under the entry "Pochta" in the *Entsiklopedicheski slovar* (St. Petersburg: F. A. Brokgaus and I. A. Efron, 1890–1907).

favorable conditions, they and other writers invested scant literary effort in their correspondence.

The violent sentimentality of A. N. Radishchev's letters reflects the changing literary scene of late eighteenth-century Russia, as this letter to his protector shows:

> But what power has the intellect over feeling? From myself I now see that reason follows feelings or is nothing other than they are; according to Helvétius's system, it revolves around one thought, and all my reasoning, all philosophy disappears, when I remember my children. Be charitable to them, dear sir; if your mercies touch and have not yet ceased to pour out onto their unhappy father, do not deprive them of the same, edify and instruct them. I feel that being deprived of their father, they are deprived of so much I cannot imagine it. . . . Before a sensitive soul I pour out my grief.[27]

Radishchev displays his own emotions and, by projecting them into his correspondent, makes the two equals on the emotional plane. Otherwise, their relationship does not differ significantly from that of Lomonosov and his Maecenas, Shuvalov. Radishchev's subjectivity does stand in contrast to the epistolary practice of Lomonosov, whose letter requesting protection revealed his emotions and character through actions—speechlessness, crying, confusion. But Radishchev's reference to Helvétius and the request in the postscript for meteorological instruments show that Radishchev's interests were not entirely exhausted by the contemplation of his own emotions. The letters to Vorontsov, like those of Lomonosov to his patron, are often either informative reports (it was part of a writer's role to educate his patron) or serious requests, with little attention to style or humor. Radishchev wrote nearly half of the letters in French, a practice common among his educated compatriots and one that seriously retarded the development of Russian letter writing. Radishchev, like Lomonosov, tended

[27] A. N. Radishchev, *Polnoye sobraniye sochineni,* 3 vols. (Moscow-Leningrad, 1938–52), III, 346. To A. R. Vorontsov, 20 October 1790.

to limit his letters to a single topic, and his adherence to this convention produced a ludicrous letter to Vorontsov (2 May 1791) in which the postscript on literature is twice as long as the body of the letter, a report on the Siberian economy.

That Russia produced few epistolary manuals during the eighteenth century bears further witness to the relative indifference of Russians to letter writing. The second book published in the new civil (as opposed to ecclesiastical) alphabet was a book of model letters translated from German, *Examples of How Various Compliments Are Written* (*Priklady, kako pishutsya komplimenty raznye,* 4 printings, 1708–25). The relatively brief span of time it was kept in print shows how difficult it was for Peter the Great to mass-produce Russians with the social graces of Voiture.[28] The title of N. I. Kurganov's famous *Primer* (*Pismovnik,* 11 editions, 1769–1837) is generally mistranslated as "handbook of sample letters," since the same Russian word, *pismo,* means both "letter" and "the ability to write." Kurganov's primer enjoyed tremendous popularity for its simplified version of Lomonosov's grammar, occasionally salacious anecdotes, collection of poetry, scientific refutation of superstitions, key to classical mythology, glossary of foreign words, and heroic tales from Russian history. Alas for our purposes, Kurganov included no model letters in this compact encyclopaedia.[29]

Ivan Sokolski, a translator and teacher of French and German at several Moscow schools, wrote the most expansive epistolary manual, *The Office and Mercantile Secretary, or a Collection of the Best and Generally Used Letters* (*Kabinetski i kupecheski sekretar ili sobraniye nailuchshikh i upotrebitelnykh pisem,* 1788). Sokolski offers over three hundred and fifty examples of congratulatory, consoling, familiar, and com-

[28] See G. A. Gukovski, *Russkaya literatura XVIII veka: Uchebnik dlya vysshikh uchebnykh zavedeni* (Moscow, 1939), pp. 11–12.

[29] For a good summary of its content and sources as well as a generous defense of it, see A. Kirpichnikov, "Kurganov i yego 'Pismovnik,' " *Istoricheski vestnik,* 1887, pp. 473–503. Kurganov's humble origin, genuine erudition, and attacks on superstition have made him a heroic figure in Soviet encyclopaedias.

mercial letters. The reader learns how to advise, request, offer services, make recommendations, praise, thank, instruct, make excuses, complain, and mock in epistolary form. Samples of each type are preceded by rules. Such proliferation of categories was common in the European manuals—it helped the reader find the model he needed, even though the categories themselves lacked mutual exclusiveness. Sokolski's models show that he leaned heavily on foreign sources for the content of his letters; he based the content on unaltered French situations and on such hoary recipes as advice to the recipient on how he should arrange his day. The program that Sokolski's imaginary father sets for his son does not differ significantly from that which Erasmus set for a student except that the father is ultimately concerned with his son's success in the civil service and not with learning for its own sake.[30]

Sokolski recommends for letters a language sometimes archaic, even by the standards of his own time, and his selection of letters shows poor taste. Nevertheless, his instructions on letter writing coincided with Western practices. Sokolski helped the merchants and lower civil servants, for whom his book was obviously intended, to ape the salon style of Western correspondence. He told his readers that they must avoid merchant-like errors, crudeness, and the style of *fermiers généraux*.[31] He introduced the essence of familiar correspondence: it should be written as artlessly as the writer speaks, but not too negligently and not as if the writer wanted it shown to the whole world.[32] Sokolski, well aware of the art this artlessness required, gave specific instructions for taming the bombastic style that had dominated eighteenth-century Russian prose—a moderate use of tropes, no forced wit, and no rhythmic constructions or alliteration.[33] Similes should be avoided "in keeping with the taste of the age," as should extremes of

---

[30] Ivan Sokolski, *Kabinetski i kupecheski sekretar ili sobraniye nailuchshikh i upotrebitelnykh pisem*, 2nd ed. (Moscow, 1795), pp. 66–68; *Epistles of Erasmus*, I, 110.

[31] Sokolski, *Kabinetski sekretar*, pp. 12, 30.

[32] *Ibid.*, pp. 9–10.

[33] *Ibid.*, p. 13.

emotion.[34] Sokolski did furnish some examples of the graceful compliments popular in European letters of the seventeenth and eighteenth centuries, but other samples, such as those lifted verbatim from contemporary epistolary novels, violate his rules by using anaphoric constructions and mythological conceits.

Sokolski presented his exhaustive account to a public unreceptive to the salon style or else unwilling to write familiar letters in its native language. Within a few years, however, the literary milieu had changed sufficiently to support a group of writers working creatively within the Western epistolary tradition.

[34] *Ibid.,* pp. 12–16.

II

Arzamas and Its Approach to Epistolary Tradition

> My plan is to settle down with my wife on the
> banks of the Rhine, where I will live quietly as a
> private person, enjoying my happiness in a circle
> of friends.
>
> Alexander I, as quoted in Ye. P. Kovalevski,
> *Graf Bludov i ego vremya,* p. 63.

A brief examination of the Arzamasians' literary milieu and aesthetic, so very different from those of eighteenth-century Russia, suggests why these talented writers devoted their creative energy to familiar letters.

The ascension of Alexander I to the Russian throne in 1801 opened a new era for Russian cultural life, which had been severely constrained during the 1790s under the increasingly repressive reigns of Catherine II (1763–96) and Paul I (1796–1801). Foreign books and travel, forbidden under Paul I, were again permitted. The censorship relaxed; a few new literary journals sprang up.

This amelioration of cultural life did not, however, prove sufficient for the development of a literary profession, independent of patronage and learned academies. A few journals of the early 1800s had the good fortune to see a third year of publication, but most did not. N. M. Karamzin, around whom the Arzamasians later rallied, founded the *Herald of Europe* (*Vestnik Evropy*) to improve Russian manners, to publish original works, and to bring Russia news of European literature and politics. It attracted a multitude of subscribers by the standards of early nineteenth-century Russia—580.[1] Luckily Karamzin and his wife owned several estates; he could not have made a living exclusively through his journalistic

[1] N. M. Karamzin, *Pisma N. M. Karamzina k I. I. Dmitriyevu,* ed. Ya. Grot and P. Pekarski (St. Petersburg, 1866), p. 123. Information on the commercial aspects of early nineteenth-century literary life may

enterprises, which he abandoned in 1803 to become the official historiographer. Nor did the book trade do much to encourage the literary profession; translations of foreign novels far outnumbered native works in the bookstores, and commercial translators occupied an unenviable social and financial position in Russia. Writers were likely to be paid in books, not currency—a fate that most of them deserved. In a situation strikingly similar to that of Imperial Rome, profits from literature generally went to publishers, not authors. No copyright laws effectively protected Russian authors until 1828. In the 1820s, Pushkin finally began to receive respectable advances on his works. But Russia's first truly professional writer had to struggle against literary pirates; a harsh censorship; and his own brother, a social lion who cut Pushkin's profits by spreading his works at literary salons before publication. During the period covered by this study, literature was not yet a profession in Russia.

Despite Alexander's leniency and the writer's inability to make a living by his pen, the imperial court failed to remain the center of Russian literature, as it had been for much of the eighteenth century. Zhukovski and Derzhavin did not greet Alexander's coronation with odes, although they held no ill will toward him. Karamzin wrote a coronation ode to Alexander calling for freedom guaranteed by the rule of law, morality at court, tranquility, and enlightenment.[2] It praised the new emperor as a "man," not a demigod, and concluded on an autobiographical note, which the eighteenth-century ode did not generally do. In the poem Karamzin carefully dis-

---

be found in S. Ya. Gessen, *Knigoizdatel A. S. Pushkin* (Leningrad, 1930); T. Grits, V. Trenin, and M. Nikitin, *Slovesnost i kommertsiya (knizhnaya lavka A. F. Smirdina)*, ed. V. B. Shklovski and B. M. Eykhenbaum (Moscow, 1929); Robert A. Maguire, *Red Virgin Soil: Soviet Literature in the 1920's* (Princeton, 1968), ch. II; A. Meynieux, *La Littérature et le métier d'écrivain en Russie avant Pouchkine* (Paris, 1966); and *Ocherki po istorii russkoy zhurnalistiki i kritiki. Tom pervi: XVIII vek i pervaya polovina XIX veka* (Leningrad, 1950).

[2] "On the Solemn Coronation of his Imperial Highness Alexander I, Autocrat of all the Russias" ("Na torzhestvennoye koronovaniye ego imperatorskogo velichestva Aleksandra I, samoderzhtsa vserossiskogo"), in N. M. Karamzin, *Polnoye sobraniye stikhotvoreni* (Moscow-Leningrad, 1966), pp. 265–70.

tinguished his praise from flattery; elsewhere, in a familiar letter, he revealed a certain distaste for the episode by finding the jeweled snuffbox that the Tsar had given him *"not very shiny."*[3] A memoirist found the odes written on this occasion "rather free, in imitation of Derzhavin."[4] Derzhavin's famous ode to Catherine II, "Felitsa" (1782) had done much to broaden the genre by including satirical details on the Empress's high officials, contrasting her noble simplicity with their vain pursuits.

By the end of the eighteenth century the thematic focus of Russian poetry had shifted from the court to country estates and circles of friends. Karamzin's Sentimentalist verse with its attention to the poet's emotions (especially melancholy) did not exhaust the interests of the period.[5] Derzhavin celebrated the joys of rural life and friendship; Dmitriyev's satirical tales showed man in a social setting, as did Karamzin's cynical "Improvement" ("Ispravleniye," 1797). Karamzin himself asserted that "man is born for society and friendship."[6]

Friendship became one of the major themes of Russian literature. The Sentimentalists' interest in the individual personality and belief in the dignity of all people, based on everyone's ability to feel and love, provided fruitful ground for the cultivation of friendship. The letters of two subsequent Arzamasians, Karamzin and Dmitriyev, are flooded with professions of it as a consolation for life's sorrows. Friendship lent its name to two of the most popular genres of the time— familiar letters (*druzheskiye,* literally "friendly") and familiar

[3] *Pisma Karamzina k Dmitriyevu,* p. 124. Underscored in the original. Catherine II had also rewarded panegyrists with gold snuffboxes.

[4] A. S. Shishkov, *Zapiski, mneniya i perepiska,* ed. and pub. N. Kiselev and Yu. Samarin (Berlin, 1870), I, 81.

[5] N. I. Mordovchenko, *Russkaya kritika pervoy chetverti XIX veka* (Moscow-Leningrad, 1959), gives an excellent analysis of Sentimentalism, but ignores other trends in Russian poetry of the period. G .P. Makogonenko, "Byl li karamzinski period v istorii russkoy literatury?" *Russkaya literatura,* 1960, no. 3, pp. 3–32, seeks to correct this imbalance. R. Neuhäuser, *Toward the Romantic Age: Essays on Sentimental and Preromantic Literature* (The Hague, 1974), offers an encyclopedic survey of the various trends in late eighteenth-century Russia.

[6] N. M. Karamzin, *Izbrannye sochineniya v dvukh tomakh,* ed. P. Berkov (Moscow-Leningrad, 1964), I, 120.

verse epistles (*druzheskiye stikhotvornye poslaniya*). Lomonosov had established the names for these genres, but it remained for the Sentimentalists to realize the literary possibilities of friendship. Among these was the cultivation of the familiar letter, which was the genre most suited to the rejection of official, panegyric literature on one hand and immediate commercial success on the other. Friendship between author and reader spread to other genres as well. No longer did the writer relate to his reader as teacher to pupil or subject to monarch, as he had in Russia during the earlier decades of the eighteenth century.[7] Karamzin's story "The Isle of Bornholm" ("Ostrov Borngolm," 1794) addressed its readers as "friends," as did many other stories and poems.

Freemasonry, strong in Russia during the second half of the eighteenth century, helped make friendship a serious intellectual concern. The Masonic idea of friendship was a more active one than that of the Sentimentalist poets, for whom friendship furnished proof of their ability to feel. The Masons sought truth and self-perfection collectively in closely knit groups of friends, whose secret discussions featured vigorous mutual criticism. Catherine the Great, fearing the revolutionary potential of secret societies, disbanded the Masonic movement, but the principle of learning in groups continued to dominate the schools in which the Masons retained their influence, such as the Nobles' Pension at Moscow University, which educated the future Arzamasians Zhukovski, Dashkov, Kavelin, Voyeykov, Zhikharev, A. I. Turgenev, and N. I. Turgenev. Several of these students formed the Friendly Literary Society (Druzheskoye literaturnoye obshchestvo)[8] to

---

[7] Gukovski, *Russkaya literatura XVIII veka* p. 506.

[8] Analyses of the group's activity appear in V. M. Istrin, "Druzheskoye literaturnoye obshchestvo," *Zhurnal ministerstva narodnogo prosveshcheniya,* 1910, no. 8, pp. 273–307; Yu. M. Lotman, "Andrey Sergeyevich Kaysarov i literaturnoobshchestvennaya borba ego vremeni," *Uchenye zapiski Tartuskogo Gosudarstvennogo Universiteta* 63 (1958), 18–76; and Marcelle Ehrhard, *V. A. Joukovski et la pré-romantisme russe* (Paris, 1938). Concentrating on political dissentions within the group, Lotman argues against any Masonic influence on its thinking. However, the group's organization and moral seriousness reveal the influence of Masonry.

41

lend each other support in their moral and literary development. They delivered solemn speeches and objected to the
frivolity of Moscow Sentimentalism, but this did not preclude
the professions of friendship that filled their correspondence.
The Masonic movement and its offshoots also cultivated feeling; its idea of friendship complemented the Sentimentalist
one and was not incompatible with it.

Friendship captivated Russian thought and literature. Even
the future Tsar, who earlier in the century would have expected to be celebrated as a demigod, was sensible to its
allure, as we see in the epigraph to this chapter. Zhukovski's
patriotic poem "A Minstrel in the Camp of the Russian War-
riors" ("Pevets vo stane russkikh voinov," 1812), unlike the
Russian military odes of the eighteenth century not only
praises the Tsar and his generals, but also extols the friendship
among the soldiers. A line from this poem, "For friendship all
there is in the world," echoed through the correspondence of
Arzamas. By 1822 Pushkin could think of no more pervasive
cliché of the period's refined periphrastic style than "friendship, that sacred feeling whose noble flame . . ." (XI, 18). In
Eugene Onegin Pushkin extinguishes the parodic poet Vladimir Lenski for his blind faith in the reality of this literary
convention. Lenski, who makes human relationships into
civilized rituals, projects his sentimental friendship into the
shallow Eugene, who treats society as a vicious competition,
and receives a bullet in return.

A change in the language of Russian literature accompanied
the movement of poetry away from the court. A convoluted,
latinate syntax and a lexicon of liturgical provenance (Church
Slavonic) had marked the lofty style of odes, epics, tragedies,
and oratorical prose. However, a wave of reaction against the
bombastic style, inappropriate to the expression of intimate
feelings and personal relationships, had steadily swelled during
the eighteenth century. Even one of its most skilled practitioners, V. K. Trediakovski, found Church Slavonic harsh

and unacceptable for secular love stories as early as 1730.[9] Letters proved the beneficiaries of this search for a less ornate style.

For help in changing the Russian literary language writers turned to the educated, Westernized portion of Russian society, whose cultural model was the French salon of the seventeenth and eighteenth centuries. The poet and educator M. N. Muravyev, whose works were later published by the Arzamasians Karamzin, Batyushkov, and Zhukovski, gives us some sense of what the Russian writer sought in the discourse of polite society: a lexicon free of technical and scholastic terminology but capable of expressing tender emotions and personal relationships; a less convoluted, shorter, and more natural period; a carefully studied "casual" manner—in other words, the style of the aristocrat of leisure and general culture, the *honnête homme*. Among the writers who mastered this style Muravyev features an epistolarian, Mme de Sévigné:

There was no man of the court or noble lady who could not express himself pleasantly and who would not have listed among his advantages the ability to write and speak his native language well. Many ladies, the ornament of their sex, poured the innate and inimitable graces of their minds into works, seemingly light and careless, but which no art could counterfeit: Mme de Sévigné, Mme de Lafayette and others. The isolated scholar could not have captured these tender turns of phrase, introduced by the usage of society.[10]

However, Russian writers found the most aristocratic layer of Russian society imitating its French counterpart only too thoroughly; aristocrats were speaking not their native language

[9] From his preface to a translation of "Voyage à l'île d'amour," in S. P. Obnorski and S. G. Barkhudarov, eds., *Khrestomatiya po istorii russkogo yazyka* (Moscow, 1948–49), vol. II, part ii, pp. 149–50.

[10] Quoted in V. V. Vinogradov, *Ocherki po istorii russkogo literaturnogo yazyka XVII–XIX vv*, 2nd ed. (Moscow, 1938), p. 173. Vinogradov provides an extensive description of the Russian salon style, pp. 148–88.

but French. This of course inhibited the growth of Russian-speaking salons on the French model, with lively discussions of all fields of knowledge. In Paris such visitors as Horace Walpole could converse on literature and politics in the language of their hosts. In Petersburg high society spoke French, which eliminated Russian literature from the topics of conversation. The opening of Tolstoy's *War and Peace* at Anna Sherer's salon accurately reflects this situation. Karamzin's essay, "Why There Are Few Authorial Talents in Russia" ("Otchego v Rossii malo avtorskikh talantov," 1802) grimly describes a lack of interaction between Russian literature and polite society. Karamzin complains that the French writer can tame his school rhetoric in the *grand monde* and can write according to its spoken usage, but the aspiring Russian author, faces a literature lacking in subtle ideas and incapable of pleasantly expressing the most ordinary thoughts. When the author turns to society he finds it speaking French, disgusted by the crudeness of the Russian literary language. He can only invent expressions and guess at the right word.[11] Karamzin's indictment was devastating, for the Enlightenment aesthetics upon which he based his criticism appealed to the consensus (taste) of society as literary arbitrator rather than to abstract rules.

During the years following Karamzin's pessimistic essay many members of high society answered the writers' interest by adopting literature as a favorite diversion. It was a truly symbiotic relationship. Literature provided appropriately entertaining genres for social occasions. Russian verse, bouts-rimés, and epigrams were read at balls, suppers, and other assemblies. Young ladies of fashion kept albums in which friends and admirers would write gallant verse, compliments, and madrigals. In such genres as familiar letters, verse satires, and comedies of manners, Russian writers treated the every-

---

[11] Karamzin, *Izbrannye sochineniya,* II, 183–87. F. F. Vigel, visiting the circles in which Karamzin moved, noted sadly that, among all these people, only Karamzin tried to speak Russian. F. F. Vigel, ed. S. Ya. Shtraykh, 2 vols. (Moscow, 1928), II, 34.

day life of polite society. Society responded by distributing and criticizing literature, a function only partially fulfilled by Russia's unstable and still immature periodical press.[12] Batyushkov settled literary disputes with his friend N. I. Gnedich by appealing to the judgment of their frequent hostess Samarina (III, 111). The Arzamasians subsequently did much to further the prestige of Russian journals, but they relied mainly on their familiar correspondence and on discussions for intelligent criticism of their works.

Several factors reinforced this lively interest in literature. Russian education of the early nineteenth century prepared the gentry for it. A knowledge of languages and literature helped the children make their way in society and in the Foreign College, the most prestigious branch of the civil service. Children learned French (less frequently German, Italian, and English) at home with tutors. The best schools prepared boys to become useful servants of the state, but this orientation did not preclude an education that focused on French literature of the age of Neoclassicism, as Vyazemski later recalled: "My mind was raised and formed in the French school. I learned other foreign languages and studied German, English, and Italian literature at various times, but these were more or less accidental acquaintances. My ties grew stronger with French literature alone, especially that of the past century."[13] Pupils of the Imperial Lycée near St. Petersburg and of the Nobles' Pension at Moscow University followed a similarly cosmopolitan curriculum, with the emphasis again on French literature and the Neoclassical aesthetics that encouraged precision and clarity.[14] Foreigners taught in these schools and directed several others; Batyushkov studied at a

[12] M. I. Aronson, "Kruzhki i salony," in M. I. Aronson and S. A. Reyser, eds., *Literaturnye kruzhki i salony* (Leningrad, 1929), p. 30.

[13] P. A. Vyazemski, *Polnoye sobraniye sochineni*, 12 vols. (St. Petersburg, 1878–96), I, lviii.

[14] The curricula of these schools are described in B. V. Tomashevski, *Pushkin*, vol. I (Moscow-Leningrad, 1956), pp. 11–15, and in Ehrhard, *V. A. Joukovski*, pp. 15–41. N. A. Hans, *History of Russian Educational Policy, 1701–1917* (New York, 1964), provides further information on Russian education during this period.

French pension in St. Petersburg; Vyazemski and Severin, at a Jesuit one.

Once a young man had finished this literary education, he found that a number of writers and cultural figures occupied prominent positions in society and government. Most writers, including the Arzamasians, belonged to the gentry. The poets Derzhavin and Dmitriyev were government ministers; A. N. Olenin (President of the Academy of Arts) and Admiral A. S. Shishkov (President of the Russian Academy) held high government posts. All liked to surround themselves with young literary people; thus, a knowledge of literature and the ability to write it—together with charm and some sort of introduction —became an *entrée* into social and governmental circles. Gnedich, a serious poet and translator of the *Iliad,* saw through this behavior: "our youth labors little specifically for literature and tries to fall in with littérateurs merely for some special ends and maybe out of having nothing else to do."[15] Gnedich himself, although of undistinguished Ukrainian origin, received a sinecure in the Public Library and a government pension through his participation in the Olenin salon.

Society turned its attention to literature and literary language not only for reasons of entertainment, education, and careerism. The intellectual conditions of Russia supported such a turn, if only by default. Although the prerequisites for a lively political debate existed—various types of resistance to Alexander's reforming posture as well as support for it—a solid, continuous tradition of political discussion did not.[16] Russians of the time tended to express political opinion in emotional terms or in bureaucratic maneuvering. Alexander's ultimate plans were a mystery to the public. Karamzin's defense of the autocracy, *Memoir on Ancient and Modern Russia* (*Zapiska o staroy i novoy Rossii,* 1811), was not published for

[15] Quoted in S. P. Zhikharev, *Zapiski sovremennika,* ed. B. M. Eykhenbaum (Moscow-Leningrad, 1955), p. 427.

[16] Richard Pipes, "The Background and Growth of Karamzin's Political Ideas down to 1810," introduction to *Karamzin's Memoir on Ancient and Modern Russia: A Translation and Analysis,* ed. and trans. Richard Pipes (Cambridge, Mass., 1959), p. 89.

over twenty years. The greatest public debate of the 1800s and 1810s—on the origins and future of the Russian literary language—was an obviously literary one, but it encompassed the cultural and political issues of the day, especially the eternal Russian problem of relations with the West. The polemical battles raged not only in articles and books but also in verse, drama, salons, closed literary circles, and familiar letters. From the quarrel emerged the subsequently typical Russian situation in which literature and literary criticism had to bear the full weight of political and social issues.

Admiral Shishkov, President of the Russian Academy, opened the debate in 1803 with his *Consideration of the Old and New Styles of the Russian Language (Rassuzhdeniya o starom i novom sloge rossiskogo yazyka)*. In it and subsequent articles the arch-conservative Shishkov took issue with the Sentimentalist, Karamzinian reforms of the language and defended Church Slavonic as the basis of the literary language and of Russian civilization. Specifically, he objected to periphrastic avoidance of concrete imagery, calques from French, and the loss of synonyms from various stylistic levels, which resulted from the use of a single style by Karamzin's imitators. Shishkov believed with his age that language could be transparent to thought and not becloud or distort it. He defended the Neoclassical norm of "clarity" and "purity" no less rigorously than the Arzamasians, but he believed that Russian based on Church Slavonic and uncorrupted by French was the surest means of achieving them.

Shishkov's polemics were not without justice and value. He appreciated the stylistic possibilities of the Russian language and Russian folklore; he also inspired essays on the history of the language. And it cannot be denied that some of Karamzin's epigones had indeed made the Sentimentalist style flaccid and monotonous. However, Shishkov's sarcasm and his unfortunate habit of arguing by innuendo inhibited and debased the controversy. He felt, wrongly, that the Sentimentalists' use of a single style rather than a hierarchy of styles reflected political egalitarianism, considered ignorance of Church Slavonic a

47

sign of apostasy, and attacked the morals of those who dared oppose him. And Shishkov's linguistic studies had a clear political purpose: believing that language was identical with thought, Shishkov felt that no Russian could conceive such a pernicious French idea as "revolution" once the French loan word for it *(revolyutsiya)* were removed from the Russian language.

The tendency of Soviet scholarship to concentrate on the conservative political implications of Shishkov's writings has illustrated the extent to which literary discussion absorbed other fields of interest in the early nineteenth century.[17] Shishkov certainly reaped political profit from his literary activities —he became Secretary of State and Minister of Education in periods of gallophobia and national conservatism—but his genuine commitment to the study of literature and literary language cannot be doubted. He continued to plod along at his etymology, eventually writing a book on it. In accordance with the fashion of the times, Shishkov wrote light verse, hired a French tutor for his nephews, translated Tasso from Italian, and lent his house for amateur theatricals.[18]

Such paradoxes thrive in an age in which respect for social obligations confounds intellectual consistency. Shishkov's formation of the "Colloquium of Lovers of the Russian Word" ("Beseda lyubiteley russkogo slova," 1811–16) hardly resolved them. The Besedists met in Derzhavin's palatial Petersburg town house, dressed in formal attire, and sat according to plan. The membership, however, was as motley as the

[17] Mordovchenko, *Russkaya kritika,* pp. 77–98, summarizes the polemic in detail. V. V. Vinogradov, *Yazyk Pushkina: Pushkin i istoriya russkogo literaturnogo yazyka* (Moscow-Leningrad, 1935), discusses its linguistic aspects. Political ramifications of the debate are analyzed in B. S. Meylakh, "A. S. Shishkov i 'Beseda lyubiteley russkogo slova,'" *Istoriya russkoy literatury,* vol. v (Moscow-Leningrad, 1941), pp. 183–97. Excerpts from the polemics of both sides appear in M. G. Zeldovich and L. Ya. Livshits, eds., *Russkaya literatura XIX v.: Khrestomatiya kriticheskikh materialov,* 3rd. ed. (Moscow, 1967), pp. 28–39.

[18] S. T. Aksakov, "Vospominaniye ob Aleksandre Semenoviche Shishkove," *Sobraniye sochineni v pyati tomakh* (Moscow, 1966), II, 258–303.

organization was rigid. It can be explained by combinations of family, class, service, and literary ties. The Beseda absorbed two groups, the Olenin salon and the Derzhavin circle, *en masse,* thus adopting some whose literary orientation and political views were not particularly conservative. S. N. Marin satirized the Emperor Paul and translated Voltaire. D. P. Gorchakov wrote blasphemous satires. P. Yu. Lvov began his literary career as a contributor to Karamzin's Sentimentalist *Moscow Journal* (*Moskovski zhurnal,* 1791–92) and did not abandon this orientation to participate in the Beseda; in the society's journal his Sentimentalist works appear alongside Shishkov's speeches and Derzhavin's essay on the ode. The zealous Arzamasians Zhikharev and Uvarov also belonged; they had relatives in the Beseda. Nor were the members of uniform social class and governmental rank, as the Soviet "vulgar sociologists" intimated.[19] I. A. Krylov, for example, was a cardsharp and a rather déclassé member of the lower gentry— as well as Russia's most brilliant fabulist.

"The Arzamas Society of Obscure People" ("Arzamasskoye obshchestvo bezvestnykh lyudey") formed officially in St. Petersburg in 1815 in reaction against Shishkov's Beseda and its members, some of whom, such as the playwright A. A. Shakhovskoy, had attacked Karamzin and Zhukovski in literary satire. Arzamas shared the interests of its time: familiar correspondence, stylistic controversy, the cult of friendship, the appeal to polite society for literary instruction, and the fashionable obsession with literature. These interests as well as a complex web of intellectual, educational, family, and service relationships had brought them together in Moscow before the War of 1812. Not all of the Arzamasians could afford to gamble away hundreds of thousands of roubles as

[19] D. Blagoy, "Sotsialno-politicheskoye litso Arzamasa," introduction to M. S. Borovkova-Maykova, ed. *"Arzamas" i "arzamasskiye" protokoly* (Leningrad, 1933), finds the Beseda's orientation conservative, feudal, typical of the upper gentry, and opposed to the French style and ideas, pp. 5–9.

Vyazemski did, but even the least affluent (such as Vigel, Zhikharev, and Severin) managed to receive a fine education and make good careers through family connections and the opportunities for advancement in literary life. During the years in which they met as a group, 1815–18, none of them was a professional writer of imaginative literature; Karamzin, Zhukovski, and Voyeykov—official historiographer, tutor to the royal family, and professor of Russian literature at Dorpat University, respectively—came the closest. The others held posts in the civil or military service, supplementing their salaries with the income from their estates.

This amateur standing and the publication of the fascinatingly frivolous minutes of their meetings has spurred no end of controversy over the seriousness and influence of Arzamas.[20] As individuals, however, their impact on the first decades of the nineteenth century cannot be denied. Pushkin, Batyushkov, and Zhukovski were the finest poets of the time. Vyazemski, Zhikharev, and Vigel wrote memoirs of enduring interest. Karamzin, Zhukovski, Vyazemski, Voyeykov, and Pushkin edited important journals, which, together with the essays of Batyushkov, Dashkov, and Uvarov, did much to shape the literary taste of the time.

As the Arzamasians did not constitute an entirely monolithic body, a brief survey of their public criticism will illustrate the approaches to literature that underlay their epistolary practice. Karamzin, like Pushkin after him, was primarily concerned with strengthening secular literature as an institution. Believing that national greatness could be achieved only through culture, he sought to encourage writers, to suggest themes for works, to find a Russian literary language capable of appealing to polite society, to prove the morality of literature, and to spread literacy and good taste. His essays are oriented toward the consumers of literature; even when he is discussing the emotions of the writer, he wonders how these

---

[20] Gillelson's studies of Vyazemski, *P. A. Vyazemski: Zhizn i tvorchestvo* (Leningrad, 1969), and Arzamas, *Molodoy Pushkin i arzamasskoy bratstvo* (Leningrad, 1974), provide summaries of the debate.

emotions will effect the reader.[21] Since squabbles of the sort that marred eighteenth-century literary life were inconsistent with the refinement of manners, and since he hoped to encourage young writers, Karamzin made it his policy not to criticize contemporary works.

Several years after Karamzin abandoned journalism, Zhukovski turned his attention to the state of Russian literature. Like Karamzin, he was concerned with questions of morality in literature; but unlike Karamzin, who had encountered a certain hostility toward imaginative literature among Masonic friends, he did not feel the need to justify all aspects of literary activity. Zhukovski's essay "On Criticism" ("O kritike," 1809) cautiously takes issue with Karamzin's refusal to criticize contemporary works. Zhukovski sets rules of impartiality and civility to forestall the objection that criticism is offensive and discouraging to young talent. He further justifies criticism by making it a branch of moral philosophy: criticism helps form moral feeling since it calls attention to beauty in art, which is analogous to the Good (moral beauty) in nature.[22]

Zhukovski went beyond Karamzin not only in justifying the criticism of living authors but also in practicing it. The respect for genres, models, rules, and such Neoclassical authorities as

[21] "Style, figures, metaphors, images, expressions—all of these touch and captivate us only when they are animated by feeling; if it does not fire the imagination of the writer, then never will my tear, never will my smile be his reward." From Karamzin's essay "What Does an Author Need?" ("Chto nuzhno avtoru," 1794), *Izbrannye sochineniya,* II, 122. This derives, by way of Boileau and French Neoclassicism, from Horace's *Ars poetica,* "Non satis est pulchra esse poemata. . . . Si vis me flere, dolendum est primum ipsi tibi." For an outline of the history of the emotions' role in literary theory, see M. H. Abrams, *The Mirror and the Lamp: Romantic Theory and the Critical Tradition* (1953; reprint, New York: Norton, 1958), chapter IV. Translations of Karamzin's essays may be found in Segel, *Literature of Eighteenth-Century Russia,* I, 427–469. English versions of Pushkin's criticism appear in Tatiana A. Wolff, ed. *Pushkin on Literature* (London, 1971) and Carl Proffer, *The Critical Prose of Alexander Pushkin with Critical Essays by Four Russian Romantic Poets* (Bloomington, 1969).

[22] V. A. Zhukovski, *Polnoye sobraniye sochineni v dvenadtsati tomakh* (St. Petersburg, 1902), IX, 96.

51

La Harpe that Zhukovski revealed in the essay on criticism is more forcefully stated in the essay "On Fables and on the Fables of Krylov" ("O basne i o basnyakh Krylova," 1809). This article, a rare example of practical criticism in the early nineteenth century, sets out the rules for fables, distinguishes several trends in the history of fable writing, and with remarkable impartiality compares the fables of La Fontaine, Dmitriyev (an Arzamasian), and Krylov (a Besedist). However, it is hardly a new direction in criticism. Curiously enough, Zhukovski, who is often called the father of Russian Romanticism, failed to use his articles and letters as a vehicle for new critical departures, and as late as 1849 he expressed respect for La Harpe even in the relaxation of his epistolary work.[23]

Batyushkov offered a third approach, "the science of the poet's life" (II, 120). Unlike Karamzin and Zhukovski, Batyushkov did not edit journals, and he wrote his essays from the poet's point of view. To him the study of rules and the observation of models were necessary for a poet, but insufficient. The poet could master the "art of expression" only by following the rule "live as you write and write as you live" (II, 120). In his essay "Something about the Poet and Poetry" ("Nechto o poete i poezii," 1815), Batyushkov manipulated the lives of a number of French, Italian, and Russian poets to show how they had followed this rule. This critical orientation toward the poet (not the work, the audience, or the subject of the work), characterized by M. H. Abrams as an "expressive theory" of literature,[24] became increasingly popular with the rise of Romanticism. But Batyushkov's letters show his continuing attachment to Neoclassical criteria. Soon after writing these articles Batyushkov redirected his attention to the poetry inspired by polite society, which had taught Russian poets "to fathom the secret play of passions, to observe manners, to

[23] V. A. Zhukovski, *Sobraniye sochineni v chetyrekh tomakh,* ed. I. M. Semenko et al. (Moscow-Leningrad, 1959–60), IV, 664. Letter to A. S. Sturdza, 10 March 1849.

[24] Abrams, *Mirror and the Lamp,* pp. 21–26.

preserve all social conditions and relationships, to speak clearly, lightly, and pleasantly" (II, 243).[25]

A fourth important critic among the Arzamasians, Vyazemski, took less interest in developing a consistent approach to literature than in using criticism as a vehicle for satire, polemics, and penetrating comments on the literary scene. Vyazemski objected to Zhukovski's reliance on rules and models (such as La Fontaine for fables). Nevertheless, in the same article Vyazemski himself proposed models (such as Karamzin and French society) and used decidedly Neoclassical criteria: proportion between thought and decoration, logic, pleasantness and usefulness of subject, and "pictures."[26] Like Batyushkov, Zhukovski, and Karamzin, he expected writers to know the language and manners of society.[27] (In a later chapter we shall study this demand for "verisimilitude" in Pushkin's letters.)

Uniting these somewhat disparate strands is a common understanding of enlightenment, which Zhukovski defines as "the art of living, the art of perfecting oneself in that circle in which the Hand of Providence has enclosed you."[28] Enlightenment is first of all something one practices oneself, living harmoniously in groups of friends and in the family circle, accepting the inevitability of many human problems, and believing that this enlightenment (learning and civility) is the only means to individual and collective progress. The seriousness of the Arzamasians' belief echoes in Karamzin's ringing

[25] "On the Influence of Light Poetry on the Language" ("O vliyanii legkoy poezii na yazyk"), 1816.

[26] Vyazemski, "Sochineniye v proze V. Zhukovskogo," *Polnoye sobraniye sochineni,* I, 260–69. For discussions of the emphasis on pictorial representation in Neoclassical criticism, see William K. Wimsatt, Jr. and Cleanth Brooks, *Literary Criticism: A Short History* (New York, 1957), pp. 252–82; and K. V. Pigarev, *Russkaya literatura i izobrazitelnoye iskusstvo, XVIII–pervaya chetvert XIX veka: Ocherki* (Moscow, 1966).

[27] For example, Vyazemski condemned a journal, *The Son of the Fatherland (Syn otechestva)* for not knowing the first rules of society. "Pismo v Parizhe," *Polnoye sobraniye sochineni,* I, 202.

[28] Zeldovich and Livshits, *Khrestomatiya,* p. 51.

53

phrases: "Let us repeat the unquestionable truth: in the nineteenth century only that nation can be great and respected that by the noble arts, literature, and learning assists the successes of mankind in its glorious course toward the goal of moral and spiritual perfection."[29]

Batyushkov's treatment of Voltaire casts this Arzamasian interpretation of enlightenment into sharper relief. Visiting the château at Cirey where Voltaire had lived with Mme du Châtelet, Batyushkov wrote a Sentimentalist hagiography of Voltaire as cultivator of the château's English garden and votary of friendship, love, the Muses, and liberty (II, 51–72). The Voltaire who inspired the French Revolution disappears. In the sphere of politics, this interpretation of the Enlightenment precluded radical transformation of existing systems and favored, as Richard Pipes has noted, a form of government that would grant the individual the security to pursue these modest pleasures.[30]

Civility and literacy cannot be imposed by governmental or authorial ukase but must be communicated to the reader by example, by the illustration of their pleasures and benefits, and by the involvement of the reader in them as a participant; hence the relationship of friendship between narrators and their created readers that we observed earlier. Familiar letters occupy a central position in such a process of enlightenment. The epistolarian generally appears cloaked in this harmonious ideal of learning and civility (as we shall see in a later chapter on characterization), but for the larger public he does so *indirectly,* in writing for his friend, not in an openly didactic, sermonical fashion. The familiar letter's intimacy and self-irony are shields against this sort of preaching.

The social situation of Arzamas combined with its intellectual position to make the familiar letter a genre of more than casual interest to the group. Letter writing is an art that an amateur can practice in the leisure that his career and social obligations afford. It became especially important to the

[29] Karamzin, *Izbrannye sochineni,* II, 198.
[30] Pipes, *Karamzin's Memoir,* pp. 36–37.

Arzamasians, whose commitment to the ideals of the Enlightenment—education, cosmopolitanism, the rule of law—in many
cases found expression through successful careers in the
Ministries of Popular Education, Foreign Affairs, and Justice,
and not through literary works of massive scale.

It is not surprising that, given their attitudes toward enlightenment, the future Arzamasians had greeted the formation
of Shishkov's xenophobic Beseda with disdain. A letter from
Severin to Vyazemski articulates their feelings:

> You want me to say something about the Beseda. . . .
> March 14 [1811] I was at the opening and first public
> meeting of this worthy society. Imagine a large hall,
> adorned with columns and many so-called visitors, in the
> middle, a table covered with a green cloth. Around the
> table sat the members, behind them, in the second row,
> the honorary members, amongst whom—Bunina and
> Volkova. That's the Beseda. The first meeting was opened
> with the works of the first section. Its chairman, the
> glorious pale figure Shishkov, read, without stopping for
> two hours, a speech on the merits of the Russian word,
> in which this rhetorician forgot the rules of logic and
> common sense. He incessantly confuses the gift of speech
> in general with the Russian language. That's awful! In
> addition, the speech was based on the comparison of
> man with animals and on the advantages of the former.
> Scoffers say that they don't see any difference between
> Shishkov and an owl, but that's a bad joke. After the
> speech Prince Gorchakov, like Count Khvostov in all
> respects, read a dithyramb to immortality, not a transla-
> tion of Delille, but his own work. Then three fables by
> Krylov rewarded us in full measure for our patience.[31]

Shishkov draws criticism for his abuse of language and
common sense, the faculties by which the age of Neoclassicism

[31] Tsentralni gosudarstvenni arkhiv literatury i iskusstva, Ostafyevski arkhiv, 195/1/2727, sheets 155–56.

distinguished men from animals—hence the comparison of Shishkov with an owl. The ironic use of "rhetorician" and "dithyramb" contrasts the pretentions of Shishkov and Gorchakov with their less than impressive achievements, accentuates their stiffness, and links them with traditions distasteful to adherants of the salon aesthetic. The formal seating, interminable speech, and division into sections seemed tasteless to those used to the movement and conversation of informal gatherings, in which everyone was expected to participate—hence the comic conjunction of columns and visitors. Comparison with Count Khvostov, an inept graphomaniac, further damns the Beseda. The poetesses Bunina and Volkova evoke scorn because a woman's place in salon culture was rarely a creative one.[32] Since Severin was writing to a friend and fellow thinker, he did not find it necessary to articulate his position in greater detail; irony and comic comparisons sufficed to illustrate his distaste for the proceedings and did not unbend his gentlemanly pose of civilized disdain.

The Arzamasians elected to make their literary society a playful one.[33] Vigel confessed: "To cut ourselves further off from the world, we renounced the names we bore in it and took new titles from Zhukovski's ballads."[34] (Zhukovski's tastefully restrained literary ballads had been the focus of Shakhovskoy's satire and ridicule.[35] The name of their society

[32] Chauncey Brewster Tinker, *The Salon and English Letters. Chapters on the Interrelations of Literature and Society in the Age of Johnson* (1915; reprint, New York, 1967), pp. 27–28. This study provides an excellent history of salon culture in Italy, France, and England.

[33] I use the analysis of play set forth in Johan Huizinga, *Homo Ludens: A Study of the Play Element in Culture* (1950; reprint, Boston, 1955).

[34] Vigel, *Zapiski,* II, 67.

[35] Shakhovskoy's comedy *A Lesson for Coquettes, Or the Spa of Lipetsk (Urok koketkam, ili Lipetskiye Vody,* 1815) ridicules the implied author of Zhukovski's ballads in the person of a tearful, sentimental, infatuated minstrel, devastated by the common sense of all around him, including the lady he writes for. Shakhovskoy's parodies

also took the Arzamasians far from the hostile literary world of St. Petersburg. Arzamas is a town in the Nizhni Novgorod (now Gorki) area.[36] Their play had its specifically delimited time and space; they defined their meeting place as anywhere (the antithesis of Beseda formality) and measured time from the literary events that led to their society's founding. Naturally, these nicknames, places, and events freely entered their letters.

Arzamas transformed the world of its enemies by allegoric fantasy, parody, satire, and travesty—techniques that also contributed to their epistolary manner. Literature played a prominent role in the social rituals of the age, and Arzamas applied literary techniques—parody and travesty—not only to the works but also to the organizing rituals of other groups. As in a learned academy, new members of Arzamas delivered eulogies, in this case to still living members of the Beseda and the Russian Academy. Dashkov's "Arzamas Cantata," sung at their meetings, parodies a patriotic cantata that Derzhavin composed for the Beseda.[37] Masonic organizations did not escape the all-inclusive spirit of parody; Arzamas kept the form (secrecy, protocols, speeches, initiation rite, and oath), but discarded the solemnity, of the Masonic content.

---

isolate the precious and fantastic elements in the lexicon of Zhukovski's ballads (roses, modest cottage, incense, temples, midnight, corpses), Zhukovski's extensive use of emotional epithets (especially "dear"), his sentimental interpretation of antiquity (the infatuated Homer sang of Achilles so that Chloe would smile), and the coyness of his fantastic ballads ("And oh! . . . everything is frightful in them; but for the dear ones all is pleasant"). To judge by the Arzamasians' outraged reaction, the parodies hit their mark. See A. A. Shakhovskoy, *Komedii, stikhotvoreniya* (Leningrad, 1961), pp. 119–264.

[36] Nabokov's keen ear finds Arzamas "a kind of incomplete anagram of Karamzin." A. S. Pushkin, *Eugene Onegin,* trans. Vladimir Nabokov, 4 vols., rev. ed., Bollingen Series LXXII (Princeton University Press, 1975) III, 172. Karamzin in fact owned an estate near the town and visited it several times during the 1810s; this association may provide the most likely explanation for the choice of the name.

[37] G. R. Derzhavin, *Stikhotvoreniya,* ed. G.A. Gukovski (Leningrad, 1933), pp. 378–79, contains Derzhavin's cantata. Dashkov's parody may be found in Aronson and Reyser, *Literaturnye kruzhki i salony,* pp. 94–95.

The formal meetings of Arzamas consisted of the reading of minutes (usually by Zhukovski), mock eulogies, welcoming speeches, and dinners of roast goose. Although the absent Moscow members V. L. Pushkin, Batyushkov, and Vyazemski provided many of the jokes and images for Arzamas, it was Zhukovski who established the characteristic Arzamasian technique: "Arzamasian criticism should ride horseback on galimatias."[38]

The Russian word *galimatiya* comes from the French word (used by Molière, Le Sage, and—in a verb derived from the noun—Rabelais) *galimatias,* meaning "a confused mixture," "grandiloquent nonsense." In Russian it conveys these same meanings, both now and at the beginning of the nineteenth century. The word captures the unfailing humorous exuberance of Arzamas and implies its harmlessness. However, Zhukovski told Karamzin that "Galimatias does not always spring from madness and does not always mean nonsense."[39] The Arzamasians' protocols, like their letters and like Pushkin's *Eugene Onegin,* constitute an all-inclusive critical survey of the literature and literary organizations of their time. The Arzamasians also took advantage of the privacy of their circle to criticize each other's works by parody and travesty. Karamzin and Zhukovski had persuaded the Arzamasians to avoid public quarrels; public criticism of the powerful Besedists might have proved disadvantageous to their careers. Open criticism of a friend would have violated the ties of friendship so sacred to the age; but the tradition of mutual criticism within circles let them vent their critical impulses against anything in view. One of the group's private targets was a public target of the Besedists: Zhukovski's ballads.

The Arzamasians' speeches translated the fantastic, folkloric elements of Zhukovski's ballads into a tradition of the supernatural that was acceptable to Neoclassicism: the allegorical apparatus of mock epics. As, for example, in Canto IV of

[38] Quoted by Dashkov in a letter to Vyazemski of 26 November 1815, "Pisma D. V. Dashkova: Vyderzhki iz starykh bumag Ostafyevskogo Arkhiva," *Russki arkhiv,* 1866, p. 499.

[39] Borovkova-Maykova, *"Arzamasskiye" protokoly,* p. 159.

Pope's "Rape of the Lock," the supernatural creatures of the protocols enter comic situations or possess petty, unattractive human features. Thus Zhukovski's ballad monsters become petulant Besedists. The Arzamasians stripped Zhukovski's supernatural of its terrors and rendered it harmless by stylistic exaggeration, which accentuated its literary, rather than its existential, nature. To the extent that the Arzamasian speeches follow typical details and events of the ballads (demons, moonlight magic, corpses rising from the dead), they are parodic. The Arzamasians loved Zhukovski as a friend and considered him a master stylist—his criticism, as we have seen, did not depart drastically from Neoclassical tenets—but antagonistic parody served them as a means of differentiating their poetic system from his. Even though the features of the ballads may have been used to ridicule the Beseda, the inseparability of the form and content of a literary work spreads the conflagration of satire from the content to the organizing form. Statements by the Arzamasians about Zhukovski's ballads support this hypothesis. From 1812–18 Batyushkov and Karamzin constantly urged him to write a long narrative poem on a subject from Russian history or something more worthy of his talents than ballads, which Batyushkov placed on a level with chapbooks, the pulp literature of that time (III, 111). Vigel's memoirs speak for the Arzamasians:

> Zhukovski took to German literature and treated us to its works, which in form and content were not quite to our taste. Nourished by the literature of the ancients and by French literature, its humble imitator . . . , we saw something monstrous in his selections. Corpses, ghosts, devils, murders illuminated by moonlight. . . . Instead of Hero, awaiting the drowning Leander with tender trepidation, he presented us the madly passionate Lenore with the leaping corpse of her lover.[40]

Parody here does not work as an accelerator of literary change, as in Tynyanov's famous theory, but as a brake.[41]

[40] Vigel, *Zapiski,* I, 343.
[41] See Tynyanov, "Stikhovye formy Nekrasova" and "Dostoyevski i Gogol (k teorii parodii)," *Arkhaisty i novatory,* pp. 399–455.

In the course of their formal meetings the Arzamasians came to create visions of visions of visions, stretching their parodistic techniques to the breaking point. By 1818 the most talented members had given their initiation speeches. As a distant relative of Shishkov (Vladimir Nabokov) notes in his commentary to *Eugene Onegin* (III, 172–73), other Arzamasians repeated the same jokes until they became stale.

A sense of victory also contributed to the downfall of the Arzamasians. Derzhavin died in 1816 and, frustrating Shishkov's hopes, did not will his home to the Beseda. The Beseda promptly folded. The other butt of Arzamas, the Russian Academy, accepted Karamzin and Zhukovski into its membership and was soon listening to Karamzin's defense of cosmopolitanism and enlightenment. Karamzin, in one of his final public appearances, 5 December 1818, told these idealizers of pre-Petrine Russia that Russia's break with the Middle Ages had been completed, that Russians write like foreigners do because they read and live as foreigners do, that languages change, that usage and not academies must produce new words.[42] In their letters, which served among other things as chronicles, the cosmopolitan Arzamasians considered this their ultimate triumph, marred only by the pedantry of an academician who objected to a French loan word in the speech.[43] But this victory mollified the Arzamasian animus against their opponents to such an extent that it could no longer serve as a unifying force.

A new political seriousness in the air helped stifle the spirit of galimatias. Officers returning from the European campaign, including M. F. Orlov, Nikita Muravyev, and N. I. Turgenev, were seized with enthusiasm for liberal institutions, secret political societies, and mass education by the Lancaster system. Through ties of family and friendship the three joined Arza-

[42] Karamzin, *Izbrannye sochineni,* II, 233–42.
[43] P. A. Vyazemski, *Ostafyevski arkhiv knyazey Vyazemskikh,* ed. V. I. Saitov, 5 vols. (St. Petersburg, 1899), I, 167. From A. I. Turgenev's letter to Vyazemski of 11 December 1818. Subsequent references to this edition will appear in the text in the form (*OA,* volume, page).

mas and immediately sought to change its direction. In his initiation speech Orlov pleaded ignorance of the struggle against the Beseda and inability to follow the joking style. He rejected the influence of frivolous French literature and called for a goal more worthy of the society.[44]

Politics began to replace literature as the most fashionable topic of conversation. Pushkin's Eugene Onegin, a young Petersburg dandy, followed the trend with his usual *savoir faire:*

> Homer, Theocritus disdaining,
> From Adam Smith he sought his training
> And was no mean economist. . . .[45]

N. I. Turgenev, not content to be a mere follower of public opinion, helped feed political controversy with his *Essay on the Theory of Taxes (Opyt o teorii nalogov,* 1818), which forcefully opposed serfdom. Karamzin, on the other hand, defended the autocracy in his history, the first volumes of which also appeared in 1818. Alexander I fed the fires with a speech to the Polish Assembly (27 March 1818) in which he declared a desire to grant Russia a constitution. Vyazemski translated this speech for publication in the Russian press. The constitution was never granted, but the possibility that it might be kept Russians busy drafting proposals for it. The letters of the Arzamasians easily absorbed these new currents, but their meetings could not, despite attempts to reorganize them around the publication of a journal.

The transfer of some members abroad on diplomatic missions, the lack of a common enemy, a sense of triumph, and the members' impatience with their own frivolity speeded the disbanding of Arzamas as a formal society, although the Arza-

[44] Borovkova-Maykova, *"Arzamasskiye" protokoly,* pp. 206–10. Frivolity can be unconscious. Orlov was connected with a secret political organization flamboyantly called the "Order of Russian Knights." See S. Ya. Borovoy's introduction to M. F. Orlov, *Kapitulyatsiya Parizha, Politicheskiye sochineniya, Pisma* (Moscow, 1963), p. 279.

[45] A. S. Pushkin, *Eugene Onegin,* trans. Walter Arndt (New York, 1963), p. 8, chapter I, stanza 7.

61

masians continued to gather casually as they had done before the War of 1812. The protocols they had written for their formal meetings had sparkled with wit and fancy, but their humor had often been juvenile, forced, or repetitive. The playfulness manifested in their gatherings, however, remains an important aspect of their relationship with familiar letters and with the concept of genre.

Early nineteenth-century Russia shared the Neoclassical passion for taxonomy, which Michel Foucault has so thoroughly described.[46] Russian theorists named a far greater number of specific genres than the tripartite classification— epic, drama, lyric—that had evolved from classical antiquity. N. I. Grech, whose combination of erudition and unoriginality makes him a useful representative of the time, proposed a typically broad definition of literature. To him it consisted of everything written; its chief branches were eloquence, history, and poetry; its related fields, grammar, aesthetics, and criticism.[47] The Arzamasians also avoided the problem of defining literature in general and thought of it as a large body of genres. They were quick to show how individual works failed to live up to genre expectations, but did little to define their genres positively. Zhukovski, as we have seen, proved an exception in his essay on fables.

During the first quarter of the nineteenth century the multiplicity of genres held dominion over practicing writers and editors, as well as theoreticians. Batyushkov, Zhukovski, Dmi-

[46] Underlying Neoclassical thought Foucault finds an epistemology conducive to taxonomy and surface descriptions (in biology), theories of exchange (in economics), and the study of general grammar (in linguistics). The advent of Romantic historicism and organicism turned these fields toward the study of the functions of invisible tissues, production by human labor, and historical linguistics. *The Order of Things: An Archaeology of the Human Sciences* (New York: Random House, 1970).

[47] N. I. Grech, *Uchebnaya kniga rossiskoy slovesnosti ili izbrannye mesta iz ruskikh sochineni i perevodov v stikhakh i proze,* 4 vols. (St. Petersburg, 1819–21), IV, 275.

triyev, and A. S. Pushkin arranged editions of their poetry according to genres, among which were elegies, verse epistles, satires, verse tales, fables, "lyric poems" (odes), madrigals, epitaphs, inscriptions, and epigrams. In 1810 Zhukovski organized a large anthology of Russian poetry by genres rather than by authors or chronology.

Not every Arzamasian agreed with Voltaire that all genres are good except the boring ones. The group tended to scorn odes and, except for Zhukovski, considered ballads beneath the dignity of talented poets. They did grow restless at times with the genres they had inherited. Batyushkov wanted to "broaden the range of the elegy" (III, 448) and did so by giving his elegies specific historical settings. Zhukovski found fables attractive because they combined the "beauties of all other genres,"[48] and he did much to popularize ballads, a type of poetry unrecognized by Neoclassicism. But none of the Arzamasians campaigned to overthrow the concept of genre itself.[49] Several important aspects of their literary situation preserved the genres more or less intact, one of the most important being the spirit of poetic play and competition.

If the modern reader seeks high seriousness, a critical relationship to surrounding reality, and expressions of the poet's soul in Russian literature of the early nineteenth century, he will find them, but he will find a significant play element as well, such as that which manifested itself in the Arzamas rituals.[50] Even such a solemn poet as Zhukovski regarded verse translation as a sort of game: "the translator of prose is a slave; the translator of verse, a competitor."[51] Translators and imitators were expected to improve upon their originals but by playing under the same rules. Writers sought to do in their

[48] Zhukovski, *Sobraniye sochineni v chetyrekh tomakh,* IV, 410.
[49] For an opposing view see Tomashevski, *Pushkin,* I, 47–48. He finds genre divisions in the 1810s "conventional" and "unclear," which would be true for genre divisions of any period, since a generic schema exists not to constrict talented writers but to be munipulated by them.
[50] Johan Huizinga sees the play element as dominating eighteenth-century culture with its salons, circles, interest in style, and graceful combination of play with seriousness. *Homo Ludens,* pp. 186–89.
[51] *Sobraniye sochineni v chetyrekh tomakh,* IV, 410.

own literature what had been done in Western literatures; Vyazemski, as we shall see, felt that the publication of Russian letters was a matter of Russian honor. The Arzamasians in fun named each other after the foreign writer most similar to each of them. Although such figures as Admiral Shishkov asked themselves what was different about Russian culture, many writers continued to support the prestige of their literature by competing on their rivals' home grounds, that is, in the recognized Neoclassical genres.

The Romantic expressive theory that a poet should write as he lives and vice versa, that poetry should express his inner life, gathered adherents among the Arzamasians,[52] but they reconciled it with describing and practicing a number of Neoclassical genres, especially when these included such loosely organized genres as verse epistles, satires, essays, and familiar letters. Batyushkov opened the first edition of his works with the poem "To His Friends" ("K druzyam"), part of which reads:

But friendship will find in exchange [for skill] feelings—
The history of my passions,
The delusions of my mind and heart,
The cares, the vanities, the griefs of former days
And the lightwinged pleasures.[53]

He clearly felt that the system of genres available to him could express the variety of his feelings and passions.

Genre criticism proved capable of resolving the potential conflict between the Neoclassical genre system and the emerging expressive theory. The poet's emotion became the defining feature of an inherited genre. Zhukovski wrote of the "good nature" of fables;[54] Vyazemski, of the "indignation" of sa-

---

[52] Batyushkov, *Sochineniya,* II, 120; V. A. Zhukovski, "Pisma-dnevniki V. A. Zhukovskogo 1814 i 1815 godov," in *Pamyati V. A. Zhukovskogo i N. V. Gogolya,* ed. P. K. Simoni, vol. I (St. Petersburg, 1907), p. 182.

[53] K. N. Batyushkov, *Polnoye sobraniye stikhotvoreni,* ed. N. V. Fridman (Moscow-Leningrad, 1964), pp. 191–92.

[54] *Sobraniye sochineni v chetyrekh tomakh,* IV, 407.

tires.[55] Grech saw that a particular feeling dominated each composition.[56] The totality of a poet's work in several genres would express his soul; thus, a poet was expected to have more than one emotion and practice more than one genre. Moreover, the salon ideal of the *honnête homme* precluded narrow specialization. Batyushkov and Vyazemski praised Voltaire for his versatility and took friends to task for generic monotony. Batyushkov used Voltaire as an authority in urging Gnedich to enjoy something besides Homer's epics (III, 68; December 1809):

> Le véritable esprit sait se plier à tout,
> On ne vit qu'à demi quand on n'a qu'un seul goût.
> "Épître à M. le comte de Maurepas"

Vyazemski felt that Zhukovski's "mystical" verse had become monotonous, and warned: "A poet should pour out his soul into a variety of vessels" (*OA*, I, 305; 9 September 1819).

From the foregoing description of their approach to literature we may conclude that the Arzamasians helped create a literary milieu and aesthetic in which the Western tradition of familiar correspondence could interest both serious writers and the reading public. Gentlemen amateurs presided over a literature dedicated to themes of friendship and independence. Writers banded together to read and criticize each other's works, participating in this activity by letter when separated from their circles. The everyday activities, impressions, and feelings of these writers became subjects for literature. Russian prose, now less bombastic because of the efforts of such writers as Karamzin, more appropriately expressed the new themes. Patriotism aroused by the Napoleonic invasion inspired many to use Russian, rather than French, in letters. The rhetorical manuals, although still required reading in schools, yielded their rule over literature to the taste of polite society. With so

[55] Vyazemski, *Polnoye sobraniye sochineni*, I, 265.
[56] Appendix II, p. 204.

many favorable conditions converging, it is not surprising to find an Arzamasian saying: "I shall write nothing but letters to friends: that is my true genre" (III, 422; late February–early March 1817 to N. I. Gnedich).[57]

The catalogue of Pushkin's library provides a useful indicator of the interest in European letters among the Arzamasians. Pushkin collected the correspondence of Cicero, Seneca, Pliny, Mme de Sévigné, Swift, Frederick II, Lomonosov, Voltaire, Grimm, Diderot, Holbach, Galiani, Byron, Coleridge, and Lamb. The pages of all but the French translations of Cicero and Seneca were cut.[58] Pushkin obviously read other books than those in his library, and he did not necessarily read all the books he owned; it is possible that pages had been cut when the volumes were bound. That he purchased so many collections of letters, however, shows the extent of his interest in the genre.

Pushkin owned no epistolary manuals. The Arzamasians scorned these recipes and other primers for the mass audience. No member of Arzamas even mentions Sokolski. They use Kurganov as a figure of fun; Dashkov, for example, accused Admiral Shishkov of seeking inspiration in Kurganov's *Primer*.[59] Pushkin made the provincial, naive narrator of his "History of the Village of Goryukhino" ("Istoriya sela Goryukhina," 1830) another admirer of Kurganov. Pushkin did have a copy of N. I. Grech's *Textbook of Russian Literature or Selected Passages from Russian Works and Translations in Verse and Prose* (part of which is translated in Appendix II), but he did not cut the few pages on letters. Grech's taste was Karamzinian, it should be noted, and his sophistication exceeded that of Kurganov and Sokolski.

---

[57] Batyushkov also planned a "short course in letters on Russian literature for people of fashion, to acquaint them with their own wealth" (III, 453). Letter to Vyazemski of 23 June 1817.

[58] B. L. Modzalevski, *Biblioteka A. S. Pushkina: Bibliograficheskoye opisaniye* (St. Petersburg, 1910).

[59] Borovkova-Maykova, *"Arzamasskiye protokoly,"* p. 199. The observation is not mere invective. Kurganov taught mathematics and navigation at the Naval Academy in St. Petersburg, where Shishkov had studied. Like Shishkov, Kurganov opposed the use of foreign loan words in Russian.

References to foreign letters in their own correspondence show how the Arzamasians related to epistolary tradition. Only Zhukovski showed any enthusiasm for Latin familiar letters. He recommended that Cicero's be translated into Russian, despite the difficulties presented by their wealth of detail on everyday Roman life.[60] Although Zhukovski himself often wrote abstract, moralizing letters, Seneca's were less to his taste than Cicero's. A. I. Turgenev upset him by implying that he was composing "epistles à la Senèque."[61]

The Arzamasians rejected the sort of politeness and precious compliments that had been popular in seventeenth-century France, perhaps because they had become fodder for popular formularies. Pushkin considered Voiture's *oeuvre* rubbish (XII, 191) and disapproved of a friend's use of the polite epistolary formulae that Voiture had favored (XIII, 75). Dashkov was even more emphatic in rejecting the formulae: "Once and for all I take the liberty of dispensing with ceremonies with you; do me a favor and yourself forget the lessons from the *Manuel de la civilité honnête et puérile* with which they plagued me when I was a child."[62]

Several Arzamasians read the letters of Mme de Maintenon but left no comments on them. Mme de Sévigné captivated Arzamas. Pushkin admired her treatment of the French peasantry; he found strength in her restraint from grief and indignation (XI, 257). Batyushkov viewed her more sentimentally—"dear, fine Sévigné (III, 51)—and as a catechism for young girls (II, 24). Vyazemski, like Batyushkov, quoted her pithy sayings.

The Arzamasians turned most readily, however, to the letters of the *philosophes,* especially to those of Voltaire, Galiani, and Grimm. Vyazemski emphasized Voltaire's role as an active spokesman for tolerance.[63] He considered Voltaire's letters to

[60] Zhukovski, *Sobraniye sochineni v chetyrekh tomakh,* IV, 657. To A. F. Fon-der-Briggen, 1 June 1846.

[61] *Ibid.,* IV, 489. To A. I. Turgenev, 4 December 1810.

[62] Tsentralni gosudarstvenni arkhiv literatury i iskusstva, Ostafyevski arkhiv, 195/1/1820.

[63] Vyazemski, "O novykh pismakh Voltera," *Polnoye sobraniye sochineni,* I, 65–66.

all recipients equally entertaining and attributed this to Voltaire's versatility.[64] Pushkin, who also reviewed Voltaire's letters, paid more attention than did Vyazemski to the letters themselves. Finding Voltaire's prose a fine example of "reasonable" (unmannered) style (XI, 18), Pushkin liked the all-encompassing humor and the judgments expressed in the correspondence. Pushkin's criticism of Voltaire as a letter writer, like Vyazemski's, considers not only style but also the self-portrait of Voltaire that emerges from his letters. From the correspondence with Frederick II, published only in 1836, Pushkin sadly concluded that Voltaire had no self-respect and hence won little respect from his contemporaries. True to the ideal of the writer's independence from patronage and the court, Pushkin himself followed the model set by Karamzin, Batyushkov, and Zhukovski at the outset of the formation of Arzamas: "the writer's real place is in his study and, ultimately, independence and self-respect alone can lift us above the trifles of life and the storms of fate" (XII, 81).

The publication in 1818 of the Abbé Galiani's extensive correspondence with French salon figures and *philosophes* delighted the Arzamasians. Karamzin and A. I. Turgenev applauded his wit and intelligence, and Vyazemski copied many of Galiani's thoughts into his notebooks. Galiani's definition of sublime oratorical talent struck a sympathetic chord with the exiled A. S. Pushkin: "c'est l'art de tout dire, sans être mis à la Bastille, dans un pays où il est défendu de rien dire."[65] Galiani's fluently expressed thought, directness, unmannered expression, and aversion to epistolary clichés prefigured the style of the Arzamasians. A. I. Turgenev thought that Vyazemski's letters would make a companion volume to Galiani's (*OA*, I, 232).

Self-characterization in a letter was, however, as important to the Arzamasians as it had been to Demetrius. Galiani, like

[64] *Ibid.*, p. 68.

[65] Ferdinando Galiani, *Correspondence avec Madame d'Épinay, Madame Necker, Madame Geoffrin, etc., Diderot, Grimm, d'Alembert, de Sartine, d'Holbach, etc.*, ed. Lucien Perey and Gaston Maugras, 2 vols. (Paris, 1889–90), II, 348. To Mme d'Épinay, 24 September 1774.

Voltaire, was judged according to the Arzamasian norm of behavior: friendship and independence. A. I. Turgenev had
charitably defended Galiani, saying that it was the fashion at
that time to be cold and for the *philosophes* to be cool toward
each other (*OA,* I, 149–50). Vyazemski nevertheless criticized
the persona of Galiani's letters for coldness and calculation:

> Sensibility was in his age and society what Liberalism
> is in our time. Grimm owed his first successes in Paris
> to the fact that he lay senseless several days out of love
> for an opera wench. Every intelligent man was the votary
> of some goddess. Thomas was the Pylades of Necker's
> wife; icy d'Alembert warmed himself with Lespinasse;
> Raynal wept burning tears over Eliza Draper; Diderot
> was a fiery furnace. Everything was ablaze with intense
> heat, perhaps counterfeit at times, but it at least proves
> that coldness was not honored then. But this Galiani at
> the deathbed of his brother sees only the dowries he will
> have to give the orphaned nieces; this Galiani, when the
> sparks of freedom began to flare up, preached autocracy;
> his friends did not call him Machiavellino in vain. And
> his last letter blazes with coldness. In his friends he saw
> acquaintances; friendship was nothing special to him. He
> enjoyed it, but was satisfied with himself. (*OA,* I, 157–58)

The Arzamasians also knew Grimm's *Correspondence lit-
teraire, philosophique et critique,* published in 1812. Its run-
ning commentary on the French literary scene helped to equip
them with their detailed knowledge of the French life and
culture of the eighteenth century. However attractive its mixture of criticism, literary gossip, epigrams, and parodies might
have been to them, this correspondence really constituted a
newsletter for royal subscribers. Perhaps because it did not
feature the personal portraits of familiar correspondence, it
failed to evoke in Arzamas such passionate quarrels as had
Voltaire's and Galiani's correspondence. A. I. Turgenev did
earn the nickname "little Grimm" for the news of literature
and scholarship that he was constantly spreading, but the Arza-

masian taste in letters was not for lengthy reports, and A. I. Turgenev himself objected to Dmitriyev's "dry chronicle of Moscow's literature" (*OA*, I, 378).

It would be naive and inaccurate to see the influence of any single writer in the Arzamasian letters, no matter how much they admired him. The Arzamasians used the general outlines of the genre as a guide and challenge to creativity, not as a straitjacket. The Arzamasians avoided epistolary clichés, jokes untied to their own circumstances, secondhand compliments, and other elements of letters that travel easily across borders and centuries. If they quoted Galiani, Voltaire, or Mme de Sévigné, they acknowledged their source—their addresses would have known it anyway.

What the Arzamasians did find in the West and hoped to import was essentially the literary milieu in which such a genre as familiar letters might prosper. At its best, literature defined as an expression of salon society with its emphasis on intelligent conversation inspired familiar letters marked by, in Pushkin's words, "true learning unburdened by pedantry, profundity of thought, playful sallies, and pictures sketched carelessly but with life and daring" (XII, 75). The growth of Russian-speaking salons on the French model was, as we have seen, impeded by the use of French at social gatherings. Nevertheless, theorists, literary circles, formal literary organizations, and hosts who received literary figures, such as A. N. Olenin and Karamzin, had begun to establish the Russian salon aesthetic by the time Arzamas was formed.

The Arzamasians' attitude toward familiar correspondence sprang from the salon adaptation of the familiar letter. They circulated each other's letters within their group. They considered letters written conversation, free and spontaneous, a special form of literature distinct from "dissertations," "sermons," "elegies," "fables," and "dry chronicles." Although everything in a letter did not need to be completely spelled out, they expected it to contain news, details, and a portrait of the writer. Letters moved them to tears and laughter. In keeping with the close relationship between literature and society, they applied social criteria to the art of writing letters. Batyushkov, for example, wrote Gnedich that not to answer letters is not to know how to live in society (III, 77).

Karamzin's wife reminded A. I. Turgenev of the familiar letter's obligatory ties to its immediate recipient:

> Et quoique vos trois lettres, que nous avons lues avec tant d'intérêt, ne contiennent rien d'individuel, vous entendant parler de vous, de ce que vous faites, on oublie ce défaut de sentiment, car pour ma part j'aimerais assez à trouver dans une épître amicale quelque chose qui m'appartienne en propre, qui ne soit que pour moi et non pour la masse.[66]

The Arzamasians generally did write for their addressees. But most of them also collected familiar letters and preserved them for a wider public, as their European counterparts had done. The only consistent exceptions were Karamzin and Bludov, who systematically destroyed the letters they received. A. I. Turgenev and Vyazemski were far from coy about their collections. Turgenev warned:

> Zhukovski liked the letter very much and wanted to take it away from me; but that would have meant taking it away from immortality, for I am saving your letters in order to publish them in time, under free skies, and to make a second volume of Galiani out of you. Mind you, be smarter and behave yourself better, that is, write more and do not joke your way out of a second page. (*OA*, I, 232; 14 May 1819)

Vyazemski, who years later published many of their letters himself, did not object: "I, too, would like you to publish my letters, not out of personal vainglory, but for the national

---

[66] N. M. Karamzin, "Pisma N. M. Karamzina k A. I. Turgenevu," *Russkaya starina,* 1899, pp. 230–31. Postscript to Karamzin's letter of 6 September 1825.

honor. It will be a long time before that happens: I confess, out of curiosity I would like to live until then" (*OA*, I, 240; 23 May 1819).

The Arzamasians, then, composed familiar letters for their immediate recipients and, ultimately, for posterity. In practice they could not simultaneously present their letters to both audiences. Tradition demanded that for modesty's sake some time elapse between the writing and the publishing of a familiar letter—otherwise the genre's illusion of intimacy would be broken. Under Nicholas I the censorship code made a delay compulsory; writers, recipients, those mentioned in letters, and the families of all parties could stop publication. The Arzamasians' letters underwent a series of metamorphoses as they moved from their immediate audience to their ultimate one.

First, the letters were exploited as handwritten forms. Batyushkov once replaced a signature with a picture of himself; others included sketches in their letters. Their calligraphic fun with letters included altering the script to fit the situation; Batyushkov wrote an ironically solemn letter to Vyazemski using the official formulae due him for his princely rank; the script was an official semiuncial one with large, heavy letters and generous spacing.[67] The Arzamasians' choice of paper and ink helped the original letters survive. Most have suffered little deterioration in the archives because they were written on good paper—fine stationery or "sugar paper" *(sakharnaya bumaga)* filched from the chancelleries.

The Arzamasians wrote legibly, at least by comparison with the drafts of their other works. They crossed out few words, apologized when they did,[68] and objected to poorly written letters.[69] Surprisingly enough, since the letters are generally quite coherent, they made few rough drafts. The paratactic and associative organization frequently employed in the letters made drafts less necessary for this type of writing than for other

[67] Batyushkov, *Sochineniya*, III, 137–38. Letter of 26 August 1811. The original is located in Tsentralni gosudarstvenni arkhiv literatury i iskusstva, Ostafyevski arkhiv, 195/1/1416.

[68] Karamzin, *Pisma Karamzina k Dmitriyevu*, p. 1.

[69] Batyushkov, *Sochineniya*, III, 558.

types, and a measure of *neglegentia epistolarum* maintained the illusion of "talking on paper." Pushkin did make some drafts in his notebooks, but these were usually for letters that were official, letters that were ultimately worked into prefaces, letters that dealt with difficult literary problems, or letters that were written immediately after trying emotional experiences when he found it difficult to keep his composure. Vyazemski, whose notebooks have also been preserved, copied some thoughts and quotations from them into his letters, but he did not draft whole letters.[70] The occasionally confused syntax of his letters confirms this observation.[71] Nor did the Arzamasians have their clerks or servants copy the finished letters to save them for posterity; they relied on their recipients for this and were not disappointed.

The rare letters that found their way into print during the decades immediately following the collapse of Arzamas constitute the next stage in the presentation of its correspondence to the Russian public. Boris Fedorov—a writer, journalist, and editor of literary collections—provided this introduction to a selection of letters that he published: "I have included letters that are especially remarkable for their content or style, curious for the biographer and observer of manners, serving (so to speak) as mirors of the feelings, thoughts, and lives of their authors."[72] As Fedorov suggests, the readers of the time turned to letters for the combination of intimacy and concrete, everyday detail they offered, a combination that had scandalized critics and readers when Pushkin offered it to them in a different genre, the verse novel *(Eugene Onegin)*. However, a comparison of Fedorov's text of Batyushkov's letter to Uvarov of May 1819 with the original reveals how little of the whole

[70] This writing of drafts and copying of sections of notebooks into letters suggests that the Arzamasians letters were not necessarily a "laboratory" for other genres but something worth composing in their own right.

[71] See, for example, Vyazemski, *Ostafyevski arkhiv*, I, 382. Letter of 26–27 December 1819.

[72] Boris Fedorov, ed., *Pamyatnik otechestvennykh muz* (St. Petersburg, 1827), p. 1.

"mirror" the collection's readers really viewed.[73] Missing from Fedorov's edition are all names but those of literary figures (Uvarov and Zhukovski); those of public officials and Uvarov's wife are excised. Batyushkov's modest hopes for Russia's enlightenment have disappeared, as have pessimistic thoughts on the state of Russian learning: "happiness and glory do not lie in barbarism despite [the opinions of] some of our blind minds, fabricators of phrases, and astrologers." A sarcastic comment on Shishkov's Russian Academy ("lies and bad syllogisms") has vanished—the Arzamasians' chief rival had by this time taken charge of censorship. Batyushkov's positive views about Zhukovski's elegy on the death of the Queen of Wurttemberg remain, but not his wish for more invention and less redundancy in the poem. The final result was a "mirror" of a mind capable of expressing only a few conventional phrases. Critical spirit and commitment to enlightenment, so important to the Arzamasians, had little place in the Russia of Nicholas I.

In the years following Nicholas' death in 1855, it gradually became easier to publish the familiar letters of Arzamas, especially since most of their writers and recipients had died. The oldest surviving Arzamasian, Vyazemski, arranged for the printing of thousands of them. Academic scholars then took over the task of gathering the letters from family archives, and by the early years of the twentieth century substantial collections of the letters of Pushkin, Batyushkov, A. I. Turgenev, N. I. Turgenev, Vyazemski, Zhukovski, Dmitriyev, Davydov, and Karamzin had been published by such prestigious organizations as the Academy of Sciences. Scholarly reverence for all of an author's writings led editors to restore many passages that had previously been deleted. Editors now omitted only the most offensive blasphemies and antigovernment sentiments. An example of their excisions is Vyazemski's

---

[73] The two versions can be found in Batyushkov, *Sochineniya*, III, 551–52 and 779–82. I do not know who abridged the letter, Fedorov, or A. I. Turgenev, who furnished Fedorov with materials for the collection.

Arzamasian advice to Zhukovski to avoid "court romanticism":

> No matter how superficial and insignificant a husband's association with wenches, the marital union still suffers from it, and sooner or later the debauchery will have its influence in the home. Our marital union is with the nation; our domestic life is in the fatherland; the Tsar's caress is a tempting whore, who leads us into sin and distracts us from our lawful obligation.[74]

The editors of scholarly editions replaced easily surmised obscenities with dashes or rows of dots. With these minor qualifications, many Arzamasian familiar letters had reached their ultimate audience.

What the Arzamasians wrote about their own familiar letters and about the European epistolary tradition shows that they considered letters a significant literary genre whose important aspects are style, persona, and content. While a genre study would be too abstract without such a summary of contemporary expectations and attitudes, the vague manner in which these attitudes are expressed makes them insufficient for defining the genre and comparing it with other forms of writing. The other aspects of our analytic scheme—selection of content, the parts of a letter, epistolary self-characterization, and principles of organization—will supplement the Arzamasians' valuable impressions.

[74] The original is in Arkhiv Pushkinskogo Doma, 27985/ccib44, sheet 3. The letter was published in *Russki arkhiv*, 1900, no. 2, pp. 181–83.

III

Content: Principles of Selection

Phoo! Prosaic nonsense,
The motley rubbish of the Flemish school!
Eugene Onegin, "Onegin's Journey," xix

A familiar letter reaches one audience at a time: immediate recipient, then the larger public. Its radical of presentation, however, is a complex one: the familiar letter traditionally caters both to its immediate recipient and to this larger public. Unlike the open letter, it is written with intimacy for an individual or small group and conveys its author's awareness of his addressee. Karamzin sought to create the illusion of familiar correspondence in his *Letters of a Russian Traveler* (*Pisma russkogo puteshestvennika,* 1791–1801) by using intimate nicknames and mentioning received letters; but he abandoned the attempt after a few pages, perhaps to avoid repetition, perhaps in accordance with the conventions of travel letters, which are concerned with the writer's relationship to what he encounters, not with his fictional recipient. However, a familiar letter, unlike the ordinary personal letter, is composed with the possibility of a larger public somewhere in the back of the author's mind. Neither of these elements of the familiar letter's radical of presentation can be ignored in describing the genre. The first encourages the writer to choose subjects of specific interest to his recipient. The second encourages him to select topics of more than passing significance, or at least to develop them in an interesting manner. His friends may be pleased to know that he is alive, well, and enjoying himself, but posterity requires something more than the bare mention of the fact. Although they are composed to seem so, familiar letters are not a "mirror" of an author's mind, as the nineteenth-century

76

editors understood that metaphor. The author himself, limited in movement by epistolary tradition, decorum, knowledge, and range of vision, holds up and maneuvers the "mirror"—a framed, uneven surface—to capture certain objects, hastily pass others by, and leave still others utterly unreflected. An investigation of these limits should help place the familiar letter among the Neoclassical genres.

Intimacy and themes proscribed in other genres proved essential in fascinating posterity.[1] Part of the pleasure that familiar letters afford derives from the reader's feeling that he has discovered something not blatantly intended for his eyes. Batyushkov, who carefully preserved and composed letters, emphasized their intimacy by playing down their interest for the general public:

> Do not give away anything for publication without my permission. I do not wish to further inform the public that on such-and-such a day I was merry, drank with you, fell in love, supped, or did not sleep at night. . . . But my scribbling will have value for my friends, and thus for me, and you occupy the first place in my heart.[2]

Avoiding the tradition of abstract moral epistles, the Arzamasians elected to convey this necessary intimacy by keeping the content of their letters close to their immediate surroundings, interests, and occupations. Specifically, they selected news, gossip, erotic themes, obscenity, and concrete detail. To judge from their comments on each other's letters and from the content of their own letters, they enjoyed receiving such details. Dashkov told Vyazemski: "You cannot doubt that all news of your domestic life is pleasant to your friends."[3]

---

[1] Karamzin, for example, thought that writing political verse was "une faute contre le goût," but he included many political statements in his letters. *Pisma N. M. Karamzina k knyazyu P. A. Vyazemskomu: 1810–1826 (iz ostafyevskogo arkhiva)* ed. N. Barsukov (St. Petersburg, 1897), p. 75. Letter of 9 April 1819.

[2] Tsentralni gosudarstvenni arkhiv literatury i iskusstva, Ostafyevski arkhiv, 195/1/1416, sheet 20. To Vyazemski, 1 August 1815.

[3] Tsentralni gosudarstvenni arkhiv literatury i iskusstva, Ostafyevski arkhiv, 195/1/1820, sheet 24. 8 March 1827.

The Arzamasians' approach to literature gave them confidence that the details of their lives and literary skirmishes would interest future readers as well as their friends. The salon aesthetic, as we have seen, encouraged the writer to focus on the life of polite society as it provided a model for civilized discourse. Neoclassical decorum precluded concrete, physical detail only in the loftier genres. A number of other genres—comedy, satire, and epigrams—shared the letter's ability to delve into the particular, physical aspects of human existence. V. L. Pushkin's comic poem, "The Dangerous Neighbor" ("Opasni sosed," 1811) is set in a brothel whose customers read the Besedists' works. Thus many of the genres at which the Arzamasians excelled—literary satires, verse novels, and epigrams—addressed specific contemporary targets. Though many of their works could not always be published immediately, the Arzamasians nevertheless circulated them in manuscript and preserved them. Bludov justified their concreteness by analogy: "Why write personal satires? Many think and say: 'only contemporaries can read them, and a poet should labor for posterity.' However, lovers of pictures even now buy portraits painted by Van Dyck."[4] The naïveté of this analogy—satire depends more on a knowledge of its subject than portraiture does—only demonstrates this Arzamasian's total faith in the deathlessness of their ephemora.

Not all possible details of everyday life entered the familiar correspondence of the Arzamasians, however. The omissions are not surprising if one remembers the letters' radical of presentation, that letters were written not only for the immediate recipient, but for a larger public as well. Fear of ridicule, as Mme de Staël rightly indicated, was a powerful inhibiting force in an aristocratic literary milieu.[5] And the

[4] "Mysli i zamechaniya grafa Bludova" in Ye. P. Kovalevski, *Sobraniye sochineni Ye. P. Kovalevskogo,* vol. I: *Graf Bludov i yego vremya* (St. Petersburg, 1871), p. 259.

[5] Germaine Necker de Staël, *Madame de Staël on Politics, Literature and National Character,* ed. and trans. Morroe Berger (New York, 1965), p. 206.

Arzamasians' familiar letters hardly illuminate their authors in a ridiculous fashion. In his letters Vyazemski barely mentions the more spectacular events of his life—his many infatuations, the destruction of all his ambitions, and his astounding losses at gambling.[6]

Moreover, the Arzamasians indulged in little gossip on the immorality of their contemporaries, although their permissive age could have provided many anecdotes. They did not, for example, mention the scandalous and prolonged affair of the Emperor with Mme Naryshkina. The Arzamasians related gossip and scandalous events swiftly and in tantalizing hints, as in this letter by Pushkin to F. F. Vigel, a homosexual:

> Of your three acquaintances, the youngest is especially fit to be used to your advantage; NB. he sleeps in the same room with his brother Mikhail, and they tumble about unmercifully—you can draw valuable conclusions from this; I leave them to your experience and good sense. (XIII, 72; October–November 1823)

Vyazemski moved with similar swiftness in this description of a courtier's activities:

> Yesterday we bade farewell to the latest ripple from the Neva, the brilliant Chernyshev, who showed rare activity and vivacity of imagination as marshal of the cotillion. His last visit to Warsaw with his wife, in which he distinguished himself by ludicrous jealousy, lay on his heart; because of this he employed all his resources on his present visit to be captivating and to atone for the past. Le ridicule est chez nous le dot, qui donne la faveur de la cour. (*OA*, I, 326; 11 October 1819, to A. I. Turgenev)

Despite his scorn for Chernyshev, Vyazemski ignored the op-

---

[6] L. Ya. Ginzburg finds this true of Vyazemski's notebooks and poetry as well. P. A. Vyazemski, *Stikhotvoreniya,* ed. and intro. L. Ya. Ginzburg (Leningrad, 1958), p. 21.

portunity to expand upon the reasons for his jealousy and focused instead on a larger social question, the ignominiousness of life at court.

The Arzamasians' sense of restraint and shame, of course, differed from ours. Just as in Neoclassical comedy, a loose decorum governed the treatment of inferiors and servants; a writer could give much more detail about his relationships with them. Karamzin the quondam Sentimentalist—who informed the public of the 1790s that inferiors have feelings too—not infrequently mentions having fractious servants whipped, sent to the army, or put in a workhouse. But even here there were limits to what the Arzamasians wished to leave for posterity. In the following letter, marked by literary self-consciousness, Pushkin reveals more of the *moeurs* of the gentry than he cared for the general public to know. Vyazemski, who published a number of Pushkin's letters in 1874, respected his friend's wish that this one remain private. It appeared only in 1906 in a scholarly edition:

My dear Vyazemski, you are silent and I am silent; and we do well—sometime we will have a chat at our leisure. But for now that is not the point. This letter will be handed to you by a very sweet and kind girl whom one of your friends indiscreetly knocked up. I rely on your philanthropy and friendship. Give her refuge in Moscow and give her as much money as she needs—and then send her to Boldino (my patrimonial estate, where there are chickens, roosters and bears). You see that one might write a whole epistle in the style of Zhukovski's "Of the Priest" here; but posterity does not need to know about our philanthropic feats.

In addition, with paternal tenderness I ask you to look after the little one to be, if it is a boy. I don't feel like sending him to the Foundling Home. But can't he be sent to some village for the meantime—say to [your] Ostafyevo? My dear fellow, I swear I am ashamed . . . but it's a little late for that now. (XIII, 274–75; April–May 1826)[7]

One might contrast this restraint with Rousseau's far greater openness; in the eighth book of his *Confessions,* he admits and defends—with a vehemence that may mask some sense of guilt—sending his illigitimate children to a foundling home.

The familiar letters of the Arzamasians allowed considerably more freedom than other genres in eroticism and obscenity, although Derzhavin's Anacreontic lyrics and Batyushkov's anthology verses were very suggestive. Except for Pushkin, however, the Arzamasian's exercised this freedom in moderation. Circulation of the letters inhibited some of it; A. I. Turgenev felt that Galiani's obscenities would prevent the "fair sex" from reading him, or admitting that they had (*OA,* I, 140). Vyazemski regretted that his obscene letters had been circulated, and he made excuses for them:

Zhukovski showed the Karamzins my letter; with him I permit myself to swear most obscenely and walk around without trousers. My conscience doesn't bother me, but I'm ashamed. However, there's no harm done. In my voice and habits there are certain bursts of Pindaric profanity. It comes from an excess of gaiety, which took refuge in the closet of unseemliness. I have no more seemly gaiety; people or circumstances devoured it, perhaps, or time, probably all three simultaneously. I am like those drunkards who have stopped drinking. You can't entice them with a good wine; they either go to a pub or sit tight with water. (*OA,* I, 186; 9 January 1819)

Obscenity did help them express scorn, disillusionment, and indignation. Depending on its cleverness and sensual vividness, it could more effectively than other linguistic resources make such a point as Pushkin's disapproval of marriage:

[7] *Letters of Alexander Pushkin,* pp. 308–9. To Vyazemski, late April–early May, 1826. The culprit was, of course, Pushkin himself.

Is it true that Baratynski is getting married? I fear for his mind. Lawful cunt is a sort of warm cap with earflaps. The whole head disappears into it. You are, perhaps, an exception. But even in your case I am convinced that you would be more intelligent if you had remained a bachelor ten more years. (XIII, 279; To Vyazemski, 15–24 May 1826)

In this wonderfully vivid simile and elsewhere, Pushkin's obscenity remains within the bounds of good-natured ribaldry, permissible in pre-Victorian times. Seldom does it exceed the standard of suggestiveness set by Sterne's *Tristram Shandy*. Only later in the century did polite society so resolutely avert its public gaze and language from the bodily pleasures and functions.

Lexical descents from the idyllic to the vulgar accompanied the shifting tones of an Arzamasian letter. Ribaldry and eroticism were important tools in their parodies. In the following letter, Batyushkov recreates the Sentimentalist dream world of noble poverty, family happiness, and hospitality by imitating the Sentimentalist style with its harmonious periods, loose syntactical connections, and classical allusions:

Let us marry, my friend, and say together: "sacred innocence, pure chastity and quiet heartfelt satisfaction, dwell together in a poor home, where there are no bronzes, no precious vessels, where the tablecloth is spread by hospitality, where Dame Fortune is not celebrated in the place of honor, but where the peaceful Penate smiles at friends and spouses, we greet you from afar!" (III, 36; to N. I. Gnedich 3 May 1809)[8]

[8] N. V. Fridman, *Proza Batyushkova* (Moscow, 1965), p. 153, analyzes the style of this passage in a similar manner without identifying the significance of the concluding line. The familiar letter's radical of presentation led the Arzamasians to exercise a certain restraint in their use of gossip and obscenity. They sometimes had to exercise a different sort of self-censorship, one unrelated to problems of literary tradition and decorum. The postal authorities and secret police fre-

He concludes by demolishing this ideal world with a tersely expressed reference to vulgar reality, the bordello district in Moscow: "but meanwhile let us go with our rouble to Kamenny Most and then turn right."

Posterity did not betray the faith of the Arzamasians in the continuing interest of particular detail. But such particularity alone was not enough, even for the readers of their time. In addition to news of the writer, Pushkin also wanted news of literature (XIII, 30) and everything that had come to the writer's mind (XIII, 193). Bare news and facts had to be developed and made tantalizing, even for a public willing to grant them an aesthetic function. V. L. Pushkin's letters feature much concrete information as well as a certain amount of bantering and play with the lexical levels of the Russian language. But his mindlessness, his habit of beginning a new topic with every sentence, and his utterly predictable opinions have kept the majority of his letters buried in the archives. The Arzamasians, quick to praise good letters, kept discreetly silent about V. L. Pushkin's.

In his attitude toward particularity, Zhukovski stood diametrically opposed to the other Arzamasians, for whom details were interesting in themselves. Concrete details had little place in his letters, except as evidence collected in sup-

---

quently inspected the letters of liberal Arzamasians during the 1820s and 1830s. A letter on atheism helped earn A. S. Pushkin a Northern exile in 1824, and criticism of the government in letters may have contributed to the dismissal of Vyazemski from his Warsaw post. Not even Pushkin's letters to his wife escaped the surveillance of the secret police, who passed some of them on to the Emperor, Nicholas I. Surveillance did not so much cause the proud, independent Arzamasians to develop an Aesopean language as it infuriated them. They could avoid prying eyes by sending letters with private parties (*s okaziey*). However, the general climate of fear and repression, of which such surveillance was but a part, inhibited the energy and high spirits they needed to write familiar letters on everyday, personal subjects as well as on political ones. This atmosphere contributed to the increasing sobriety in their letters during the 1820s and 1830s. Pushkin told Vyazemski that only the letters he sent with private parties were composed "with his hair down" (XIII, 85 and 98).

port of a point or as material for metaphors. His religious
background and his education had accustomed him to thinking in abstractions and in set moral categories.[9] Unlike Dashkov and the other Arzamasians, who found pleasure in
domestic news, Zhukovski took his pleasure in reflection.[10]
Shortly before his death, Zhukovski clearly articulated his interests and abilities:

> My memoirs . . . could only be psychological, that is,
> a history of my soul; my life has been poor in events of
> interest to posterity; and those events I could describe
> would be, naturally, poorly described; by nature I never
> had a practical view of life or people; I would describe
> what was real in a fantastic manner; there would be
> faces without form, and, truly, my memory has lost nine-
> tenths of the details; and what would be the account of a
> life without live details? (To P. A. Pletnev, 6 March
> 1850)[11]

Zhukovski was not only indifferent to everyday things and
events; he felt that they threatened and obscured the essential
goodness of people. He wrote that the trifles of everyday life
had killed Pushkin and that life had covered A. I. Turgenev
with dust, which fell away from him as he entered life eternal.[12]
"Dust" in this case exemplifies Zhukovski's allegorical use of
the physical world. While lacking in concrete detail, Zhukovski's letters still differ from sermons, legal briefs, and disquisitions on moral problems. His bantering, playing with style,
and attempting to capture the attention of his addressees, whom
he treats as intellectual equals rather than parishioners or
pupils—all of these bring his letters within the generic
boundaries of familiar letter writing. This conclusion to a
long letter is typical of his epistolary manner:

[9] L. Ya. Ginzburg, *O psikhologicheskoy proze* (Leningrad, 1971), pp.
40–41.
[10] Zhukovski, *Sobraniye sochineni v chetyrekh tomakh*, IV, 457. To
A. I. Turgenev, 11 September 1805.
[11] *Ibid.*, p. 668.
[12] *Ibid.*, pp. 537, 632, 651, 653.

But I have filled up nearly four pages and have said very little about what I previously thought. I have chattered too much, but I assure you that I have said everything that you should accept, and, it seems, everything I have said will always remain with me, all the more because I have thought and said everything without my previous enthusiasm, which was so flighty and changeable; from this, however, you should not conclude that I wish to reject enthusiasm entirely; on the contrary I wish to strengthen it, to implant it, knock off only some of its wings, make it calmer, more constant: I want it to illuminate me, not blind me. Friendship must do this; *one person* will not be so daring, but that which will inflame and will be inflaming for *many at the same time* will not seem an empty dream, but something reasonable and well-grounded. Do you see that I want to be an enthusiast by reason? C'est une rareté!

I put off until the next post what I wanted to tell you about myself, that is about my character, about my goal in life, in general about my *private* life apart from our *common* life, which friendship must give us. (To A. I. Turgenev, 11 September 1805)[13]

Zhukovski's mixed metaphor (implant, wings) shows his cavalier attitude toward the things of this world. I shall examine how his way of talking about himself differs from that of the other Arzamasians in the next section.

Zhukovski's letters, with their concentration on processes of thought and feeling and their relative indifference to concrete details, are closely connected with his meditational verse. The letters of the other Arzamasians, with their concrete detail and ties to an immediate situation outside themselves, have more in common with their verse epistles and satires. Zhukovski's poetic response to a letter he received from Batyushkov in August, 1819, illustrates their differing approaches to a single problem: describing the beauty of a natural scene. It

[13] *Ibid.*, pp. 456–57.

also reveals the extent to which the Arzamasians depended on each other for poetic stimuli. Not only genre but also the interests and philosophies of the two writers dictate the difference in their relationship to details.

Batyushkov reported his impressions from the island of Ischia with the enthusiasm of someone whose most oft-repeated phrases include "I saw . . ."; he plotted entire essays around the sights he encountered during his peregrinations: "A Stroll around Moscow" ("Progulka po Moskve," 1810–12) and "A Stroll in the Academy of Arts" (Progulka v Akademiyu Khudozhestv," 1814), for example. In this letter he pays tribute to the magnificent spectacle with an extensive list of all he could see:

> I am enjoying the most magnificent spectacle in the world: in front of me in the distance lies Sorrento—cradle of that man [Tasso] to whom I am obliged for the best delights of my life; then Vesuvius, which at night casts out a quiet flame like a lantern; the heights of Naples, crowned with castles; then Cumae, where Aeneas or Virgil wandered; Baiae, now mournful, once luxurious; Misena, Puzzoli; and at the end of the horizon, mountain ranges separating Campagnia from Abruzzi and Apulia. The view from my terrace is not limited to this; if I turn my gaze to the North, I see Gaeta, the summits of Terracina, and the whole coast stretching toward Rome and disappearing into the blue of the Tyrrhenian Sea. From the mountains of this island lie before me the island of Procida, as if in my palm; to the South, Capri, where the evil Tiberius lived (evil Tiberius —an epithet of Shalikov's); the Pontine Islands to the North and the island of Ponza, where, according to antiquarians, dwelled Circe—don't tell this to Kapnist [who thought her island was in the Black Sea]. At night the sky is covered with an astonishing brilliance; the Milky Way looks different here, incomparably clearer. In the direction of Rome, a terrible comet rises out of the sea, about which we worry little. (III, 559–60)

A list of attractions not being enough for an Arzamasian letter, Batyushkov relates them to his literary likes (Tasso, Virgil) and dislikes (the Sentimentalist poet, Shalikov), then attempts to convey the emotional yield from what he has seen (admitting that it depends on associations from the past), and involves Zhukovski in the situation by a challenge:

> Such pictures would put your imagination to shame. Nature is a great poet, and I rejoice to find in my heart feeling for these great spectacles; unfortunately I can never find the strength to express what I feel: for this your talent is necessary. But memories of every type give ineffable charm to this land and bring even greater satisfaction to the heart than the beauty of the views.

Zhukovski, who once wrote that his mind was a steel that had to strike a flint before giving off sparks,[14] set down his poem "The Inexpressible (a Fragment)" also in August 1819. He did not publish it until 1827, which, together with its abstract nature, has prevented scholars from seeing its connection with the letter, although both appeared in the same literary collection.[15] Only faint traces of the beauty that Batyushkov saw remain in the poem (the sunset, the flame, the water, the shores); these and Zhukovski's italics and demonstratives relate the poem to Batyushkov's letter:

The Inexpressible (a Fragment)

What is our earthly language beside marvelous nature?
With what careless and easy freedom
She scattered beauty everywhere
And harmonized the diverse with oneness!
But where, what brush portrayed her?
With great effort inspiration
Barely succeeds in seizing a single trait . . .
But can one render the living with the dead?

[14] *Ibid.*, p. 544. To Gogol, 6 February 1847.
[15] *Pamyatnik otechestvennykh muz.*

Who can re-create creation in words?
Is the inexpressible subject to expression?
Holy secrets, only the heart knows you.
Do we not often in the majestic hour
Of evening transfiguration of the earth—
When the soul, confused by prophecy,
Is filled with a great vision
And is borne away into the infinite,
And painful emotion wrings the breast—
Wish to hold back the beautiful from flight,
Wish to name the unnamed,
And enfeebled art keeps silent?
What is visible to the eyes—
This flame of clouds,
Flying about the quiet sky,
This trembling of the shining waters,
These pictures of shores
In the conflagration of a splendid sunset—
These *traits so vivid,*
Winged thought seizes them easily,
And there are *words* for their *shining* beauty.
But what is merged with this shining beauty—
This thing so vague, so disturbing to us,
This voice of something fascinating
That can be heeded only by the soul,
This striving for the distant,
This greeting from something that has escaped
(Like the breath that flies up suddenly
From the meadow of one's homeland,
Where there was once a flower,
Holy youth, where hope lived),
This memory whispering to the soul
About the dear joy and grief of former days,
This sacred thing descending from on high,
This presence of the Creator in creation—
What language is there for them? . . . The soul soars on high,

All the unbounded is compressed into a single sigh.
And only silence speaks clearly.[16]

[16] "Nevyrazimoye (Otryvok)," *Sobraniye sochineni v chetyrekh tomakh*, I, 336–37.

Что наш язык земной пред дивною природой?
С какой небрежною и легкою свободой
Она рассыпала повсюду красоту
И разновидное с единством согласила!
Но где, какая кисть ее изобразила?
Едва-едва одну ее черту
С усилием поймать удасться вдохновенью ...
Но льзя ли в мертвое живое передать?
Кто мог создание в словах пересоздать?
Невыразимое подвластно ль выраженью? ...
Святые таинства, лишь сердце знает вас.
Не часто ли в величественный час
Вечернего земли преображенья,
Когда душа смятенная полна
Пророчеством великого виденья
И в беспределное унесена,—
Спирается в груди болезненное чувство,
Хотим прекрасное в полете удержать,
Ненареченному хотим названье дать—
И обессиленно безмолвствует искусство?
Что видимо очам—сей пламень облаков,
По небу тихому летящих,
Сие дрожанье вод блестящих,
Сии картины берегов
В пожаре пышного заката—
Сии столь *яркие черты*—
Легко их ловит мысль крылата,
И есть *слова* для их *блестящей* красоты.
Но то, что слито с сей блестящей красотою—
Сие столь смутное, волнующее нас,
Сей внемлемый одной душою
Обворожающего глас,
Сие к далекому стремленье,
Сей миновавшего привет
(Как прилетевшее незапно дуновенье
От луга родины, где был когда-то цвет,
Святая молодость, где жило упованье),
Сие шепнувшие душе воспоминанье
О милом радостном и скорбном старины,
Сия сходящая святыня с вышины,
Сие присутствие создателя в созданье—
Какой для них язык? ... Горе душа летит,
Все необъятное в единый вздох теснится,
И лишь молчание понятно говорит.

89

The poem makes light of Batyushkov's challenge to Zhukov-ski's pictorial imagination: there *are* words to express visible beauty, thought can seize it. The poem moves beyond nature as Batyushkov empirically understood it to the sacred force that both created nature and is present in it. Because Zhukov-ski does go beyond Batyushkov's visible world, it is appropriate that he replace the movements of the eye with those of the heart and soul. The poet answers the challenge to find a way of expressing his feelings upon seeing such a view by listing aspects of the complex, contradictory emotional process of contemplating a scene of natural beauty: pain, confusion, helplessness, fascination, longing for the past and its associations, desire for an understanding of the force that has given form to the scene. Specific historical and literary references disappear. Zhukovski uses height and distance, which have spatial meaning in Batyushkov's letter, metaphorically. No words can fix the effects of such a scene on the observer, and Zhukovski must resolve the rush of questions, exclamations, emotions, and impressions, magnificently marshaled by the poem's syntax, in a sigh, which upholds the logic of the concluding oxymoron.

A brief outline of Karamzin's protean epistolary practice will help bring the Arzamasians' principles of selection of content into focus. Karamzin belonged to an earlier generation than did most of the group, and his forty-year correspondence with Dmitriyev illustrates the transition from Sentimentalist letter-writing to the Arzamasian style. Before 1790 Karamzin's letters expand upon the elegiac themes of his Sentimentalist verse, much of which was written for inclusion in the letters. They project an image of Karamzin as a poet and friend who is little concerned with the details of everyday life. The only imagery in the following letter is culled from the pastoral—spring, birds, meadows, stream:

> I rejoice that you are satisfied with your life or have ceased to be bored. I hope that the coming of spring will

have a healing influence on your health. Everything will soon come to life. Soon the birds, joining in choirs, will sing a song of praise to spring. My friend! Shall we really go about hanging our heads? Shall we really not take part in the universal happiness, and, knitting our brows say:

Everywhere, everywhere we see happiness,
Everywhere merriment alone;
But we, weighed down with sorrow,
Dejectedly wander about the forests—
We find no pleasure in the meadows;
Looking into a stream, we shed tears;
With our tears we trouble the water.
We disturb it with our sighs.

Farewell, my friend, farewell! I live as before; there is no important change in my life. (2 March 1788)[17]

The prose of this letter, less bombastic than that of Lomonosov's epistle dedicatory, which was quoted in the first chapter,

[17] *Pisma Karamzina k Dmitriyevu*, pp. 5–6.

Любезный друг Иван Иванович!

Радуюсь, что ты доволен своею жизнью, или перестал скучать. Надеюсь, что приближение весны имеет целебное влияние на твое здоровье. Все скоро оживится. Скоро птицы, соединясь в хоры, воспоют хвалебную песнь весне. Мой друг! не уже ли мы с тобою будем ходить повеся голову? не уже ли не возмем участия во всеобщей радости, и, наморщив лоб, скажем:

Везде, везде мы видим радость,
Везде веселие одно;
Но мы, печалью отягченны,
Уныло бродим по лесам,—
В лугах утехи не находим;—
Смотря в ручей, мы слезы льем;
Слезами воду возмущаем,
Волнуем вздохами ее.—

Прости, мой друг, прости! Я живу по прежнему; нет никакой важной перемены в жизни моей.
Покорнейший твой слуга
и верный друг
Н. Карамзин

is nevertheless carefully orchestrated in both sound (skoro . . . khory; vospoyut . . . pesn vesne—compare the translation "sing a song of praise to spring") and syntax (the anaphoric "shall we really . . . shall we really"). These devices carry over into the verse. At the same time the lines in iambic tetrameter remain unrhymed, and this refusal to employ a common distinguishing feature of verse helps merge prose and verse into a harmonious whole. Prose and verse also join in expressing the same theme: the poets' elegiac separation from the universal ("everything," "everywhere") joy of spring. Their tears are but an imperceptible contribution to the stream of happiness; they "disturb" and "trouble" nature's cycles only as these are embodied in their own lives. Dmitriyev's mere satisfaction and Karamzin's unchanging life frame the composition and emphasize the disharmony with nature.

Karamzin's subsequent epistolary practice laid the groundwork for that of the future Arzamasians. It illustrates the extent to which the content of their letters was concerned with their immediate surroundings, interests, and occupations. From 1792 to 1802 Karamzin actively engaged in editing journals and literary collections. "I must work more for my purse," he told Dmitriyev.[18] Fine sentiments of former letters yield to references, sometimes spiteful, to journalistic competitors. As in the letter that follows, lengthy passages on friendship are reduced to brief salutations and conclusions; literary opinions replace the poems once composed for letters; and material delights prove more attractive than the contemplation of emotions. Karamzin's style also becomes terser and features a number of one-sentence topics.

> After an eight-week illness I take up my quill for the first time to write you, my dear friend, Ivan Ivanovich.
>
> Thank you for your two notes. The latest one grieved me with its news of your poor health. As for your poor economy—hope, hope! However, when there is coffee to spare, macaroni now and then, and blancmange, one can

---

[18] *Pisma Karamzina k Dmitriyevu*, p. 84. 10 December 1797.

endure philosophically. Moneylenders? Have you really lost your talent for making them laugh and sending them home unpaid but content? For my part, with this letter I am sending you Neledinski-Meletski's songs as sustenence for your purse. Print the *Songbook* and gather money from the public! Or have you already abandoned your intention? Please let me know. I saw Bulgakov not long ago, but we were prevented from conversing on the usefulness of human shit. What a man. You did well to give the issues [of my journal] to Avdotya Dmitriyevna; they were really sent for her. I will send the June issue with the September one, which is already printed. I want to put the continuation and ending of "Liodor" in the October and November issues. Thank you for the verses. They are not up to your "Dove," but they are good, especially the apostrophe to the swallow in these lines:

"Whether roses breathe over my grave
Or wormwood grows on it," and so forth.

Did you know, my friend, that Nikolev was offended by your "Hymn to Ecstasy?" I assured him that the author was not thinking of him. How is our Gavrila Romanovich [Derzhavin]? Does he remember us from time to time? Farewell, dear one! My hand still shakes from weakness. Your friend. (21 October 1792)[19]

The concrete detail, mild obscenity, and references to Karamzin's and Dmitriyev's daily activities illustrate the Arzamasian letter's use of content to convey intimacy and to give the reader the impression that he has discovered something not directly intended for posterity. Of course, the effect depends on a number of other epistolary techniques as well: paratactic construction; Karamzin's portrait of himself as Epicurean friend, not preceptor; unobtrusive closure resulting from a final return to the opening theme (illness); and elliptical, seemingly artless syntax, which is in its novelty for Russian prose a

[19] *Ibid.*, pp. 31–32.

skillful and radical deformation of the carefully orchestrated rhetorical syntax that was so prevalent in Karamzin's youth. In this letter Karamzin avoided the anaphoric and chiastic constructions of his earlier letter.[20]

Both Karamzin and Dmitriyev lived in Moscow for a number of years and did not correspond. When they again exchanged letters, from 1810 to 1826, Karamzin selected content for his letters consistent with his interests of that period: his health, his historical research, his material circumstances, and the royal family.[21] He could now say: "I do not want to write for the bookstalls; I want to write for posterity."[22] The authorial image of his letters becomes that of the Tsar's independent advisor, grateful for the favor shown him, but not so bound to events at court as to abandon his historical studies.

[20] Further discussion of the stylistic problems raised here appears in Chapter VII, below.

[21] Dmitriyev's account of a visit to Petersburg in 1822 confirms this summary of Karamzin's interests: "the court, rarely and superficially history, and town news were the only subjects of our conversations; not once did his heart seek mine. I was sure of his love, but felt sad. ..." I. I. Dmitriyev, *Sochineniya,* ed. A. A. Floridov, 2 vols. (St. Petersburg, 1895), II, 150–51.

[22] *Pisma Karamzina k Dmitriyevu,* p. 180. 20 April 1814.

IV

Characterization and Caricature

[Your] life has been a very funny epigram, but it
should be a lofty epic.
From a letter by Zhukovski to A. S. Pushkin,
9 August 1825.

It is unlikely that any Russian psychological novelist ever
echoed Dostoyevski's alleged tribute to Gogol, "We have all
emerged from under the frock coats of the Arzamasians."
Nevertheless, characterization of themselves, their recipients,
and others played a large part in the Arzamasians' letters, and
a variety of the methods they used to this end have survived
in later practice.

The most thoroughly characterized figure in a letter is the
author, whether he is presented by self-conscious description
or must be extrapolated from his interests, ideas, or style. Self-
characterization has remained a central preoccupation of the
familiar letter writer since the time of Demetrius. To characterize themselves most of the Arzamasians wrote letters that
accounted for a typical day of the period in which they were
writing. The habitualized present of such accounts permitted
the writer to compose a harmonious, complete description of
himself without breaking the familiar letter's close connection
with the events of the moment. The depiction is both timeless
and immediate. A comparison of the typical days of some
Arzamasians shows the various ways in which they produced
this effect. Vyazemski said of the following description of a
typical day by Karamzin that it was one of his best pages and
presented him in his entirety:[1]

[1] P. A. Vyazemski, "O pismakh Karamzina," *Torzhestvennoye sobraniye Akademii Nauk 1 dekabrya 1866 goda v pamyat stoletney
godovshchiny rozhdeniya N. M. Karamzina* (St. Petersburg, 1867), p.
27.

In reply to your dear letter I shall say in accordance with the old Latin proverb that one does not dispute tastes; I really enjoy the quiet, isolated life here when I am well and have no anxieties of the heart. All the hours of the day are occupied in a pleasant manner: at nine o'clock in the morning I wander the dry (even in bad weather) roads around the beautiful, not misty lake, celebrated in [Mme d'Épignay's] Conversations d'Émilie; at eleven o'clock I breakfast with my family and work with enjoyment until two, still finding in myself soul and imagination; at two o'clock—on horseback, regardless of rain or snow; I shake, I sway—and am cheerful; I return with an appetite, eat dinner with my dear ones, nap in the armchair, and in the evening darkness I walk another hour in the garden, look at the lights of houses in the distance, listen to the little bells of people galloping along the highway and often to the cry of an owl; I return refreshed and read newspapers, non-Russian journals, a non-Russian book; at nine o'clock we drink tea at the round table, and from ten to eleven-thirty, always regretting that the evenings are short, the two girls, my wife, and I read Walter Scott—novels, but with innocent food for the imagination and heart. I know no boredom or yawning, and I thank God . . . I am so immobile that I have only once been to [the palace at] Gatchina, despite my heartfelt love for the Empress. My work has again become blissful for me. . . . In my quiet ecstasy I think not of contemporaries, nor of posterity; I am independent and enjoy only my work, my love for the fatherland, and for humanity. . . . In a word, I am a perfect Count Khvostov in my ardor for the Muses or the Muse. (22 October 1825)[2]

In describing his actions and attitudes, Karamzin manages to characterize himself as living up to the norms that have constantly appeared in this study: independence from the court;

[2] *Pisma Karamzina k Dmitriyevu*, pp. 407–8. That Karamzin had to make excuses for reading novels shows the low regard in which they were held.

capacity for love and friendship; love of literature; good taste; a harmonious balance of mental, physical, and emotional activities; and a relieving sense of self-irony, which he reveals in comparing himself to the hapless graphomaniac Khvostov (a member of Shishkov's Beseda) and in painting an unheroic equestrian portrait of himself. No Arzamasians reading this monumental account could accuse Karamzin, as they had accused Galiani and Voltaire, of coldness or lack of independence. And no minute of Karamzin's typical day fails to exemplify Zhukovski's definition of Enlightenment: "the art of living."

Batyushkov, a younger, more playful Arzamasian, described his own typical day to N. I. Gnedich in answer to the charge that the cause of his illnesses was idleness:

"Idleness and inaction is [*sic*] the mother of everything, including illnesses." This is what you write me, industrious bee! But here there are a multitude of grammatical mistakes. . . . The sense of it sins against truth, first of all because I am not idle:

In a day there are 24 hours.

Of these I pass 10 or 12 in bed, occupied with sleep and dreams.

Ibid. . . 1 hour I smoke tobacco.

1 hour I dress myself.

3 hours I practice the art, called *il dolce far niente,* of killing time.

1—I eat dinner.

1—my stomach digests the food.

¼ hour I look at the sunset. This time, you will say, is lost. Not true! Ozerov always followed the sun beyond the horizon, and he writes better verses than mine, and he is more active than both you and me.

¾ of an hour each day must be deducted for certain natural needs, by which Mistress Nature, as if in punishment for excessive activity and for the good of mankind, condemned heroes, enemies of mankind, idlers, judges, and bad writers to spend in walking up and down the stairs, in the cloakroom, etc., etc., etc. Oh, Humanité!

1 hour I use for remembering friends, of which I think of you for a half-hour.

1 hour I occupy with the dogs, and they are live, practical friendship, and, by the grace of heaven, I have three of them: two white ones, one black. P. S. The ears of one are sore, and the poor thing tosses her head a great deal.

½ hour I read Tasso

½—I repent that I translated him.

3 hours I yawn in expectation of night.

Notice, oh my friend, that all people wait for night like a blessing, all in general and I am a human being!

In all, 24 hours.

From this it follows that I am not idle; that you consider distraction activity, for you in the city of Saint Peter have no time to think about what you are doing every day; that for me and for you and for all equally time comes and passes equally:

Eheu fugaces, Postume, Postume... that my illnesses are not from laziness, no, but my laziness is from the illnesses, for rheumatism deprives one of the power not only to reflect, but to think, etc. (III, 101–03; 30 September 1810)

Batyushkov was fond of quoting Buffon's maxim that "le style est l'homme même." In this passage he characterizes himself as playful Epicurean with his frivolously logical style, his hyperbolic confirmation of Gnedich's charges, and his mixture of everyday details, sentiments, and literary references. When he was writing this passage, Batyushkov was reading Montaigne with great enjoyment, and echoes of Montaigne's techniques and themes—quotation from Horace, willingness to talk about the bodily functions, playing with pets, and scepticism toward mindless activity—reinforce the authorial image that Batyushkov constructed. With Arzamasian self-irony, Batyushkov, who enjoyed one of his most creative years in 1810, pretends to devote no time to poetry. This casual attitude toward literary creativity, as we shall see, often distinguished the Arzamasian epistolary persona. Writing was one of the activities that perfected the individual, but not the only one.

Describing his quest for moral perfection, Zhukovski moved from the habitual—and idealized—present of the other Arzamasians' typical days to the future:

> Here are my daily pursuits:
>
> 1. *A collection of religious concepts.* I must make a confession to you. I cannot be a hypocrite before you. I do not have what is called a complete understanding of religion. But I wish to believe and will have a pure faith, worthy of man and God. In this you are my surety. Sincerity in this wish is sufficient. I will spiritually seek conviction, that faith which is necessary for happiness, which perfects the heart. . . .
>
> 2. *Reading of the Moralists.* I want to make *my grafts* every day without fail, that is, every day to graft onto somebody else's good thought some of my own. A collection of these thoughts for you. Every day must be marked by its own special thought.
>
> 3. *Each day two or three pages of prose* about anything at all. In time this will constitute decent material for a journal. . . .
>
> 4. *Each day without fail* [*I will*] *write in verse,* and everything will be recopied for you.
>
> 5. *Reading books on education.* Before taking action, one must gather together one's thoughts, even those of others if one has none of one's own. From these materials [I shall] in time make up letters about education and letters to Dunyasha about her children. A fine *pamphlet* (?) might come of it.
>
> 6. [*I will*] *take notes on my day.* This is for you. The bad and the good uncovered before my friend, before my conscience, before my second Providence. Look, what a mass of pursuits, and in all of this, you, my friend, my benefactress, are my resuscitator, encourager, and witness. Here is the

99

arrangement of hours, so that you will know how I am occupied at every moment:

6 o'clock. Read holy scripture, etc., and your notebook.

7
8 } Prose (letters).

9　Walk.

10
11 } Verses (letters).
12

1
2 } Materials for an epic on Vladimir.

3
4 } Free activity. It would not be bad to sleep a bit.
5

6　Walk.

7
8 } Read moralistic books and about education.
9

10　Notes on the day.[3]

Zhukovski characterizes himself by his mental and moral strivings (not by his actual pursuits), by the solemnity of his reading material, and by his capacity for active friendship. There is feeble Arzamasian self-irony in his admission that he might have to take a nap in the afternoon. Unlike Batyushkov and Karamzin, he assigns little importance to physical activity, the emotions, and the world of objects.

Pushkin's brief list of activities does not erect such a monument as the other three. It characterizes its author by his move-

---

[3] Zhukovski, "Pisma-dnevniki V. A. Zhukovskogo 1814 i 1815 godov," pp. 183–84. Zhukovski composed these so-called letter-diaries for his beloved half-niece M. A. Protasova. Difficulties in communicating with her led him to assemble the letters in little booklets until such time as they could be delivered. I feel justified in treating them as letters not only because Zhukovski did, but also because their constant awareness of a recipient distinguishes them from a diary. Zhukovski seems to have made no greater attempt to avoid repetition between the "letter-entries" than he did in successive letters to his other recipients. The "letter-entries" closely resemble the letters of Zhukovski described above, Chapter III, pp. 83–85.

ments and reading: "Do you know my pursuits? Before dinner I write memoirs, I dine late; after dinner I ride horseback, in the evening I listen to fairy tales, and by this compensate for the insufficiencies of my damned upbringing" (XIII, 121; November 1824, to L. S. Pushkin).

The authorial image of an Arzamasian letter required, as these examples suggest, modesty and self-depreciation to rescue it from pomposity. The Arzamasians had passed through Sentimentalism with some worldly cynicism intact. They joked about a variety of matters, some quite tragic. Upon hearing about the dreadful Petersburg flood of 1824, later the subject of his poem "The Bronze Horseman," Pushkin remarked, "Voilà une belle occasion à vos dames de faire bidet," and expressed fears for the city's wine cellars (XIII, 122; November 1824 to L. S. Pushkin). Soon, however, realizing that it was not so funny as it had seemed, he was sending money anonymously to the victims (XIII, 127; 4 December 1824 to L. S. and O. S. Pushkin). A. I. Turgenev combined cynicism with charity in a similar manner in his relations with the drunkard-poet Milonov, whom he had employed in spite of his weakness. Here he impales the unfortunate on some Arzamasian puns:

> In Vienna ("Ein Conversationsblatt") they are translating the drunk Milonov, whom I had to turn out of my department. Enivré de sa gloire littéraire et autres he now hangs about the guardhouses and drinks up his life and talent with the prisoners. They recently said that he is in the stronghold. Since everything is strong there except the drinks, that will probably sober him up, or else he will die of the drought, from which the fields and forests around Petersburg are now burning. (*OA*, I, 281; 5 August 1819)

During a more sentimental period of his life Turgenev had reacted with righteous indignation against such callousness on the part of a fellow student:

> Oh cold little soul! Is there any human feeling here (not to speak of brotherly feeling) to make such parallels? And

101

he writes his father a letter with the same cold expressions, and, moreover, in rhetorical figures. Why did you not die, cold-blooded frog. . . .[4]

Although few such scruples restrained their sense of humor, the Arzamasians did balance their harshness with accounts of charitable deeds and warm sentiments. Indeed, some such sentiments were expected of them, especially in professions of friendship, and, if the occasion demanded it, they did not hesitate to reveal their emotions.

From the use of the word "confession" in Zhukovski's typical day and from the letters themselves, it is readily apparent that in their letters the Arzamasians had little intention of revealing such shameful events and making such intense analyses of themselves as Rousseau had done in his confessions. Little intrudes into their other correspondence to add warts to the portraits they sketched in letters about their typical days. In a letter to Vyazemski, however, A. I. Turgenev fills in some of the details about the activities of Zhukovski and Pushkin that they neglected:

> You alone have not given in to that idle laziness that, like a dread destroyer of all that is beautiful and every talent, soars above Zhukovski, Pushkin, etc., etc. You demand Zhukovski's verses, but where will you seize this magnet that should raise you? He himself reposes with the grammar or sits at the Grand Prince's rich table and then yawns in anticipation of inspiration. Pushkin in the morning tells Zhukovski where he did not sleep the whole night; he visits whorehouses, me, and Princess Golitsyna, and in the evening sometimes plays "bank." (*OA*, I, 119; 4 September 1818)

The Arzamasians themselves expressed scepticism that the true image of a writer could be extracted from his writings, even though they thought that one should write as he lives. Batyush-

[4] Quoted in V. M. Istrin, "Russkiye studenty v Gettingene v 1802–4 gg.," *Zhurnal ministerstva narodnogo prosveshcheniya*, XXVIII (1910), no. 7, Otd. 2, p. 102.

kov confided to a friend that he feared to write sincerely, that it would be impossible to tell of all he thought and did anyway (III, 220; 30 June 1813, to E. G. Pushkina). Vyazemski, who knew that he did not always act as he wrote and wished to be judged by posterity for his writings alone (*OA*, I, 230; 18 April 1819), doubted the verisimilitude of the portrait of the author in Batyushkov's works: "Is Batyushkov in fact what he is in his verses? There is absolutely no voluptuousness in him" (*OA*, I, 382; 26–27 December 1819). The authorial images projected by the letters may have reflected the ideals by which the Arzamasians sought to live. This is certainly true of Zhukovski's strictly organized typical day of the future. Whether or not the Arzamasians actually succeeded in living by these ideals is a problem for their biographers. The uniformity of their authorial images should lead us to suspect a literary pose. As we saw in the last chapter, they rejected such detail as would make them seem ridiculous to posterity. Writers and the public did consider the familiar letter a nonfictional genre; it remained for Gogol to add extensive mystification to its possibilities.[5] But one does well to consider a point raised by Northrop Frye in connection with autobiography: "most . . . are inspired by a creative, and therefore fictional, impulse to select only those events and experiences in the writer's life that go to build up one integrated pattern."[6]

The authorial image that the Arzamasians presented in their letters varied, as we have seen, but it had certain basic characteristics that constitute the norm against which they judged others—capacity for love and friendship, love of literature, good taste, delight in the pleasures of the mind and flesh, frankness, self-irony, a variety of interests, civility, and a sense of humor. Karamzin's typical day provided the most inclusive list of these traits.

The authorial image projected by a letter could also contain features characteristic of other genres—the pose of effortless creation and laziness of a verse epistle, the righteous indigna-

[5] Todd, "Gogol's Epistolary Writing," p. 69.
[6] Frye, *Anatomy of Criticism*, p. 307.

tion of a bitter satire, the patriotism of a panegyric ode, the melancholy of an elegy. Much of the freedom and sincerity traditionally attributed to familiar letters, as opposed to other genres, results from their authors' being able to present themselves in such a combination of moods and poses, acquiring authenticity from their use of specific detail and self-irony.

The writer's relationship with his recipient further complicates the image he projects. Accustomed to pouring out aspects of himself into various poetic genres, an Arzamasian further divided himself among his recipients. Social etiquette became literary etiquette for this aspect of letter writing. As they would have done in polite conversation, the Arzamasians remembered the interests and capabilities of their addressees and tailored their letters accordingly. A. I. Turgenev spoke openly of this practice to Vyazemski:

> With Dmitriyev I correspond almost weekly, sometimes even twice a week, but in a different manner and not without cause; only with you can I speak directly from the heart on everything that comes to mind and pours from the pen *without difficulty*. With him I am only a reviewer of foreign and sometimes Russian literature. (*OA*, I, 293; 19 August 1819)

One might well suspect that Turgenev invented the comparison as a means of demonstrating his friendship with Vyazemski; it serves that purpose admirably. But Dmitriyev's age and stiffness of manner did not permit the free and easy address that distinguishes Turgenev's letters to Vyazemski. The formality of this opening and its bureaucratic lexicon typify letters to Dmitriyev: "Dear sir, Ivan Ivanovich. I hasten to forward Your Excellency the verses recited in the local gymnasium and others by the same author, recited in the Masonic lodge. To these latter I append one strophe for your attention alone."[7]

[7] A. I. Turgenev, "Pisma A. I. Turgeneva k I. I. Dmitriyevu," *Russki arkhiv*, 1867, pp. 639–40.

Vyazemski met the requirement that a letter be tailored for its recipient by writing what he thought his friends needed to hear. He loved to argue with and exhort his correspondents, as this passage from a letter to Zhukovski illustrates:

Your misfortune is that you carry your poetry with you everywhere. Jasmine is jasmine even in a stable, but what benefit is there from it. Just think, what have you done for your own glory and the Fatherland's in the course of these last five or six years? You cast several flowers at idols, sooner or later they must fade; that is not the place for them. Do not forget, moreover, that you have reached the age of manhood; now it is time to carve away for posterity. Tell me in good conscience, can you take on important work in such surroundings as those in which you are quivering? Minerva did not spring from a powdered head. Powder dries the brain, believe me. (16 February 1822)[8]

By "idols" Vyazemski meant the royal family, for whom Zhukovski had written verses in the early 1820s. "Powder" refers to the powdered wig of Zhukovski's costume for court events, as Vyazemski imagined it. At this time Zhukovski was a tutor to members of the royal family, and Vyazemski feared for his authorial independence.

Pushkin was the most protean of the Arzamasians in joining his epistolary persona to the interests of his recipients. As the occasion demands, he appears as sentimental friend, ardent lover, practical husband, stern philosopher, or carefree rake. In the two familiar letters that follow, written at approximately the same time (October 1824), Pushkin makes personal requests using different literary personae, two varieties of the carefree poet. In this letter to P. A. Pletnev—a mild-mannered poet and publisher whose taste was somewhat old-fashioned— Pushkin employs a verse compliment, classical conceits, and references to the literary people and events that interested

[8] P. A. Vyazemski, "Pisma k V. A. Zhukovskomu," *Russki arkhiv*, 1900, p. 183.

Pletnev. Not only the subject, but also the bland style and image of the poet coincide with Pletnev's poetic preferences:

> You published my uncle;
> The creator of "The Dangerous Neighbor"
> Was very worthy of that,
> Although the defunct Beseda
> Did not take notice of it.—
> Now publish me, friend,
> The fruits of my vain labors,
> But for Phoebus' sake, my Pletnev,
> When will you be your own publisher?

> I am nonchalantly and joyously relying on you with respect to my Onegin!—Summon my Areopagus: you, Zhukovski, Gnedich, and Delvig—I await your verdict and will accept the decision with humility. (Late October 1824)[9]

For N. V. Vsevolozhski, a leader of the "Green Lamp" (a theatrical and drinking society), Pushkin modifies the image of the carefree poet. Classical conceits and sentimental compliments yield to specific reminiscences of physical pleasures. Concomitantly, poetry becomes a less serious matter; recreation of the irreverent, politically liberal manner of the "Green Lamp" replaces stylization of Sentimentalist poetic friendship:

> I cannot believe that you have forgotten me, dear Vsevolozhski—you remember Pushkin, who spent so many happy hours with you—Pushkin, whom you saw both drunk and in love, not always faithful to your Saturdays, but your devoted comrade in the theatre, the confidant of your pranks; Pushkin, who sobered you up on Good Friday and led you by the hand into the church of

---

[9] I have used the reading of this letter published in A. S. Pushkin, *Sobraniye sochineni v desyati tomakh* (Moscow: GIKhL, 1959–62), IX, 112.

the theatrical management to pray to the Lord God and to stare at [the ballerina] Ovoshnikova. This very Pushkin has the honor to remind you now of his existence and to set about a certain matter which concerns him closely. . . . Do you remember that I half-sold, half lost to you at cards the manuscript of my verses? For you know that bad luck at gambling gives rise to recklessness. I repented, but too late—now I have decided to atone for my sins, beginning with my verses, the greater part of which are beneath mediocrity and are only fit for complete destruction, several of which I would like to save. Dear Vsevolozhski, the Tsar will not give me my freedom! Sell me back my manuscript for the same price of 1000 rubles (I know that you will not quarrel with me; I would not want to take them for nothing). I will send you the money with gratitude as soon as I make it—I hope that my verses will not become stale at Slenin's bookstore. Think it over and send a reply. I embrace you, my joy; I also embrace your tiny Vsevolod. Someday we shall see each other. . . . Someday. . . . (XIII, 115; late October 1824).[10]

The Arzamasians also modified their epistolary personae in keeping with changes in their interests, attitudes, and (in Batyushkov's unfortunate case) mental health. The two forces of human change they most readily acknowledged were the individual's will to change and education, here applied by Batyushkov to Pushkin: "It would not be a bad idea to lock him up in Göttingen and feed him milk soup and logic for three years or so. Nothing decent will ever come of him unless he wants it himself" (III, 533; 10 September 1818, to A. I. Turgenev). The will to perfect oneself seemed an effective force to them, especially to Zhukovski, because they believed in the possibility of individual independence and self-discipline and because they considered seriously no forces of social determinism except education. The Arzamasians did not seek

---

[10] *Letters of Alexander Pushkin*, pp. 184–85.

the causes of human change in any depth. On the one hand, they focused their letters on the events and conditions of the moment, and, on the other, they expressed interests and characteristics that they hoped were unchanging—capacity for friendship, love of literature, and good taste. Vyazemski's account of the fate of his "seemly gaiety" is as complex an explanation of human development as their letters provide: "people or circumstances devoured it, perhaps, or time, probably all three simultaneously." Change, then, results from some combination of social interaction, fate, and the mere passage of time. The problem did not particularly interest Vyazemski in this case, and his analysis concludes with one of the entertaining, if intellectually unsatisfying, analogies to which the Arzamasians frequently resorted in their letters: "I am like those drunkards who have stopped drinking. You cannot entice them with a good wine; they either go to a pub or sit tight with water." (*OA*, I, 186; 9 January 1819)

The Arzamasians described their correspondents and others in their letters by the same means they employed for self-characterization: comparison with a norm; metaphor and analogy; and lists of interests, attitudes, and activities. By comparing Pushkin's life to an epigram and wishing it would become an epic poem,[11] Zhukovski provides an example of their habit of viewing character in terms of the plots and poses of the various literary genres. The brevity of the familiar letter encourages such terse characterization, and, given the Arzamasians' general indifference to the processes of human change, the letter proved adequate for such character description as they desired. Batyushkov's portrayal of V. L. Pushkin illustrates this brevity: "He is stupid and sharp, malicious and good-natured, merry and ponderous; in a single word, Pushkin is a living antithesis" (III, 132). Six adjectives and a rhetorical term suffice.

[11] In A. S. Pushkin, *Polnoye sobraniye sochineni*, XIII, 204. 9 August 1825.

108

Because the Arzamasians did not write letters for immediate distribution to a larger public, they did not generally conceal the people they were describing behind Greek names or smooth their outlines into the generalized shapes of Neoclassical "characters." Specificity marked the genre to the extent that letter writers used real names and tried to capture the individual features of real people. The Arzamasians did occasionally characterize each other with only the name of a classical prototype, but they did it in an ironic manner. When Vyazemski objected to being called the "grandson of Aristippus," Batyushkov justified the description by a playfully condescending, tongue-tied explanation:

> But why not call you the grandson of Aristippus or of Anacreon or of the devil if you wish? This does not mean, that is, that you are the grandson, actually, that is, and that your father was named Aristippych or Anakreonych, but it means that you, that is, have qualities, as if something characteristic, that is, amiability, or a fondness for getting drunk at the wrong times etc., etc., etc. (III, 168; 19 December 1811)[12]

The Arzamasians administered rebukes to each other and even insulted recipients, but they generally relieved this harshness by offering assurances of friendship or by delivering the insults in such exaggerated style that they became more funny than stinging. When Vyazemski's sarcastic references to Zhukovski's "court romanticism" became unbearably harsh, Zhukovski pleaded:

> I would not want your treatment of me to resemble your treatment of Vas. Lvovich [Pushkin]; I would not wish to be always inseparable from a *caricature* in your mind. The habit of [making] such jokes can turn into a way of thinking. . . . A tender solicitousness is necessary in friendship. I should not be a buffoon to you, let us leave

[12] Further discussion of the use of classical prototypes appears in Chapter VI, p. 145.

that for [the meetings of] Arzamas; in other moments imagine me not according to the protocols. . . . And do not forget that you are writing Turgenev! He is too careless on this score. He needs a witty letter to carry in his bosom and read to everyone he comes across. . . . The main thing that is unpleasant is that Turgenev *reads* these letters and that nobody stops him from reading them. . . . Stop sharpening your pen on me, brother! It's sharp enough as it is![13]

As Zhukovski suggests, the Arzamasians frequently wrote of each other using the caricatures of their protocols—Pushkin's frivolity, A. I. Turgenev's gluttony, or Zhukovski's otherworldliness. Because of his physical unattractiveness, marital difficulties, and eccentricity, V. L. Pushkin evoked the cruelest caricatures, such as this one by Batyushkov:

Pushkin . . . with his curly head, in an English frock coat with a pair of madrigals in his trousers and a long impromptu, prepared at breakfast on the day before, an impromptu copied out of some *Almanach des Muses,* appears in society at about nine o'clock, drinks tea, pronounces French guttural r's, inveighs against the Slavophiles [Shishkov's followers], lauds La Harpe's psalter and his pale beauty, and, finally, when night is falling over the towers of the Fortress of Peter and Paul and midnight is striking, our Pushkin, who never eats supper, *pian pianino* returns home to the embraces of his Penelope-Robin-redbreast and . . . with the help of the Muses and Phoebus Apollo does what he did nine months before that day or night in which he called himself the father of his offspring for the first time, and, like Hector, pressed his new Astyanax to his breast. (III, 152; November 1811, to Vyazemski)[14]

[13] Quoted in Gillelson, *P. A. Vyazemski,* p. 53.
[14] The Italian *pian pianino* ("gently," "softly") puns on the Russian adjective "drunk" *(pyan).*

By the vividness of their writing, the Arzamasians engraved these essentially static caricatures and authorial images on the minds of posterity and of each other. Zhukovski, who foresaw the possibility and protested against it, was not exempt from thinking in caricatures and passing them on to posterity. His portrait of A. I. Turgenev carelessly reading their letters to passers-by allows us to see none of Turgenev's greater virtues, such as his diligence at finding valuable historical documents, his philanthropy, or his administrative ability. To Vyazemski, writing as late as 1866, Pushkin remained the "favorite pupil of Karamzin and Zhukovski"[15]—feeble commemoration indeed for Russia's national poet. Only in arranging the posthumous publication of Pushkin's manuscripts did Zhukovski penetrate Pushkin's pose of effortless creation: "with what labor he wrote his light, flying verses! There is no line that had not been several times scribbled over."[16]

[15] "O pismakh Karamzina," p. 31.
[16] Zhukovski, *Sobraniye sochineni v chetyrekh tomakh,* IV, 631. 12 March 1837, to I. I. Dmitriyev.

V

Literary Criticism in the Letters of Arzamas

> In a good poem I notice everything and let noth-
> ing pass without criticism.
>> From a letter by Karamzin to Dmitriyev, 6
>> September 1794

The familiar letters of the Arzamasians are to a great extent
works of literature about literature, and this feature in large
part won them the attention of posterity. N. L. Stepanov felt
that their "shuffling" of literary and intimate material made
all of their material literary by contagion.[1] They feature
various types of criticism, literary theory, discussions of the
writing process, and many verse inserts. As we have seen, the
Arzamasians could not view nature or make requests without
referring to literature. Indeed, literary criticism is frequently
the thread that sews their seemingly chaotic letters together,
and an investigation of the familiar letter's methods of literary
criticism will help define it as a genre.

A number of considerations made letters an important
vehicle for the literary criticism of the Arzamasians. An alter-
native medium, journalistic criticism, was poorly developed
and, as we have mentioned, feebly supported by the small
cultivated public. Neoclassical attitudes further constrained
open criticism; close analyses and rigid attention to rules
risked ridicule for academic pedantry. Polemics evoked
memories of the degrading Grub Street activities of the
eighteenth century and threatened the civility that Karamzin
had hoped to spread through journalism. Growing scepticism
about the validity of rules and an awareness of the relativity
of taste made public criticism pretentious in the eyes of some.

---

[1] Stepanov, "Druzheskoye pismo nachala XIX v.," p. 85.

112

Fear of hurting the feelings of well-meaning amateurs led Karamzin to reject criticism of living Russian authors.[2] Since writers tended to be gentlemen amateurs of all ranks and since the number of writers was small, the author one might want to criticize was often a relative, friend, or superior in the service, such as Admiral Shishkov. Bonds of friendship prevented writers from criticizing their friends publicly. Like the other Arzamasians, Pushkin did not always find Zhukovski's poetry and ideas attractive, but he loyally defended his friend against public criticism:

> I do not quite agree with [Bestuzhev's] stern sentence against Zhukovski. Why should we bite the breasts of our wet nurse? Because we have cut our teeth? Whatever you say, Zhukovski had a decisive influence on the spirit of our literature; moreover, the style of his translations will forever remain the model. (XIII, 135; 25 January 1825)

Public criticism could even be physically hazardous in such an unsophisticated milieu. Karamzin reported—alas without dénouement—the story of a frustrated poet who challenged a critic to a duel.[3]

The relative importance of these social and intellectual factors varied from instance to instance, but the multitude of obstacles drove much criticism underground. Arzamas included many of the best poets and critics of the early nineteenth century; most of their comments on each other's work and on the ideas of such highly placed figures as Shishkov are expressed exclusively in their letters. The Arzamasians wrote their letters for equals; the genre required this relationship between author and recipient. There was no need to feed pabulum to unsophisticated readers. Because letters were not written for the immediate public, the Arzamasians could follow the tradition of friendly criticism, instilled in them in schools and literary circles, and dissect their friends' works in a sensible, hard-headed manner. The ultimate audience of the letters,

[2] Karamzin, *Izbrannye sochineniya*, II, 176.
[3] *Pisma Karamzina k Dmitriyevu*, p. 56.

posterity, would understand that the Arzamasians had not criticized their friends in public. Only Vyazemski among the active Arzamasians wrote about his friends' works, but he used his articles on Pushkin, Zhukovski, and Dmitriyev more as a pretext for waging polemical warfare against their detractors than as a vehicle for close analyses of their works. His essay on Zhukovski's prose, for example, devotes nearly as much space to attacking critical clichés as it does to discussing its ostensible subject.

Letters were not only a useful or necessary medium for Arzamasian literary criticism, they were also an adequate one, especially for Vyazemski, the member of the group whose essays most closely fit Dr. Johnson's definition: "a loose sally of the mind; an irregular indigested piece; not a regular and orderly composition."[4] Bantering, verbal fireworks, polemics with the reader, digressiveness, and a mixture of news with terse analysis characterize both Vyazemski's essays and his familiar letters on literary topics, although the letters are more obscene and specific in their criticism. Like Batyushkov, Vyazemski published some of his first articles in epistolary form to justify the liberties he took. His contemporary, Grech, wrote that the "external form of a letter" could be selected to give the author "more freedom in arranging and expressing his thoughts."[5] Later Vyazemski kept the disorderly organization without the epistolary motivation because it suited the resolutely unsystematic, "empirical" criticism that he, like the other Arzamasians, practiced in opposition to what Pushkin called the "abstract philosophy of the Germans" (XII, 65).

The Arzamasians devoted little space to literary theory in their letters except briefly in support of an argument or in criticism of a third party. Since they shared many of the same Neoclassical views on literature, they did not feel the need to

---

[4] Samuel Johnson, *Johnson's Dictionary: A Modern Selection,* ed. E. L. McAdam, Jr. and George Milne (New York, 1965), p. 167.

[5] Appendix II, p. 207. Pushkin accepted the loose organization of Chaadayev's philosophical letters because "le genre excuse et authorise cette négligence et ce laisser-aller" (XIV, 187). 6 July 1831.

articulate them; as Batyushkov wrote Gnedich about philosophy in general: "I know your thoughts, you know mine, and thus I have told you this in passing" (III, 57; 1 November 1809). Their letters, like their articles, were more apt to present the process of thinking than its carefully wrought products. In the 1820s a new generation of Russian critics, sympathetic to Schelling and the Schlegels, began to call for systematic literary theory and reserved the term "thought" for finished products. But the Arzamasians were content to consider their loosely organized letters and essays "thought." Pushkin, understanding "metaphysical" as simply "expressing abstract concepts,"[6] credited Vyazemski's letters with giving birth to the Russian metaphysical language (XIII, 44; 1 September 1822). He praised Vyazemski's essays for bearing the mark of a fine, observant, original mind and for making the reader think, even when he disagreed with Vyazemski's ideas (XI, 97).[7]

Despite the absence of abstract theorizing, one can extract a coherent set of Neoclassical criteria from the Arzamasians' articles and letters: taste, smoothness, pleasantness, style, verisimilitude, thought, clarity, accuracy, correct diction, common sense, strength, movement, contrast, pictures, imagination (as a combining, not a synthesizing facility), and feeling.[8] The letters that follow illustrate what was meant by these terms. In their public criticism, the Arzamasians, perhaps

[6] V. V. Vinogradov, ed., *Slovar yazyka Pushkina* (Moscow, 1956–61).

[7] In a devastating rebuttal of N. A. Polevoy's critique of *Eugene Onegin,* D. V. Venevitinov, a representative of this new generation, commented, "Let us abandon this trivial dissection of each sentence. In an article in which the author did not propose to himself a single *goal,* in which he did not rely on a *single fundamental thought,* how can one not encounter mistakes of this sort?" D. V. Venevitinov, *Polnoye sobraniye sochineni,* ed. B. V. Smirenski (Moscow-Leningrad, 1934), p. 222.

[8] For a discussion of these terms in Western Neoclassical criticism see Wimsatt and Brooks, *Literary Criticism,* pp. 174–336. Taking her chapter title ("The School of Harmonious Precision") from an expression of A. S. Pushkin's, L. Ya. Ginzburg analyzes the application of this Neoclassical aesthetic to Russian poetry of the early nineteenth century, *O lirike,* 2nd ed. (Leningrad, 1974), pp. 19–50.

115

fearing the charge of pedantry and not wishing to associate themselves with pedestrian reviewers, did not apply these criteria to the close analysis of literary works but rather expressed their impressions or addressed themselves to larger cultural problems. Vyazemski, for example, objected to Zhukovski's rigorous description of the fable as a genre.[9] He preferred to practice in public this sort of impressionistic criticism:

> Lomonsov in his verses is more an orator, Derzhavin is always and everywhere a poet. Both are sometimes on the same height; but the former ascends gradually and with noticeable difficulty, the latter rapidly and unnoticeably soars up to it. Lomonosov in his good strophes swims like a majestic swan; Derzhavin soars like a bold eagle. The one captivates us with symmetry and calmness of movement; the other staggers us with unexpected bursts. . . .[10]

In the appropriate place, familiar correspondence, Vyazemski was no less specific than Zhukovski, as we see from his comments on Batyushkov's verse epistle, "My Penates" ("Moi penaty," 1811–12):

> After you call us [the addressees, Zhukovski and Vyazemski] "carefree fortunates" you entreat Zhukovski to lay aside the "burden of sorrows," and consequently you were talking nonsense. You order a certain Vyazemski to avoid *him or it* [the neuter-masculine genitive singular, *ego*]. Which one? Happiness? Zhukovski? Joy? Time? Then you call this same Vyazemski Aristotle's grandson. Why Aristotle's? I don't know, will Vyazemski know, will anyone at all know! Apart from these trifles everything is fine! Still, excessive repetitions in certain places don't appeal to me, as for example in two neighboring

[9] Vyazemski, "Sochineniye v proze V. Zhukovskogo," *Polnoye sobraniye sochineni*, I, 264.
[10] Vyazemski, "O Derzhavine," *Polnoye sobraniye sochineni*, I, 19.

lines: "crown, crown, wine, wine. . . ." (9 December 1811)[11]

The difference between the two critics was not one of theory, but tactics: Zhukovski discussed rules and fine points publicly; Vyazemski imposed the rules of logic, grammar, and consistency in private, before his friend had published the epistle.

It is instructive to compare Karamzin's journalistic criticism with his epistolary criticism. Among the Arzamasians Karamzin was the most sceptical toward public criticism of living authors. Only in reviewing translations did he permit himself close analysis. In one review he took a translator of Voltaire's *Henriade* to task for a bad job and showed the public precisely where the translator had butchered the original. However, more typical of Karamzin's public criticism is this review of a translation of Sterne's *Tristram Shandy:*

> Incomparable Sterne! In what scholarly university did you learn to feel so tenderly? What rhetorical manual revealed to you the secret of stirring the finest fibres of our hearts with a pair of words? What musician commands the sounds of his strings as skillfully as you command our feelings?
>
> How many times have I read "Le Fever!" And how many times have my tears poured onto the sheets of that history! Perhaps many readers of the *Moscow Journal* have read it previously in some foreign language; but can one read "Le Fever" at any time without new heartfelt satisfaction? The translation is not my own; I only read it against the English original. Perhaps some of the beauty of the original is lost, but the reader can correct it in his heart.[12]

[11] P. A. Vyazemski, Letters to K. N. Batyushkov, Arkhiv Pushkinskogo Doma, Arkhiv K. N. Batyushkova, fond 19, no. 28, sheet 1.
[12] N. M. Karamzin, *Izbrannye sochineniya,* II, 117. This introductory comment was composed in 1792.

A precise list of the translator's failures would have been inconsistent with the reviewer's pose as a person of tender sensibility and would have served to ally him with the very academic institutions and rhetorical manuals he found so inadequate.

However vague his public criticism may have been, Karamzin the letter-writer could tell his friend Dmitriyev, "In a good poem I notice everything and let nothing pass without criticism."[13] In the following letter he not only states his criteria (logic, smoothness, pleasantness), but also gives concrete examples of their application:

> The skylark [Dmitriyev's fable "The Skylark, Its Children, and the Husbandman"] is very good. I would wish that the line "and did not think about love" were smoother and that instead of *vstrepenyas* ["having shaken its wings"] you placed another word: one must say *vstrepenuvshis* ["having shaken its wings"]. Do not change "the dear little bird"—for God's sake do not change it! Your advisors may be good on other occasions, but in this case they are wrong. The noun "dear little bird" [*pichuzhechka*] is exquisitely pleasant to me because I used to hear it from good swains in the open field. It arouses in our soul two dear ideas: *freedom* and *rural simplicity*. It is impossible to capture a better word for the tone of your fable. "Little bird" [*ptichka*] almost always calls to mind a cage, and hence bondage. "A feathered one" is something quite indefinite. Hearing this word, you do not yet know what is being talked about— an ostrich or a hummingbird.[14]

Karamzin desired the substitution of the stylistically neutral *vstrepenuvshis* for the more colloquial *vstrepenyas* (both gerunds here mean "having shaken its wings") in keeping with the norms of his time.[15] The substitution of one diminutive of

---

[13] *Pisma Karamzina k Dmitriyevu,* p. 50.

[14] *Ibid.,* pp. 38–40. 22 June 1793.

[15] V. V. Vinogradov and N. Yu. Shvedova, *Ocherki po istoricheskoy grammatike russkogo yazyka XIX veka* (Moscow, 1964), II, 178–79.

"bird" for another is not dictated or even discussed by grammars or rhetorical manuals. Karamzin advised the change because of the associations the words evoked (freedom, simplicity, cage) and because of the scene that caused the positive association (swains in the open field).[16] His decision was not only personal and subjective, it was temporary as well. In his famous story "Poor Liza" ("Bednaya Liza," 1792) Karamzin had associated "little birds" (*ptichki*) with freedom, gaiety, and open spaces: "There a young monk, with pale face and languid gaze, looks at the field through the grating of his window and sees the merry little birds, freely floating on a sea of air."[17]

Karamzin goes on to articulate his criteria for distinguishing the lofty from the low. He bases them not on the lexical levels of the language, as Lomonosov had done in his "Introduction to the Use of Church Books in the Russian Language" ("Predisloviye o polze knig tserkovnykh v rossiskom yazyke," 1758), but on associations with concrete visual images:

That which does not communicate to us a bad idea is not low. The same peasant says "dear little bird" and "fellow" [*paren*]; the first is pleasant, the second repulsive. With the first words I imagine a beautiful summer day, a green tree in a blooming meadow, a bird's nest, a fluttering robin or chiffchaff, and an easy-going swain, who with quiet satisfaction looks upon nature and says: "what a nest! What a dear little bird!" With the second word there appears in my thoughts a stout peasant who scratches himself in an unseemly manner or wipes his damp moustache with his sleeve, saying: "Hey, fellow!

[16] Lomonosov did give a chart and rules in his rhetorical manual (2nd version, 1748) to help its readers select images ("primary and secondary ideas") to accompany particular concepts ("terms"). For example, "obstacle" (term) attaches itself to "winter" (primary idea), then to "frost, snow, hail, trees without fruit or leaves, the retreat of the sun" (secondary ideas). Karamzin seems to have known the English Empiricists at first hand; Lomonosov knew of Empiricism through Christian Wolff's *Psychologia Empirica* and incorporated some of it into his manual. Lomonosov, *Sochineniya*, III, 97–104 and notes.

[17] Karamzin, *Izbrannye sochineniya*, I, 606.

What kvas!" One must confess that this is nothing of interest to our soul! And so, my dear Ivan, is it not possible to use some other word in place of "fellow"?

Karamzin continues with a logical analysis of the fable's ending: "the moral in the conclusion seems unclear to me. From the fable it follows that one should not rely on others' help; why then is it said, "Do not always be hasty in your intentions?" But this is very far from the mark and obscure. These are my very, very unimportant comments."

The epistolary nature of Karamzin's criticism does not rest only in its specificity and in its casual disregard for previous practice, although these are important features of it. The very aims and strategy of such epistolary criticism differ from those of journalistic criticism. The public critic can infect the reader with his emotions, as Karamzin did in the introduction to Sterne, by using exclamations, rhetorical questions, and anaphoric constructions; but these devices are too pompous for a letter. He can ignore the translator's blunders, which are beyond repair and, in some cases, would not ruin the reader's enjoyment of the work. Dmitriyev, however, had not submitted his mistakes to the public. There was time to repair them, if Karamzin could persuade him to accept suggestions without hurting his feelings. Specific criticisms, such as these comments by Karamzin on Prince Golitsyn's translation of Voltaire's *Henriade,* would have been too blunt for a letter to Dmitriyev:

Is there the smoothness, precision, pleasantness, and strength of the original in the translation? According to the rules of grammar, the relative pronoun *which* should have been used in the first hemistich in place of *who.* Where did *perfidy* come from in the first line? It is not in the original. And can one *destroy perfidy?* The second line is such that one would not want to read another —*to get the French kingdom.* Moreover, it is not expressed here that the French crown belonged to Henri by right of inheritance.[18]

[18] *Ibid.,* II, 98.

120

This serves admirably to frighten off potential purchasers of the translation, and it applies the same criteria as the letter to Dmitriyev (precise diction, logic, pleasantness), but it lacks the familiar letter's regard for friendship.

In his letter to Dmitriyev, Karamzin softens his criticisms by five techniques: framing, praise, extravagance of imagery, expressions of friendship, and modesty. The last two techniques maintain the equality of writer and recipient necessary in a letter: Karamzin does not address Dmitriyev as would a schoolmaster or haughty critic.

Karamzin frames his criticisms of Dmitriyev with two passages that mock a journalistic rival, A. I. Klushin, about whom Dmitriyev had written an epigram:

> The ode with a *cart* is like a cart of firewood, and firewood, as is well known, is put to good use. One can and should make other use of the political verses—forgive me this gallicism [*faire usage de*]. The paper on which they are written is rather soft. I suspect that the author wished to dig up the laurel wreath of Vasili Trediakovski, lying in dust and ashes—dig it up and place it on his own empty head. . . .
>
> Your epigram on the odic nonsense is worth printing beneath this great work of Klushin's mind. Should someone ask then, "Why did Klushin write the ode on man?" I would reply, "so that Dmitriyev could compose a fine epigram on him."

These framing passages accentuate Dmitriyev's talent. Beside Karamzin's viciousness toward Klushin, expressed in a scatological hint, his criticism of Dmitriyev appears mild indeed. He is not suggesting, after all, that Dmitriyev's verse should be burned or used as toilet paper; and he does not put Dmitriyev on a level with Trediakovski, the early eighteenth-century odist and a favorite butt of the Arzamasians' jokes.

Karamzin's success both in keeping Dmitriyev's friendship and in persuading him to make the suggested changes in the fable demonstrates his skill as an epistolary critic.

121

In analyzing Griboyedov's comedy, *Woe from Wit* (*Gore ot uma,* 1823–27), Pushkin illustrates another of the Arzamasians' Neoclassical criteria, verisimilitude. Pushkin read the play in manuscript—censorship did not permit publication of a full text until 1862—and sent his comments to A. A. Bestuzhev, a fellow writer and friend of Griboyedov. Pushkin begins his commentary by pledging allegiance to the tradition of genre criticism: "One must judge a dramatic writer according to the laws he himself acknowledges. Consequently I condemn neither the plan, nor the initial situation, nor the conventions observed in Griboyedov's comedy" (XIII, 138; late January 1825). Griboyedov had called his verse drama a comedy and had respected the conventional unities of time and place in it. The plot centers around an idealistic, impatient young man's failure at love and involves social criticism of Moscow high society; it unfolds in the home of the girl the young man loves during the course of a single day. Pushkin, as B. P. Gorodetski has noted, did not mistake Griboyedov's play for one of the popular farces that occupied the Russian stage at the time. Pushkin judged the play as what he called elsewhere "high comedy": comedy based on the development of characters (XI, 178).[19] Griboyedov's goal, continues Pushkin's letter, was "characterization and a sharp picture of manners." Within the limits of his generic expectations, however, Pushkin had some serious reservations: "Sofiya [the heroine] is sketched unclearly: half a whore, half a Moscow *cousine*" (XIII, 138). It was, of course, historically possible, given the Platonic nature of contemporary Sentimentalist love, that a young girl could entertain a young man in her bedroom all night without injury to her virtue. But Neoclassical "verisimilitude"—in accordance with the ninth chapter of Aristotle's *Poetics*—was not based on historical truth. As the movement's chief legislator,

---

[19] B. P. Gorodetski, "K otsenke Pushkinym komedii Griboyedova 'Gore ot uma,' " *Russkaya literatura,* 1970, no. 3, p. 35. For an excellent discussion of Griboyedov's play in the context of Neoclassical comedy, see D. J. Welch, *Russian Comedy 1765–1823* 'S-Gravenhage, 1966).

Boileau, wrote in "L'Art poétique": "Le vrai peut quelquefois n'être pas vraisemblable." The compromising situations in which Griboyedov places his heroine at the beginning and end of the play make Sofiya unbelievable as a virtuous young heroine within the traditions of this genre. Critics awarded the quality of verisimilitude with respect to the idealized relationships of polite society as they had been canonized in Neoclassical literature, not in accordance with historical aberrations from that movement's idea of "general nature." Griboyedov's other characters, psychologically and historically convincing by the subsequent standards of literary Realism,[20] ran afoul of similar criticism by Pushkin:

> Molchalin is not distinctly base enough. . . . Now a question. In the comedy *Woe from Wit* who is the most intelligent character? The answer: Griboyedov. And do you know who Chatski [the hero] is? A fiery, noble, and good fellow who has spent some time with a very intelligent man (namely with Griboyedov) and has filled himself with his thoughts, witticisms, and satiric observations. Everything he says is very intelligent, but to whom does he say all of this? To Famusov [Sofiya's father]? To Skalozub [a *miles gloriosus*]? To Molchalin [Chatski's rival]? This is unforgivable. The first sign of an intelligent man is to know at first glance with whom he's dealing and not to cast pearls before Repetilov [an informer] and others like him. By the way, what is Repetilov? In him there are 2, 3, 10 characters. Why make him vile? It's enough that he's empty-headed and stupid with such ingenuousness; it's enough that he confesses his stupidity every minute. (XIII, 138)

Pushkin, prompted by the generic title and unities of Griboyedov's play, expected minor characters to be simply delineated and the intelligent hero to be as versed in the ways of social intercourse as Pushkin himself was. Pushkin's foot-

[20] The novelist I. A. Goncharov's fine essay, "A Million Torments" ("Milyon terzani," 1871), is eloquent testimony to this.

note to his comment on Chatski is instructive in this regard; it compares Griboyedov's hero unfavorably with the villain of Gresset's Neoclassical comedy, *Le Méchant* (1745): "Gresset's hero Cléon doesn't show off his intelligence before Géronte or Chloé" (XIII, 138). That Pushkin could compare Griboyedov's hero with Gresset's troublemaker shows that he was in this case the prisoner of the generic approach to literature. Both Chatski and Cléon try to break up romances, but the former acts out of memory for a past love, the latter for the sake of perverse amusement. Griboyedov had taken a traditional comedy type, the obstacle to love, and made him his hero; Pushkin failed to appreciate the resulting complexity of Chatski's characterization. Chatski's love makes him lose self-control and deprives him of the ability to persuade others to share his social criticism; Chatski's social concerns in turn lend his abortive profession of love a harsh satiric tone that has entirely the wrong effect upon Sofiya, whose taste runs to the quiet, sentimental types who would normally be the successful young lovers of Russian comedy. But Chatski is hardly a rational troublemaker in the mold of Cléon.

Pushkin's comments on the love situation in the play further reveal his conventional expectations:

> Among the masterful features of this charming comedy is Chatski's disbelief in Sofiya's love for Molchalin— charming!—and how natural! This is what the whole comedy should have turned on, but Griboyedov evidently didn't want it—his will be done.

Griboyedov had taken the timeless love situation that Pushkin wanted and shaped it in terms of the dilemma that faced the young reformers of his time: how can one persuade a self-idealizing society to transform itself without violating the proprieties of that society and being excluded from it. Any deviation from the normal social relationships was considered insane or comic by that society; Chatski's ideas make him appear insane, and, ironically, the more he tries to participate in that society (through his love for Sofiya) the more frustrated and "insane" he becomes. It is a brilliant stroke on Griboyedov's part that it is Sofiya who starts the rumor of Chatski's insanity.

Pushkin, whose novel *Eugene Onegin* quotes *Woe from Wit* and casts similar illumination on the viciousness of polite society, did like Griboyedov's play. He concluded his criticism with the following gracious mollification:

> Of the verses I shall say nothing—half of them are bound to become proverbs. Show this to Griboyedov. Perhaps I am mistaken in something. While listening to his comedy I was not criticizing but enjoying myself. These observations came to mind afterward, when I could no longer check on them. At least I am speaking directly, without beating around the bush, as to a truly talented person. (XIII, 139)

Almost simultaneously with this criticism of *Woe from Wit* for its lack of verisimilitude Pushkin was writing a self-styled "Romantic tragedy," *Boris Godunov,* in which he broke the unities of time and place with a vengeance, leapt from the comic to the tragic with Shakespearean freedom, and tried to re-create the cultural situation of seventeenth-century Russia and Poland through painstaking research. In the haste of his epistolary criticism Pushkin, who boldly signaled his own dramatic innovation by his choice of subject and form, failed to see the full originality of Griboyedov's design. More than Pushkin's public essays, however, the letter allows us to see precisely what a critic raised in the Neoclassical tradition expected in the way of dramatic characterization and plotting.

Together with close analysis of their friends' works, the Arzamasians generally reserved criticism by parody and travesty for their familiar correspondence, although, as we have seen, they made use of these techniques in the protocols of their meetings as well. In a recent essay, A. Morozov has distinguished three varieties of parody: parody that is humorous

125

or joking, and friendly or neutral toward the parodied work; parody that is satiric and antagonistic to the parodied work; and parody that uses the original work against something other than a work of literature.[21] The Arzamasian protocols would fall into the second and third categories: they parody Zhukovski's ballads and, at the same time, use them against Shishkov and his Beseda. Placing a work in one of these categories raises the difficult problem of determining a writer's intentions, unless one understands "writer" as the implied author who can be extrapolated from the parody itself. But Morozov's scheme provides useful distinctions for our discussion.

Frequently the parodying of a line or two, or even a stanza, served to tease one's recipient or give a literary cast to a non-literary subject. Pushkin used some lines from Dmitriyev's poem "To Masha" in a passage on his desire to leave Russia:

> We live in a sorry age, but when I imagine London, railroads, steamboats, English journals and Parisian theaters and whorehouses, my God-forsaken [estate] Mikhaylovskoye bores and enrages me. In the fourth canto of *Onegin* I depicted my life [of provincial boredom]; sometime you will read it and ask with your dear smile: "Where is my poet? Talent is conspicuous in him." You will hear, dear one, in reply: "He made off to Paris and will never return to damned Russia"—well done, smart fellow. (XIII, 280; 27 May 1826)[22]

On one level, Pushkin's quotation represents the humorous appropriation of literary material, Morozov's joking parody. However, it is also a round in the continuous sparring of Pushkin and Vyazemski over Dmitriyev. Pushkin, who did not

---

[21] A. A. Morozov, "Parodiya kak literaturni zhanr (k teorii parodii)," *Russkaya literatura*, 1960, no. 1, p. 68.

[22] The parodied lines from Dmitriyev's poem are: "You will read these lines with a dear smile and ask: 'Where is my poet? Talents are conspicuous in him.' You will hear, dear one, in reply: 'The unfortunate are of few years; he is no more!' " I. I. Dmitriyev, "K Mashe" (1803), *Polnoye sobraniye stikhotvoreni*, ed. G. P. Makogonenko (Leningrad, 1967), p. 340.

care for Dmitriyev's work, reminded Vyazemski of that fact by parodying a few lines of one of Dmitriyev's poems and destroying their elegiac mood.

In another example of epistolary denigration, Batyushkov tailored the sublime imagery of odes to fit an account of the Petersburg literary scene during the Napoleonic invasion. The phrase "home of the sun" (*solntsev dom*) belongs to Derzhavin, one of the greatest Russian odists:

> Shall I speak now of our Petersburg acquaintances, about Baty, about Tamerlane, about Genghis Khan, the poet [D. I. Khvostov] who annihilated Racine, Boileau, La Fontaine, and others? Shall I tell you that he wrote an ode on the peace with the Turks; an ode, yes, an ode, *in this day and year!* Shall I tell you of our society, all of whose members, like Horace's wise or just man, are calm and writing during the destruction of the spheres:
>
>> Terrible thunder crashes everywhere,
>> The sea is hurled up to the sky in mountains,
>> The furious elements quarrel,
>> And the *distant home of the sun*
>> And the stars fall in rows.
>> They are calm behind their desks.
>> They are calm. They have pens,
>> They have paper, and—all is well!
>> They neither hear nor see
>> And all the while they write with goose feathers.
>
> (III, 199; 9 August 1812, to Dashkov)

This example of literary parody is more complete than is Pushkin's treatment of Dmitriyev. It calls attention to the ode's shuffling of grandiose natural scenes with the line "the sea is hurled up to the sky in mountains." Batyushkov then turns the parody against the official writers of odes, far removed from the dangers of battle. Batyushkov's parody is antagonistic toward the genre (Morozov's satiric parody) and toward its practitioners (Morozov's parodic use).

127

It is strikingly illustrative of the flexible relationship of these poets toward literary conventions that Batyushkov himself later used the sublime imagery that he had parodied to describe a storm in a poem, "The Song of Harold the Bold" ("Pesn Garalda Smelogo," 1816). In describing his work on the poem to Vyazemski, Batyushkov travesties his own poem with verse inserts. Taking advantage of the familiar letter's connection with the situation of the moment, he places blame for his disillusionment with this favorite pre-Romantic theme on his rheumatism. His travesty thus becomes less an attack on the poetic fashion than a reflection of his momentary mental state, and, as we shall see, a fulfillment of epistolary convention.

Yesterday morning, reading *La Gaule poétique,* I took it into my head to attack Harold the Bold, that is, I translated about twenty lines, but I worked myself into such a passion that my leg began to hurt. I ran out of poetic steam, and I saw a small change in my hero. When I read of the Scandinavian's exploits,

> I thought I saw in him a hero
> In a magnificent helmet
> With a finely decorated saber in his hand
> And in greaves of ancient shape.
> I thought: in his fiery eyes
> Must shine calmness of soul,
> In his lofty gait, heroism,
> And on his lips, conviction.

But having closed the book, I saw quite the opposite! The fine ideal disappeared,

> And before me
> Suddenly appeared . . . a simple Finn:
> With hair hanging to his shoulders
> And a rude voice,
> And the whole hero—a perfect Finn.

128

That was a small transformation. The hero began to act: to walk, eat, and drink. He dined in an unusually poetic manner:

> He began to skin a piece of raw mutton
> With his fingernails.
> He swallowed it like a beast of the forest
> And wiped off his hands on his hair.

I said not a word. To each his own. Homer's heroes and our Kalmuks did it this way on bivouac. But this is what made me lose patience: before the Finn stood the skull of a slain enemy, mounted with silver, and a bucket of wine. Imagine what he did!

> He seized the skull in his bloody fingers,
> Poured wine into it
> And tossed it all off . . .
> Not moving his lips.

I awoke and gave myself my word of honor never to sing of such monsters, and I advise you not to. (III, 371–72; February 1816)

The Viking chieftain's performance of bodily functions undermines the complex (flashing eyes, calm soul) conception of him as both tender lover and warrior prince, which Batyushkov had extracted from his reading. The French original had endowed Harold with the conventional sensibility of salon society; Batyushkov stripped away the sensibility when he evaluated Harold's behavior according to the manners of salon society. Transposed from the poem to the familiar letter, a genre capable of dealing practically with such everyday activities as eating, Harold can no longer maintain his lofty pose, and he becomes a travesty of his poetic self. Verse that the younger Arzamasians wrote for their letters—unlike the elegiac poetry in Karamzin's early correspondence—is almost invariably ribald or parodistic.

Batyushkov's verse did not become more "realistic" in any meaningful sense after this letter was written (February 1816),

129

and it seems unlikely that general disillusionment with the conventions of early nineteenth-century verse inspired his travesty. It is probably more accurate to view his transfer of a lofty topic to a vulgar plane as a convention of familiar letters. The genre required of its persona, as we have seen, self-irony and self-depreciation in order to keep the author of the letter on the same level as its recipient. One means for a practicing poet to accomplish this was to present the act of creation as something casual, effortless, or matter-of-fact. Another means was to present oneself as a normal human being, subject to physical suffering, and simultaneously to present the act of creation as a messy, difficult affair—as Batyushkov has done here in travestying his own work because of a bad dream. The Arzamasians consistently chose organic metaphors for the creative process that would convey self-depreciation and a sense of the human, vulnerable nature of creation—sweat, excrement, sperm, diarrhea, belching, dirty linen.

Discussion of the following letter by Pushkin gives us the opportunity to review some features of the genre that we have observed in the chapters on selection of content, characterization, and literary criticism:

> In the wilds, tormented by a life of fasting,
> With an exhausted stomach
> I do not soar, I perch like an eagle,
> And am ill of diarrheic idleness.
>
> I am guarding my supply of paper;
> Free from the strain of inspiration,
> I rarely walk upon Parnassus,
> And only out of great necessity.
>
> But your ingenious manure
> Tickles my nose pleasantly;
> It reminds me of Khvostov,
> The father of toothy pigeons,
> And calls my spirit anew
> To the defecation of former days.

130

Thank you, my dear fellow, and I kiss you on your poetic little cunt. Since I have been in Mikhaylovskoye I have guffawed only twice: at your critique of the "New Poetics of Fables" and at the dedication of your shit to shit. How can I help loving you? How can I help groveling before you? However, I am ready to grovel, but no matter what you say I shall not copy—it would be the death of me, and nothing else.

Congratulate me, my joy, on my romantic tragedy. In it the principal personage is Boris—Godunov! My tragedy is finished; I reread it aloud, alone, and I clapped my hands and shouted, 'yes, Pushkin, yes, you son of a bitch!' My holy fool is a very funny young fellow. Marina will make you get a hard on—because she is a Pole and very good looking (of the type of Katerina Orlova, have I told you?). The others are very nice, too, except for Captain Margeret, who swears obscenely all the time—the censorship won't pass him. Zhukovski says that the Tsar will forgive me, as a result of my tragedy— hardly, my dear one. Although it is written in a good spirit, there's no way I could hide my ears completely under the pointed cap of the holy fool. They stick out! Your criticism of Krylov is killingly funny: be quiet, I know that myself, but that rat is an old crony of mine. I have called him a representative of the essence of the Russian people—I don't vouch that it does not stink in some respects. In antiquity our common people were called *smerd* [stench] (cf. Mr. Karamzin). The point is that Krylov is a most original carcass, Count Orlov is a fool, but we are dolts, etc., etc.

I wrote you from Pskov a killingly funny letter, but I burned it up. The bishop there, Father Eugene, received me as the father of Eugene [Onegin]. The governor was also extremely gracious. He gave me his own verses, sir, to correct. What do you think of that! Farewell, my dear one. (XIII, 239–40; 7 November 1825)[23]

[23] *Letters of Alexander Pushkin*, pp. 261–62. I have altered Shaw's translation of the verse opening.

131

Pushkin opens *ex abrupto* with no epistolary formula, not even "dear friend." The verse travesties one of his favorite lyric themes, the return of poetic inspiration. In "The Prophet" ("Prorok," 1826), Pushkin presented inspiration as divine in nature; in "I remember a miraculous instant" ("Ya pomnyu chudnoye mgnoveniye," 1825), he linked inspiration with the return of a beautiful woman. Here, the conventions of an Arzamasian familiar letter lead Pushkin to give the poetic inspiration a vulgar origin, a similarly vulgar bit of epistolary doggerel that Vyazemski had sent to Pushkin.[24] The reference in Pushkin's poem to D. I. Khvostov, a favorite target of the Arzamasians, opens the theme of fables that helps thread the seemingly chaotic letter together. To the delight of his opponents, Khvostov had destroyed the fable convention—animals keep their natural shape, but behave like humans—by giving his pigeon human physical features: a set of powerful teeth.

The manner of this polemic reveals a method of epistolary criticism unexploited in Karamzin's letter to Dmitriyev: partial agreement. J. Thomas Shaw explains this device in a gloss of lines 39–44:

> Pushkin was amused at the way Vyazemski in his letter had objected that to present the "lackey" Krylov as typical of the Russian people would be like painting a person's backside as the differentiating human characteristic. Pushkin manages to agree and at the same time remain of the same opinion, by quoting the concluding lines from Krylov's "Council of Mice" (1811). In this poem, the mice had decided that mice with the longest tails had the most intelligence, and they called a council of the most intelligent mice, according to this standard. A tailless rat appeared. When one of the young mice objected, a gray old mouse made the rejoinder Pushkin quotes here ["That rat is an old crony of mine"].[25]

[24] Vyazemski's letter appears in A. S. Pushkin, *Polnoye sobraniye sochineni*, XIII, 238–39.

[25] *Letters of Alexander Pushkin*, p. 295.

Pushkin conceals his stubborn disagreement behind verbal fireworks as well as humor: the pun on "essence" and the recurring mention of an Orlov, this time not a beautiful woman (as in line 30), but the publisher of French and Italian editions of Krylov's fables.

Like Karamzin, Pushkin uses the theme of friendship to conceal disagreement, but he gives it a much more extravagant expression: endowing Vyazemski, a hero of the War of 1812, with what Russian dictionaries periphrastically call "a female reproductive member" as the seat of his poetic inspiration. This, like other obscenities in the letter, serves to make it intimate and to give future readers the impression that they have found something so scabrous that it was not intended for their eyes.

Pushkin employs both devices of epistolary self-depreciation referred to in connection with Batyushkov's travesty: dismissal of his poetry as excrement, and description of the process of creation as jolly and carefree. One would never guess from the way Pushkin talks about his Romantic tragedy, *Boris Godunov,* that painstaking research and months of creative effort went into writing it. The principal characters of Pushkin's tragedy—Boris, who challenges history, and the Pretender, who becomes its instrument—vanish. The familiar letter brings lesser figures to the foreground. The infantile holy fool that Pushkin mentions appears in but one brief scene, begs for pennies, and dares condemn the Tsar only because he is mad. That Pushkin jokingly appoints him *raisonneur* is a telling commentary on the poet's place in the world.

In this letter Pushkin plays his epistolary role of gaiety amidst the events that helped destroy him: exile, censorship, surveillance, dependence on the Tsar's mercy. The seriousness of these events is concealed behind references to literature. And references to the literature he took so seriously are interspersed with details that do not allow the recipient to take it too seriously— an obscenely swearing minor character, a voluptuous Pole, a scribbling governor, and a holy fool.

133

VI

Style and the Illusion of Conversational Speech

> I lack even my own simplicity for
> correspondence.
> From a letter by A. S. Pushkin to Vyazemski,
> 1 December 1826

The familiar letters of the Arzamasians have largely eluded the attention of Russia's numerous experts in stylistic analysis, although these scholars have exhaustively studied other genres of the period.[1] For theories of epistolary style we must return to the literary theoreticians of the eighteenth and early nineteenth centuries who set a stylistic norm for letters: colloquial language. However, in his own practice Lomonosov showed that the lexical levels he assigned could not accurately express the interests of an intelligent person. The Arzamasians did not observe his restrictions; they ranged over all the levels of the Russian language. Sokolski allowed the letter writer more freedom: "Since one speaks of different subjects in letters, one can not always write them in a single style. One must always coordinate his expressions with the character of the material and the dignity of the individual."[2] Even Sokolski's broader recommendation of appropriateness could not suffice for the Arzamasians. Appropriateness does not explain why Batyushkov chose to write a simple request for tobacco in a lofty style culled from the Koran, classical mythology, and obscure Church Slavonic

---

[1] On this score too, only the letters of Pushkin have been analyzed to any significant extent. V. A. Malakhovski, "Yazyk pisem Pushkina," *Izvestiya Akademii Nauk, SSSR, Otdeleniye Obshchestvennykh Nauk,* 1937, pp. 503–68, investigates such problems as the orthography, morphology, and lexical levels of Pushkin's letters. He supplies a thorough list of Pushkin's statements about the Russian language, which, while rarely concerning letters, shows Pushkin's interest in style and in the possibilities of language.

[2] Sokolski, *Kabinetski sekretar,* p. 12.

(III, 320) or why the others made seemingly unmotivated stylistic outbursts, puns, and witticisms. Plato's theory that all young creatures need to leap may be as good as any.[3] One of the basic principles guiding the Arzamasians' choice of style, then, is simply a desire to play with the resources of the language, to enjoy themselves, and to write for the fun of it. Such style-consciousness and the use of letters as a form of civilized recreation had marked epistolary tradition since classical antiquity and should not be ignored by scholars.

The Arzamasians' exuberance did, however, have starting points, methods, and directions, although these could be altered at any point. Many features of their culteral situation made the Arzamasians highly sensitive to points of style. Lomonosov's theory of three styles, the controversies of the eighteenth century, their experience in the civil service, and the quarrel between the supporters of Shishkov and Karamzin had trained the Arzamasians to think of the Russian literary language in terms of the origins and lexical levels of individual words—native Russian, chancellery, Church Slavonic, or foreign; their Neoclassical predilection for taxonomy encouraged them to assign each word and construction to one of these categories. The insistence on precision that marked their criticism further concentrated their attention on individual words, as we have seen from the examples in the last chapter. The epigrams and humorous poetry they wrote required the ability to play with the different meanings of a single word. Their familiarity with foreign languages made them conscious of the strengths and weaknesses of their own. Bludov, Dashkov, Severin, Karamzin, Zhukovski, and Vyazemski translated important documents of state; many of the others translated imaginative literature. As we have seen, they made style an integral part of characterization ("le style est l'homme même") and political controversy (Arzamas vs. the Beseda). All of these factors combined to make the Arzamasians extremely style-conscious and gave them considerable control over the resources available to them. An appropriate way to approach the style of their letters is to ask what the tendencies are in their use of each lexical level,

[3] *Laws,* quoted in Huizinga, *Homo Ludens,* p. 37.

what varieties of syntax predominate in their letters, and how the illusion of conversation on paper is maintained and destroyed.

The initiative for selecting a particular lexical level usually came from the topic under discussion, but exuberance could seize control at some point, making the style so obtrusive that it would be unwise to connect technique with "realistic" harmonizing of style and content.[4] The Arzamasians often used the chancellery style in an "unrealistic" manner. Pushkin's formal letter to his uncle (quoted in the Introduction) provides a good example. A financial matter evoked some elements of officialese; Pushkin's sense of stylistic fun led him to expand them into a parody of an entire legal petition.[5] Besides transforming the personal, potentially humiliating request into an amusing familiar letter, the style is important in itself.

[4] As is well known, Soviet critics find "realism" in works of every age, from medieval *vitae* to works of the present day. Fridman sees Batyushkov's letters as a "school for realistic writing," *Proza Batyushkova*, p. 150, but here and elsewhere he uses the term so broadly that it lacks any useful meaning. Realia of everyday life enter letters freely, but accompanied by such literary and stylistic self-consciousness that nobody could possibly mistake a passage containing them for a passage from Turgenev or Tolstoy.

[5] In the following Russian text of Pushkin's letter, I have underscored elements of officialese (the English text appears on pp. 11–12):

1811 года дядя мой Василий Львович, *по благорасположению своему* ко мне и ко всей семьи моей, во время путешествия из Москву в С.П.Б., взял у меня *взаймы 100 рублей ассигн.*, данных мне на орехи покойной бабушкой моей Варварой Васильевной Чичериной и покойной тетушкой Анной Львовною. Свидетелем *оного займа* был известный Игнатий; но и сам Василий Львович, по благородству сердца своего, от *оного* не откажется. Так как *оному* прошло уже более 10 лет без всякого с моей стороны *взыскания* или *предъявления*, и как я потерял уже все *законное право* на *взыскание выше упомянутых 100 рублей* (с *процентами* за 14 лет; что *составляет* более *200 рублей*), то униженно молю его *высокоблагородие, милостивого государя* дядю моего заплатить мне *сии 200 рублей* по долгу христианскому—получить же *оные* деньги *уполномочиваю* князя Петра Андреевича Вяземского, известного литератора.
Коллежский секретарь Александр

Сергеев сын Пушкин

A second lexical level of the Russian language, Church Slavonic, served the Arzamasians in letters in ways unrelated to religion. In the poetry of the time as well, words of Church Slavonic origin carried connotations of loftiness and seriousness, furnished "poetical" variants of everyday words, helped approximate the rhetoric of the Koran (which was much admired by pre-Romantic poets), merged with imagery from classical mythology, and entered blasphemous verses.[6] Several of these uses of Church Slavonic advance Batyushkov's request for tobacco:

> I most humbly beg you, dear comrade and brother on Helicon, to descend from the Parnassian heights to the shop of Abdul-Kuchu-Sair-Ibrahim and take two pounds of tobacco from him for a poor poet; let the Prophet reward you for this service, let roses and jasmine be born under your feet, and rhymes flow from your pen, like rose oil flows for the just from bejeweled vessels in the vale of peace, and let a bold, sober Yakovlev play your Agamemnon! . . . That is the most impossible miracle of all. (III, 320; June 1815, to M. E. Lobanov)

The imagery from Greek mythology is suggested by the Neoclassical tastes of his recipient, that from Islamic writing by the Turkish tobacco. Batyushkov's enthusiasm led him to give the request the rhetorical cadence and solemnity of the florid "Eastern style" by using such Church Slavonicisms and archaisms as the dual number, *pod stopama tvoima* ("under your feet") and the optative, *da . . . da . . .* ("let . . . let . . .").

Not infrequently the Arzamasians—especially Vyazemski, Pushkin, and Batyushkov—used Church Slavonicisms to blasphemous, humorous ends in their letters. The practice proceeded naturally from the libertinism of their youth and proved a means of puncturing the darkness and pomposity that often surrounded them. Pushkin, for example, relieved the boredom of exile by playing a trick on the local priest. He reported the scene with appropriate Church Slavonic terminology:

[6] Vinogradov, *Yazyk Pushkina,* pp. 76–91.

Today is the anniversary of Byron's death—I have ordered a mass this evening for the repose of his soul. My priest was astonished at my piety, and gave me part of the host from the mass for the repose of God's servant, the Boyar Georgi. (XIII, 160; 7 April 1825, to Vyazemski)[7]

The familiar letter's stylistic capabilities are fully reflected in the fact that it also permitted the Arzamasians nonhumorous uses for Church Slavonic. As it had done in eighteenth-century odes and tragedies, the style conveyed in their letters emotional intensity. Batyushkov, shocked out of his accustomed gaiety and self-irony by the destruction of Moscow, adapted an oath from Psalm 137 with unwonted but appropriate solemnity: "Oh beautiful Moscow! Let my tongue cleave to the roof of my mouth and let my right hand wither away, if I forget you, oh Jerusalem!" (III, 220; 4 March 1813, to E. G. Pushkina). Predictably, Church Slavonic also helped the Arzamasians express religious matters. A. I. Turgenev states his views with much Church Slavonic in addition to Arzamasian puns, lowly imagery, a neologism (*yakobinstvuyesh*), and a line from Dmitriyev's historical ode, "Yermak:"

I spoke as a disciple of Jacobi; and you, as a cutthroat of the eighteenth century; and, finally, you are playing the Jacobin. . . . Your carcase remains with its nature; what is earthly will go into the earth, but from your sensorium and from your nature will separate that which must return to the Essence and Source. "Therefore He is almighty" and not mixed with nature, but, without separating Himself from it, He fills it and you for the time allotted it and you. Here there is none of your pantheism, but one

---

[7] *Letters of Alexander Pushkin*, p. 213. The Russian reads as follows; I have underscored the Church Slavonicisms (perceived as such in Pushkin's time).

Нынче день смерти Байрона—я заказал с вечера *обедню за упокой его души*. Мой *поп* удивился моей набожности и вручил мне *просвиру*, вынутую *за упокой раба Божия* боярина *Георгия*.

eternal outpouring of light and life from the Being without beginning, one *fiat* said in time and continuing:

Until the spheres wither and time falls under the scythe. I too do not understand God, but I sometimes feel; and You are a poet and want to be a pantheist. Let Khvostov be of one essence with his own guts, but you be above their stench, and give off fragrant scents in the heavenly ether. Do not forget what is close to man and his heart, life the life of the soul, which sometimes even while still in this shell takes leave ever so slightly of what is earthly, is elevated toward the heavenly, and drowns in delights inaccessible to pantheism (*OA*, i, 242; 27 May 1819).[8]

As in Pushkin's description of the mass for Byron, the Church Slavonicisms here are used terminologically, and not, as Shishkov had recommended, as the chief lexical source for themes other than religion. The rest of the letter also demonstrates that the Arzamasians refused to be bound by his understanding of stylistic purity. Immediately after the sermon on the immanence and transcendence of God, which includes a typically Arzamasian reference to literature (Khvostov), Turgenev motivates a shift to temporal topics by a shift of location: "I began at home, and I will finish in the State Council." The final section of the letter employs the fate of Speranski, the liberal minister exiled to Siberia, as an exemplum. Turgenev again admonishes Vyazemski, this time using straightforward syntax, a macaronic style, and more mundane imagery:

From Kazan I just now received a letter from Speranski. His conclusion: "farewell until Tobolsk." That moved me. Just imagine, he taught himself German in Penza and asks for the loftiest German literature. Sapienti sat! Bear this in mind, and let Warsaw be your Penza, because

[8] The elements of Church Slavonic diction—perceived as such in Turgenev's time—would include: *Sushchestvo-Istochnik* (Essence and Source), *"Zane On vsemogushchi"* ("Therefore He is almighty"), *Sushchestvo predvechnoye* ("eternal Essence"), *dokol* ("until"), *odno-sushchestvenny* ("of one essence"), *gorni* ("heavenly").

maybe you will succeed in writing me from Tobolsk [in Siberia]. But the Council's pen, comme de raison, doesn't write. (*OA*, I, 243)

A third lexical source, foreign languages, enters the letters of the Arzamasians frequently. It's use varies by topic, writer, and momentary whim. Before the Napoleonic invasion V. L. Pushkin and Severin wrote entire letters to Vyazemski in French; thereafter, they limited letters in French to official documents and correspondence with women. The diplomatic corps and the upper civil service used French for business purposes. The French formulae for expressing gallantry and abstract sentiments were more developed than the corresponding Russian ones. In the early 1820s Pushkin wrote:

Our prose is so little cultivated that even in simple correspondence we are forced to *create* turns of phrase for explaining the most ordinary concepts; and our laziness expresses itself more willingly in a foreign language whose mechanical forms have long been prepared and are known to everyone. (XI, 21)

Once married, Pushkin abandoned the gallantry of courtship and ceased writing his bride in French; Russian was more than adequate for everyday, practical matters. He wrote to men in Russian as a rule and expressed irritation when his brother wrote to him in French. Nevertheless, he himself used French in an important letter to the Russian philosopher Chaadayev, saying that he was more at home in it than in Russian (XIV, 187; 6 July 1831). While this admission may have been a gesture of solidarity with his Westward-looking friend, there was considerable truth in it. French was the language in which the Arzamasians did most of their political, philosophical, historical, and critical reading. When the Arzamasians wrote essays and letters on these topics, they naturally included individual French terms as well as quotations.

Since the Arzamasians knew French better than other foreign languages, it is not surprising that it should occur more

140

frequently than other foreign languages in their letters and for a greater variety of reasons. French, the language of high society, helped Pushkin express the cruelty and cynicism of that class. He used French for flippant remarks, such as the one he made on the Petersburg flood, for his deadliest insults, for challenges to duels, and for cynical advice to his brother:

Vous êtes dans l'âge où l'on doit songer à la carrière que l'on doit parcourir; je vous ai dit les raisons pourquoi l'état militaire me parait préférable à tous les autres. En tout cas votre conduite va décider pour longtemps de votre réputation et peut-être de votre bonheur.

Vous aurez affaire aux hommes que vous ne connaissez pas encore. Commencez toujours par en penser tout le mal imaginable: vous n'en rabattrez pas de beaucoup.— Ne les jugez pas par votre coeur, que je crois noble et bon et qui de plus est encore jeune; méprisez-les le plus poliment qu'il vous sera possible: c'est le moyen de se tenir en garde contre les petits prejugés et les petites passions qui vont vous froisser à votre entrée dans le monde.

Soyez froide avec tout le monde: la familiarité nuit toujours; mais surtout gardez-vous de vous y abandonner avec vos supérieurs, quelles que soient leurs avances. Ceux-ci vous dépassent bien vite et sont bien aises de vous avilir au moment où l'on s'y attend le moins.

Point de petits soins, défiez vous de la bienveillance dont vous pouvez être susceptible: les hommes ne la comprennent pas et la prennent volontiers pour de la bassesse, toujours charmés de juger des autres par eux-mêmes.

N'acceptez jamais de bienfaits. Un bienfair pour la plupart du temps est une perfidie.—Point de protection, car elle asservit et dégrade.

J'aurais voulu vous prémunir contre les séductions de l'amitié, mais je n'ai pas le courage de vous endurcir l'âme dans l'âge de ses plus douces illusions. Ce que j'ai à vous dire à l'égard des femmes serait parfaitement inutile. Je vous observerai seulement, que moins on aime une femme et plus on est sûr de l'avoir. Mais cette jouissance est digne d'un vieux sapajou du 18 siècle. À l'égard de celle que vous aimerez, je souhaite de tout mon coeur que vous l'ayez.

N'oubliez jamais l'offence volontaire; peu ou point de paroles et ne vengez jamais l'injure par l'injure.

Si l'état de votre fortune ou bie les circonstances ne vous permettent pas de briller, ne tâchez pas de pallier vos privations, affectez plûtot l'excès contraire: le cynisme dans son âpreté en impose à la frivolité de l'opinion, au lieu que les petites friponneries de la vanité nous rendent ridicules et méprisables.

N'empruntez jamais, souffrez plûtot la misère; croyez qu'elle n'est pas aussi terrible qu'on se la peint et surtout que la certitude où l'on peut se voir d'être malhonnête ou d'être pris pour tel.

Pushkin concludes the letter with an attempt to balance the cynical self-portrait and to justify his cynicism; personal experience and the desire to help his brother made him write it:

Les principes que je vous propose, je les dois à une douloureuse expérience. Puissiez-vous les adopter sans jamais y être constraint. Ils peuvent vous sauver des jours d'angoisse et de rage. Un jour vous entendrez ma confession; elle pourra coûter à ma vanité; mais ce n'est pas ce qui m'arrêtait lorsqu'il s'agit de l'intérêt de votre vie. (XIII, 49–50; September–October 1822)

The shameful confession has not come down to us, and, knowing the decorum that governed Arzamasian familiar letters, we may safely assume that Pushkin never committed it to paper.

Not long afterward, in *Eugene Onegin,* Pushkin translated his advice into the medium of Russian verse. The letter writer's worldly cynicism becomes that of the novel's narrator toward women:

> The less we love her, the more surely
> We stand to gain a woman's heart[9]

and toward friendship:

> There is no despicable lie
> By curs in attics fabricated
> And by the leisured mob inflated,
> There's never a transparent sham
> Or slimy gutter epigram
> That your good friends (with smiling faces,
> Without a sly or evil thought)
> To decent people are not caught
> Repeating in a hundred places.

As did Pushkin in his letter, the narrator presents and justifies his cynicism by hinting at some bitter experience of his own:

> What friends they were to me, my friends!
> They cannot lightly make amends.

Concluding his refusal of Tatiana, Eugene employs the same pattern of cynicism, disillusionment, and desire to help a younger person that Pushkin used at the close of the letter to his brother:

> "Spent dreams, spent years there's no reliving,
> I can't rejuvenate my soul. . . .
> A brother's love is in my giving,
> And, yet, perhaps a fonder toll.
> Don't chafe at one last admonition:

[9] From the book *Eugene Onegin* by Alexander Pushkin, translated by Walter Arndt. Copyright (©) 1963 by Walter Arndt. Reprinted by permission of the publishers, E. P. Dutton & Co., Inc. This and the following passages are from the fourth chapter, stanzas 7–19, pp. 89–93.

As this monograph was about to go to press, I. A. Paperno published a fine article on the epistolary use of French in Pushkin's time. Ms. Paperno gives interesting examples in which French phrases serve to comment on the narrative level of a letter otherwise written in Russian. I. A. Paperno, "O dvuyazychnoy perepiske pushkinskoy pory," *Uchenye zapiski Tartuskogo Gosudarstvennogo Universiteta*, 358 (1975), *Trudy po russkoy i slavyanskoy filologii*, XXIV, pp. 148–56.

Your age may render the transition
From dream to dream as light and brief
As a young tree renews its leaf
With each returning vernal season.
Thus doubtless Heaven has decreed.
You will love others . . . But you need
To temper tenderness with reason;
Men will not always spare you so,
And inexperience leads to woe."

The passage from letter to verse novel is difficult to chart and includes many excursions by Pushkin into other works and forms. Pushkin read Byron and Constant in French, and found that their treatment of society echoed his own experience; he sent his brother a stylization of their insights, which he was simultaneously developing in his lyrics and narrative poems.[10] In *Eugene Onegin* Pushkin drew upon these authors and his epistolary ability as he cast a momentarily sympathetic light on disagreeable coldness and misanthropy. Letter writing—with its poses and sense of audience—provided him practice in rhetorical effect.

Returning to the Arzamasians' epistolary use of foreign languages, one finds that social terminology—when there was no ready Russian equivalent—remained in French, as when Batyushkov told Gnedich, "society, or an even more significant word, *urbanité,* is not your least advantage" (III, 47; 19 September 1809). French was also the foreign language in which jokes and puns were most frequently made, as we have seen from A. I. Turgenev's comment on the drunkard Milonov— "enivré de sa gloire littéraire."

Less familiar foreign languages furnished the Arzamasians with sayings and quotations. A. I. Turgenev often repeated his favorite lines from Horace and the *Aeneid;* Batyushkov in-

---

[10] For accounts of Pushkin's appropriation of these writers' works see Anna Akhmatova, " 'Adolf' Benzhamena Konstana v tvorchestve Pushkina," *Vremennik Pushkinskoy Komissii Akademii Nauk SSSR* I (1936), 91–114; and V. M. Zhirmunski, *Bayron i Pushkin (iz istorii romanticheskoy poemy)* (Leningrad, 1924).

cluded brief passages from the Italian poets he translated and phrases such as *dolce far niente* that would have been known to his recipients. They rarely borrowed from English or German.[11]

Western culture figured stylistically in the Arzamasians' letters as a source of neologisms and antique or mythological names. We have already encountered the mythological names as a means of characterization. Their number was as limited as it was predictable, and the individual writers showed no appreciable variations in the deployment of them. A harsh critic was a Zoilus; a rich patron, a Maecenas; an Epicurean poet, an Anacreon. Themistocles, Horace, Orpheus, Philoctetes, Catullus, Phoebus, Castor, Pollux, Hercules, and a few others complete the roster. As periphrastic constructions gradually went out of fashion, these tags became rarer and rarer in the letters. Pushkin used them considerably less than Batyushkov. The Arzamasians did not weave them into elaborate conceits. If they survived, it was because they could be used ironically, and in this form they figured in the comic genres of Neoclassical literature. By 1814 Batyushkov, who had previously defended them with tongue in cheek, came out against the periphrastic prose style.[12] By 1821, after being hailed as a "grandson of Anacreon" in a poem by Pletnev, Batyushkov indignantly rejected them: "my ancestor was not Anacreon, but a brigadier under Peter I, a man of stern temper and firm spirit" (III, 567; 21 July 1821, to Gnedich).

Western concepts provided neologisms for Russian by the addition of several highly productive suffixes. All the letter-writing Arzamasians, including Zhukovski and Karamzin, contributed to this importation. The suffixes *-stvo* (creating abstract nouns) and *-nichat* and *-ovat* (both producing verbs, sometimes with a pejorative coloration) formed a number of such neologisms from Western culture, such as *mefistofelstvo,*

[11] Malakhovski found that Pushkin used some Polish and Ukrainian words in fun and a few Italian, German, and English words as terms, "Yazyk pisem Pushkina," pp. 522–29.

[12] Tsentralni gosudarstvenni arkhiv literatury i iskusstva, Ostafyevski arkhiv, 195/1/1416, sheet 67^v. 27 July 1814 to Vyazemski.

donkishotstvo, volterstvovat, makhiavelstvovat, arlekinstvovat, liberalnichat, and *afishnichat* ("to play Mephistopheles/Don Quixote/Voltaire/Machiavelli/Harlequin," "to act the liberal," and "to advertise"). The Arzamasians applied the same suffixes to native words or the names of Russian writers, such as *vasilil-vovnichat* ("to behave like Vasili Lvovich Pushkin") or *voyey-kovstvovat* ("to write like Voyeykov").

As their wealth of everyday detail and occasional obscenities suggest, the Arzamasians made extensive use of colloquial Russian in their letters. The conversational norm for letters made this desirable, as did Karamzin's wish that writers would write as they speak. Dialectal Russian and the language of folk-lore, on the other hand, appeared infrequently in their letters except for popular sayings that could contribute to the illusion of conversation on paper, and could provide the worldly, popular wisdom that Demetrius thought appropriate for letters.[13]

Lexical levels were not the only tools by which the Arzamasians created the illusion of conversation. Thematic resources, punctuation, syntax, orthography, and the overall context of Russian prose at the beginning of the nineteenth century played important roles. The Arzamasians, of course, knew that they were creating an illusion and that a letter could imitate, but not replace, oral speech.[14] However, the enthusiastic response of their subsequent readers bears witness to the success of their imitation.

The Church Slavonicisms, chancellery terms, and foreign borrowings in the letters did not necessarily break the illusion. They were more often than not terminological in nature or else colored by the light irony of polite discourse. Subject to con-

[13] Demetrius, *On Style,* pp. 443–45. Vyazemski and Pushkin used Russian proverbs; Karamzin preferred French and Italian ones, sometimes translated into Russian, as at the head of his description of his typical day.
[14] A. S. Pushkin, *Polnoye sobraniye sochineni,* XIII, 10; *Pisma Karamzina k Dmitriyevu,* p. 298.

versational syntax with its ellipses, coordinate conjunctions, interruptions, and short sentences, phrases from these non-colloquial lexical levels could add necessary content to intelligent conversation without making it seem overly pompous. In short phrases they belonged to conversational Russian usage.

A letter, as Grech noted, differs from the one side of a conversation it imitates by being written, not spoken, and by lacking the expressiveness of vocal intonation and physical gestures.[15] The Arzamasians sought to overcome all of these obstacles. Like other epistolarians from Cicero's time on, they described the process of letter writing as "talking," "conversing," and "chattering," not only as "writing" and "scribbling." To give the letter some of the immediacy and haphazard nature of conversation, they referred to such events as interruptions that were occurring simultaneously with the writing of the letter. They approximated the intonations of conversation by using interjections and particles, by punctuating with question and exclamation marks, and by underscoring words for emphasis. Questions, of course, involved the recipient in the subject and solicited replies. Consciously or unconsciously, the Arzamasians sometimes wrote words according to their own pronunciation rather than according to the rules of orthography. They often ended letters with the standard Russian epistolary gestures—embracing, kissing—or included bodily gestures in the content of the letter. Batyushkov illustrates this technique in a letter to Gnedich: "I received your charter, the speech written with a stylus on Egyptian parchment, I received it, I read it, . . . and first shrugged my shoulders, then said: 'it is forgivable for him to deceive himself, he loves me and wishes me well' " (III, 66–67; December 1809).

The illusion of conversational speech is also created by syntax such as that which Batyushkov uses here: short phrases in subject-predicate order, lacking causal conjunctions, participles, gerunds, and other features of more formal writing. In combination with quick changes of subject, this structure could lend letters the speed of conversation.

[15] Appendix II, p. 204.

The context of early nineteenth-century Russian prose does much to explain why these letters seemed conversational to contemporaries and subsequent readers. Against the background of other varieties of Russian prose—ecclesiastical works, Shishkov's Slavonicized proclamations during the War of 1812,[16] the stiff and formal language of the chancelleries, and the rhetorical orchestration of Sentimentalist outpourings (such as Karamzin's introduction to Sterne)—Arzamasian letters could not help but appear conversational.

It must be noted, however, that the letters of the Arzamasians employ comparatively less conversational syntax than do certain verse genres of their time. They exploit fewer varieties of particles and interjections than do Krylov's fables, Griboyedov's *Woe from Wit,* and the passages in Pushkin's *Eugene Onegin* concerning Tatiana and the peasants. Pushkin's letters surpass those of the other Arzamasians in their use of conversational syntax and lexicon, yet he reserved such colloquial verbal interjections as *pryg* ("jumped") and *khvat* ("grabbed") for *Eugene Onegin* and did not use them in his letters. The syntax of Krylov, Griboyedov, and Pushkin's Tatiana is consistently elliptic and free from causal conjunctions and participles, and it makes greater use of the infinitive constructions characteristic of conversational Russian.[17] The following lines from Tatiana's dream use some features of this conversational syntax rarely encountered in letters:

> Tatiana v les; medved za neyu. (v, xiv)
> Tatiana *akh!*—a on revet. (v, xii)[18]

---

[16] Arzamasian D. V. Dashkov characterized the style of Shishkov and his party as "a gloomy labyrinth of Slavonic periods, spreading their feeble members from page to page." Borovkova-Maykova, *"Arzamasskiye" protokoly,* p. 145.

[17] Malakhovski does not treat the syntax of Pushkin's letters. Lists of the stylistic (including syntactic) peculiarities of Krylov and Griboyedov may be found in G. I. Shklarevski, *Istoriya russkogo literaturnogo yazyka (vtoraya polovina* XVIII *v.–*XIX *v.)* (Kharkov, 1967), pp. 61–70 and 80–86. Shklarevski believes that poetic forms, not letters, were the "laboratory" in which the limitations of the Sentimentalist style were overcome, pp. 80–81.

[18] "Tatiana runs into the forest; the bear follows behind her." "Tatiana cries ah!—and he roars." *Revet* is an infinitive here, not the third person singular finite form.

It is not surprising that the poetic speech appropriate to a folksy narrator of fables, the satirized characters of Moscow society, and a provincial girl should be closer to Russian colloquial syntax than the familiar letters of the educated, Western-oriented Arzamasians. Their thought occasionally required the resources of formal, logical writing, as A. I. Turgenev's inquiry into the nature of God illustrates, and short conversational sentences could be inadequate to contain it. In 1823 Vyazemski confessed to Zhukovski: "The chief fault (at least in my eyes) of my prose is the length of my periods: you could run up the Tower of Ivan the Great with asthma more quickly than you could read through my nonstop sentences."[19]

Playfulness as well as logical argument evoked complex, non-colloquial syntax. The principle of stylistic exaggeration, which we observed in the selection of individual words from various lexical levels, also applied to syntax. The Arzamasians occasionally deployed syntactic complexity as well as footnotes, drawings, and Sternean references to the letter as a written object to break the genre's illusion of conversational speech, thus creating a certain tension between this illusion and stylistic obtrusiveness.

Vyazemski, who enjoyed arguing by extensive analogies, provides an illustration of this tension:

One must not dwell for long in the world of dreams and one must not forget that we, although endowed with an immortal soul, nevertheless have some part in bestiality, and, perhaps, a large one. Zhukovski despises bestiality altogether; this is fatal. One can keep a swine in an orderly pen; but in order for it to be healthy and stout one must permit it to wallow sometimes in the mud and to eat manure. And a man, who would out of excessive respect for this quite honorable, naturally [sic], animal keep it in a fragrant hothouse, feed it pineapples and wild oranges, bath it in rosewater, and bed it down on a couch bestrewn with jasmine, would soon tire his honorable idol to death. You laugh, Turgenev, and say: "He is surely

---

[19] Vyazemski, "Pisma k Zhukovskomu," p. 185.

writing in his sleep or Shalikov [a Sentimentalist poet] is dictating to him." Laugh, if you like, but really, my nonsense is not without truth. (*OA*, I, 14; April 1813)

Vyazemski's logical syntax with its long periods and concessive ("although") and final ("in order for") subordinate clauses threatens the illusion of conversational speech. Extravagant literary imagery (rosewater, jasmine) does not lend the passage an everyday, conversational air. Nevertheless, the imagery from colloquial Russian and the imagined reply of Turgenev serve to reorient this passage toward conversation. Such a device as the imagined reply, unavailable to Lomonosov in the eighteenth century, allowed the Arzamasians to maintain the genre's traditional ties to discourse without limiting themselves to simple syntax, as Lomonosov had done in the letter to Shuvalov on the death of Richmann.[20]

A long letter by Batyushkov to Gnedich illustrates the Arzamasians' modulation of lexical levels and types of syntax. Batyushkov opens with long sentences, one of which is organized by anaphora. Even here, however, everyday imagery and parenthetic comments partially recall the letter's traditional imitation of conversation:

I see, dear friend, that with you one needs logic and the most subtle dialectics, and I therefore fear that you will attach yourself to my words. You reproach me for laziness! you, who lie from morning to night and do only what is pleasant to you, you, whose belly is dearer than fame itself, you, who write your friend only laconic replies to his long letters, in a word, you, Gnedich—while I am unfortunate (I don't want to add another word), while I sit alone inside four walls, in the most boring isolation, in such quiet that each beat of the balance of my pocket watch is repeated clearly and resonantly in my hearing, while I have no hope of leaving here. No, it would be better to wish me that

[20] Chapter I, pp. 28–30.

150

firmness of spirit that I often lack, being (the gods are at fault!) sensible to affliction; I swear by Heaven to you that it's been long since I've known joy. This is my position. I love you, and I do not grieve those whom I love with long and fruitless stories, and, moreover, why should I cry to you? Even without that your eyes hurt, and down my long eyelashes there often, very often, wind tears, which nobody except God sees.

This emotional outpouring yields to a series of shorter sentences and questions that give a sense of the absent interlocutor's presence in the writer's mind. The questions are no longer rhetorical, but serve to solicit answers, as they might in conversation. "Peter" is slang for St. Petersburg. Placing the adjectives after the noun ("reasons") in the last line gives the impression of conversational afterthought, as does the repetition of "many things," modified by "very."

What shall I do? How shall I begin? I want to write Olenin again. Let him refuse me, his refusal is easier to bear than another's because I love him and am obliged to him for many things, very many things. Once more, and for the last time, I shall ask to be posted abroad. I have a hundred reasons for it. And I do not intend to serve with you in Peter. And for that there are a million reasons, strong and important.

Batyushkov continues in the same key with questions, exclamations, and colloquial constructions (*vzdumal,* "come up with an idea," and *davay pisat,* "write away"). The "why" in the third line acts as the question of an imagined interlocutor—a conversational device in tension with the anaphoric construction, "even I."

Would you believe it? I have been living here four months and during these four months have gone almost nowhere. Why? I came up with the idea that I should write in prose if I want to be useful in the service, and write away!—I wrote heaps and would have written still

151

more, unfortunate [that I am]! Even I could think that talent without intrigues, without crawling, without any calculation could be of use to us! Even I could still build castles in the sky and chase smoke! Now, having abandoned everything, I am reading Montaine, who teaches some to live and others to await death.

Batyushkov's syntax becomes more formal again, and he employs a long quotation, but he gives the passage a conversational cast by presenting it as a reply to Gnedich ("you advise me"), by the verb that introduces the quotation ("listen"), by a mildly suggestive pun, by the unsteady sequence of the first three sentences, and by the swift change of subject in the second paragraph.

And you advise me to translate Tasso—in this state. I don't know, but even this Tasso distresses me. Let's listen to La Harpe's panegyric to Colardeau: "Son âme (l'âme de Colardeau) semblait se ranimer un moment pour la gloire et la reconnaissance, mais ce dernier rayon allait bientôt s'éteindre dans la tombe. . . . Il avait traduit quelques chants du Tasse. Y avait-il une fatalité attachée à ce nom?" I know the value of your praise, and I know that friendship could not so blind you as to praise something bad. But I also know that my pelvis or Tasso [*Taz ili Tass*] is not so good as you think. But even if it were good, what benefit would I derive from it. If my affairs (of which it is repulsive for me not only to speak but to hear) go better, will I be more or less happy? Or are we living in the age of Louis [XIV], in which one could endure unhappiness for glory, suffer and forget one's suffering?

Unfortunately I am neither babbler nor genius, and I therefore ask you to abandon my Tasso, which I truly would burn if I knew that it was here only. But I am glad that you liked my verses in the *Herald*. They were written long ago; this is most evident.

With a cavalier disregard for transitions Batyushkov next introduces the following anecdote. Only some lines later do we learn that it is connected with the theme of laziness, which opened the letter. He relates the anecdote with syntax that is neither conversational nor rhetorically organized but playfully confused and disjointed (he used the same style in a letter to Vyazemski quoted earlier).[21] Batyushkov finishes the anecdote so quickly that it has no chance to develop into a chronologically ordered narrative of any length. The quotations from Parny, Horace, and Mirabeau spill out in such rapid and easy succession that they seem casually appropriated, as they might be in the talk of literary people, not marshaled in a pedantic manner. Batyushkov reinforces this impression by thematic means: by abbreviating the passage from Horace's first satire ("Quid rides? Mutato nomine de te Fabula narratur."), by ending Parny's verse with a casual "and so forth," and by passing off the quotation from Mirabeau as something just remembered, not learned by rote.

> Shall I tell you an anecdote? Nik. Naz. Muravyev, a very honest man about whom I truly will say nothing bad, for he does not deserve it, finally, Nikolay Nazaryevich, waxing indignant with me because I did not wish to write anything in the chancellery (I was seventeen years old), told this to the late Mikhail Nikitich [Muravyev], and, in order to bear out his words and prove that I am an idler, brought him my epistle to you, which had these well-known lines from Parny as an epigraph:
>
>> Le ciel, qui voulait mon bonheur,
>> Avait mis au fond de mon coeur
>> La paresse et l'insouciance—and so forth.

What did Mikhail Nikitich [himself a poet] do? He laughed and kept the verses for himself. Quid rides? Fabula de te narratur. This is your history. And what really does my laziness mean? [It is] the laziness of a man who sits entire nights at his books, writes, reads, or reasons! No, said Mirabeau, and Mirabeau knew what he was saying,

---

[21] Chapter IV, p. 109.

if I built mills or breweries, were a salesman, deceived and confessed, then truly I would be known as an honest and active man. Do not think that I have taken Mirabeau's words as a rule: I read this two years ago and am bringing it forward from memory. By the way, I have warm rooms, three dogs for company, a tolerable appetite, and in place of a thermometer a silver ruble, left over from the Swedish campaign; with it one won't die of hunger, and if one goes mad, that's a trifle! Ah, circumstances, circumstances, you make great men!

Batyushkov's shift from the first person to the indefinite pronoun ("one") distances him and the reader from his greatest fears—poverty and the insanity that was soon to overtake him. In the opening lines of the next paragraph he articulates this movement away from personal themes. He concludes the letter with a rush of exclamations, questions, and terse sentences, each seeming to take up a new topic. I quote the rest of the letter in its entirety, not because it sets Batyushkov's mind and epistolary talent off to best advantage, but because it demonstrates how uninteresting the letters of the Arzamasians would have been, had they limited themselves to the mere imitation of everyday speech with its syntactic and lexical devices.

But I don't want to be like an old woman, and you are no doctor, hence, enough talk about myself. Lvova married Lvov. I don't understand that at all. Leonid writes me very amusingly—but not a word about that. For pity's sake, Fedor Petrovich [Lvov] has ten children. Miracles! My letter is very boring. Therefore I enclose a letter by Prince Vyazemski, which will truly make you laugh. But send it back to me, for I need it. I know nothing of Zhukovski. I spent three weeks with him at Karamzin's, and on the next day or on the day after that he left for the country. He's in Belevo, probably sick or writing. Send something for *The Herald* [*of Europe,* which Zhukovski edited], and I'll write him. Peace to Benitski's dust. He was intelligent, and he died! Aren't you ashamed not to have written a line in his praise, not in verse, but in prose?

Why not inform people that a certain Benitski lived and wrote "On the Next Day?" Why not put this biographical notice in *The Herald* and not in the journal of the manufacturer Izmaylov? Awake, Brutus! What else has Shikhmatov [a Besedist] scribbled? I read Kachenovski's review in the journal, but I haven't seen his poems and I don't want to see them. Ask Izmaylov to send me the *Flower-bed*;[22] I haven't received it since April or May, and it is good for [passing time in] the country. Have mercy on me, send some books and more stationery, about five rubles' worth. I have nothing to write on. Farewell.

What a letter-writer I am! What can I write to Baranov, and what sort of politics is that? Oh, you people! Or have I no mind and reason, and have you become too clever by half, learned ones! What are you doing? Are you translating Homer? I am rereading him now and envy you, envy you because you have perpetual nourishment. For God's sake write some more about Ivan Matveyevich, what is he doing and how? I love that man because he, it seems, loves me. Vyazemski's letter is very funny, isn't it? Greet Polozov and tell him from me: "The hell with you!" Greet Samarina: I grow radiant in soul when I recall her. The Nilovs are ingrates. Haven't you seen Petin? There's a good friend! (III, 62–66; December 1809)

Batyushkov created the desired illusion of conversational speech by colloquial syntax and lexical elements, exclamations, nonrhetorical questions, imagined replies by the absent interlocutor, and intimate themes. They sustained the illusion while he playfully set passages in rhetorically organized and hyperbolically disjointed syntax. His refusal to employ a single mood or structural principle breaks up the letter and prevents it from seeming to be an obvious monologue. Methods of thematic transition can also create the illusion of unforced, colloquial speech, but this concerns organizational principles other than syntax.

[22] The *Flower-bed* (*Tsvetnik*) was a journal that published the works of Batyushkov's St. Petersburg friends.

VII

Organizational Principles of the Familiar Letter

> Here I allow myself a brief digression.
> A. S. Pushkin, *Roslavlev*

Epistolary tradition offered the Arzamasians many examples of letters on a single topic, such as those by Voiture, Lomonosov, and Radishchev. Indeed, unity of topic seems to have been virtually obligatory in eighteenth-century Russian letters. However, Grech, a contemporary of the Arzamasians, allowed several subjects in a letter, if the letter could remain a coherent whole, and he based the letter's unity on its governing emotion.[1] The Arzamasians themselves favored less obviously organized compositions. They rarely allowed a single topic or principle of organization to dominate their letters. Anecdotes arranged in temporal sequence, travel descriptions, logical arguments, and wit (exploiting associations with a single theme) combined with other topics and principles of organization. Similarly, a single feeling—whether wartime patriotic ecstasy, friendship, disillusionment, boredom, or cynicism—seldom governed their letters.

Pushkin's account to Zhukovski of his parental difficulties is perhaps the tersest narrative in an Arzamasian letter. But this letter could hardly be called familiar as we have been using that term. The events it relates are far too personal for circulation, and it lacks literary self-consciousness and comic relief. The various forms of the verb "to beat" (*bil, khotel bit, mog pribit*) convey the terror and confusion of Pushkin's father, not playful Arzamasian punning. Pushkin moves from event to event in chronological order without his accustomed epistolary digressiveness.

[1] Appendix II, pp. 204–5.

Dear fellow, I fall back upon you. Judge my position. Upon arriving here I was met by all as well as could be, but soon everything changed. My father, frightened by my exile, has been constantly reiterating that the same fate awaits him. Peshchurov, appointed to keep me under surveillance, had the audacity to offer my father the office of opening my correspondence, in short, of being my spy. My father's irascibility and irritable sensibility would not permit me to speak frankly with him; I decided to keep silent. My father began to reproach my brother to the effect that I was teaching him godlessness. I still kept silent. They received a document concerning me. Finally, desiring to remove myself from this painful position, I went to my father, I asked his permission to speak frankly. ... My father flared up. I bowed, mounted a horse and left. My father summoned my brother and ordered him to have nothing to do avec ce monstre, ce fils dénaturé ... (Zhukovski, consider my position and judge). My head began to seethe. I went to my father, I found him with my mother, and I blurted out everything that had been bothering me for three whole months. I ended by saying that I was talking to him for the last time. My father, taking advantage of the absence of witnesses, dashed out and declared to the whole household that "*I had beat him, wanted to beat him, raised my hand threateningly, could have beaten him. ...*" I am not justifying myself to you. But just what does he want for me, in accusing me of a felony? The mines of Siberia and deprivation of noble rank? Save me, either with a fortress or with the Solovetski Monastery [on the White Sea]. I'll tell you nothing of what my brother and sister are enduring on account of me. Once more, save me.

Oct. 31.   A. P.

Hurry: my father's accusation is known to the whole household. Nobody believes it, but everyone is repeating it. The neighbors know. I do not wish to make explanations to them. If it should reach the government, judge what would happen. To try and prove my father's slander in court would be horrible for me, but there is no court for me. I am hors la loi.

P. S. You should know that I have already written a letter to the governor, in which I ask him about the fortress, without saying anything about my reasons. P. A. Osipova, at whose house I am writing you these lines, has persuaded me to take you into confidence. I confess, I am a little vexed at myself, and, my dear fellow, my head is going round and round. (xiii, 116–17; 31 October 1824)

Like Lomonosov's letter to Shuvalov, this letter reduces epistolary formulae to a bare minimum. Only its appeals to the recipient, brief salutation, and closing ("dear fellow") distinguish it from a legal deposition. Although Pushkin employs terse sentences of conversational length, the syntax of the letter uses a number of participles, gerunds, and compound conjunctions more typical of formal than conversational Russian. Unlike Lomonosov, Pushkin states his confusion ("my head is going round and round") and does not show it by confused statements; he had written a rough draft for the letter to help get his thoughts in order and to lend it some of the restraint he admired in Mme de Sévigné.[2] He rarely wrote drafts for familiar correspondence. Instead of using the postscript for a separate topic, as Radishchev frequently did, Pushkin uses it to reinforce the letter's sense of urgency and to relate the story to his condition, location, and mood at the time of writing.

Another possible method of epistolary organization is witwriting; Vincent Voiture's defense of the conjunction *car* is an example.[3] Vyazemski spins the body of the following letter out of the Russian saying "to beat at the ice like a fish," building his opinion of Turgenev's actions and a description of his plans for the day on other associations with fish:

I was in grief, in trouble, and am now struggling hard [literally, beating at the ice like a fish] and, consequently, I

[2] Chapter ii, p. 67.
[3] Chapter i, pp. 23–25.

deserve forgiveness if I have written rarely; but your Excellency, who drains the cup of happiness and delights to the dregs every day, rejoices, like a fish in the sun, swims in pleasures like a carp in a pond, and à propos of fish, is as mute with his friends as they are—it is unforgivable and sinful of you to forget those who remember and love you, even in the midst of spiritual suffering, even in the midst of heavy and dull cares. Farewell, fat and speechless Excellency-sterlet! Today I will admire your image at the brigadier's table of his Excellency, Count Fedor Andreyevich Tolstoy.

> He is like a sterlet in every respect.
> He, like it, is dumb and mute and fair—

Verses for the portrait of Aleksandr Ivanovich Turgenev. (*OA*, I, 39–40; 29 January 1816)

Vyazemski had opened with some bantering on the state of their correspondence in which he did not employ fish imagery, and thus his letter is not exclusively a wit letter on the theme of fish. The Arzamasians plaited parts of their letters from wit or puns, but unlike Voiture they did not sustain them throughout whole letters, most of which were twice as long as this one. In this restraint their epistolary practice parallels their poetry, in which they generally limited wit writing to epigrams and did not use it for longer lyrics. In a letter such elaborate weaving could have undermined the illusion of conversation and seemed ponderous, overly contrived.

The Arzamasians transformed travel letters, traditionally built around a single topic, into familiar letters with literary self-consciousness, intimate references, and conversational devices, as Batyushkov's letter to Zhukovski from the Island of Ischia illustrated. That letter began with a long passage on their correspondence and concluded with a series of greetings and questions for fellow Arzamasians.[4]

---

[4] Batyushkov's letter (abridged) appears above, Chapter III, pp. 86–87.

Such greetings and questions are omitted from Batyushkov's account of the Russian army's entry into Paris, but his letter hardly features the impersonal quality of a public travel description, as Batyushkov refers to Arzamasian literature and themes and involves his recipient in the conclusion. He opens by establishing his point of view within the Parisian crowd, not above it:

> Finally we are in Paris. Imagine now a sea of people in the streets. Windows, fences, roofs, the trees of the boulevard, everything, everything was covered by people of both sexes. Everyone was waving his hands, nodding his head, everyone was in convulsions, everyone was shouting, "Vive Alexandre, vivent les Russes! Vive Guillaume, vive l'empereur d'Autriche! Vive Louis, vive le roi, vive la paix!"

Batyushkov next enters the scene with a speaking part to satisfy the curiosity of the Parisians. His account, reminiscent in its ironic commentary of Sterne's *Sentimental Journey,* seeks out the frivolous aspects of the grand historical scene. The cosmopolitan Batyushkov, schooled in a French pension and raised on French literature, watches himself become an object of curiosity to the Parisians, who appear provincial and naive in his description. As in the previous passage, he renders the confusion of the scene by treating the crowd as a crowd, not as a group of individuals.

> Everyone was shouting, no, howling and roaring: "Montrez nous le beau, le magnanime Alexandre!" "Messieurs le voilà en habit vert, avec le roi de Prusse." "Vous êtes bien obligeant, mon officier," and, holding me by the stirrups, they shout: "Vive Alexandre, à bas le tyran!" "Ah, qu'ils sont beaux, ces Russes." "Mais, monsieur, on vous prendrait pour un Français." "You do me great honor, dear sir, in truth I am not worthy of it!" "But you have no accent," and after this, "Vive Alexandre, vivent les Russes, les héros du Nord!"
>
> The Tsar, among the wave of people, stopped at the

Champs Élysées. Past him marched the armies in perfect order. The people were in ecstasy, and my Cossack [batman], shaking his head, said to me, "Your honor, they've gone mad." "Long ago," I replied, dying with laughter.

But my head began to spin from the noise. I dismounted, and the people surrounded both me and the horse and began to examine us. Numbered among them were respectable people and pretty women, who for hors d'oeuvres asked me odd questions: why do I have fair hair, why is it long. "In Paris one has it shorter. The expert Dulong will cut your hair fashionably," said the women, "and ever so well." "Look, he's wearing a ring. Evidently they wear rings in Russia. The uniform is very plain! C'est le bon genre! What a long horse! From the steppes, cheval du désert. Step aside, sirs, the artillery! What long cannon, longer than ours. Ah, bon dieu, quel Calmok!" And then, "Vive le roi, la paix! Mais avouez, mon officier, que Paris est bien beau?" "What fair hair you have!" "From the snow," said an old man, shrugging his shoulders. I know not whether from the heat or snow, I thought, but you, my friends, have long been at odds with good sense.

From these "hors d'oeuvres" Batyushkov shifts to reflections on the historical events that had occasioned the entry into Paris. But even here the Arzamasian familiar letter calls attention to physical pleasure (charming women) and the more ludicrous aspects of the scene (the crowd's failure to overturn a statue):

Note that there were dreadful faces in the crowd, terrible physiognomies, which quickly remind one of Marats and Dantons, in rags, in large caps and hats, and alongside them pretty children and the most charming women.

We turned left toward the Place de Vandôme [sic], where the crowd increased from hour to hour. On this square had been erected a monument to the Grande Armée. A glorious Trajan column! I was seeing it for the first time and at such a moment! The people, encircling it from all sides, shouted incessantly: "À bas le tyran!" One daredevil climbed to the top and placed a rope around Napoleon's feet; a bronze statue to him crowns the column. "Put it on the tyrant's neck," shouted the people. "Why are you doing this?" "He climbed high!" they replied to me. "Very well, fine. Now pull him down; we'll smash him into smithereens, but the reliefs will stay. We bought them with blood, the blood of our grenadiers. Let our descendants admire them!" But on the first day they couldn't break the bronze Napoleon; we set a sentry at the column. On the plaque below I read: Napolio, Imp. Aug. monumentum and so forth. Vanity of vanities! Vanity, my friend! From his hand have fallen both sword and victory! And that very mob that greeted the victor on this square, that very mob—unstable, ungrateful—cast a rope around the neck of Napolio Imp. Aug. That very madman who shouted, "Hang the king with the entrails of the priests" a few years ago, that very madman is now shouting, "Russians, our saviours, give us the Bourbons! Cast the tyrant down! What good are victories to us? Trade, trade!"

Batyushkov discontinues his reflections to catalogue the pleasures of the city. He concludes with the line from V. L. Pushkin's comic poem "The Dangerous Neighbor" in which the hero is about to couple with a prostitute:

Oh, the wondrous Parisians, a people worthy of pity and laughter! My head was spinning incessantly from the noise; what would there be at the Palais-Royal, where dinner and comrades awaited me? Past the Théâtre Français I fought my way to the Palais-Royal, into the focal point of the noise, bustle, wenches, news, luxury, poverty, debauchery. Whoever hasn't seen the Palais-Royal can have no conception of it. In the best coffee-house, or, rather, restaurant, at the glorious Very, we ate oysters and washed them down with champagne, drunk to the health of our sovereign, our good tsar. Having rested a little we walked about the shops and coffeehouses, cellars, taverns, chestnut braziers, and so forth. Night found me amidst the Palais-Royal. Then a new phenomenon: the nymphs of joy, whose shamelessness surpasses everything. It was not the officers who chased them, but they the officers. This continued until midnight to the noise of the crowd, to the sound of glasses in the nearby coffeehouses, to the sound of harps and violins. . . . Everything was whirling until:

> The light in the bowl went out, and the bed
> [lit. trunk] stood near.

Oh, Pushkin, Pushkin!

After some news of Napoleon's flight Batyushkov concludes the letter:

Most of all I wish to see the theater and the glorious [tragedien] Talma, who, as Chateaubriand writes, taught Napoleon how to sit on the throne with the pomposity appropriate in the emperor of a great people. La grande nation! Le grand homme! Le grand siècle! All hollow words, my friend, with which our tutors used to frighten us. (III, 252–56; 27 March 1814, to N. I. Gnedich)

The description—with its shifting scenes, thoughts, and topics—is not organized merely by the chronology of Batyushkov's stay in Paris. It follows a trajectory of perception and generalization as Batyushkov separates himself from the chaotic scene through irony (his observation of the frivolous Parisians) and reflection (the historical role of the Parisian mob) before entering the city's life of pleasure. The last lines serve as a coda, joining the themes of pleasure, vanity, and historical upheaval.

Most frequently the Arzamasian letters include more than one principle of construction, one tone, and one topic. The genre's imitation of the spontaneity of conversation, stylistic freedom, closeness to the events of the moment, awareness of the recipient's interests, literary self-consciousness, and self-irony all impose requirements that virtually preclude taut, unified compositions. Pushkin's letter to Vyazemski of 7 November 1825 simultaneously replied to one by Vyazemski and moved through various topics, joined together by their literary associations.[5] A. I. Turgenev's letter of 27 May 1819 began with a joke, followed a pun into a serious theological discussion, and changed to secular topics as its writer moved from home to office.[6]

The letters are frequently paratactic in structure; their topics follow one upon the other in apparently unmotivated sequence. Letters that reply to other letters sometimes fall into this pattern; topics and questions in another letter may govern their order, or they may answer the points of the other letter in a different sequence. A. I. Turgenev, who confessed that he could not write without Vyazemski's letters in front of him (*OA*, I, 271) conscientiously replied to his recipient's points, but in no particular order. Once Vyazemski sent him a numbered list of requests:

Why won't you send me: (1) my rank; (2) Karamzin's "Speech"; (3) your brother's book; (4) the rescript to Vyazmitinov; (5) your Bible Society speech on serfdom; (6) the reward for the doctor with character;[7] (7) patience and fortitude against the enemies who surround me under the command of generalissimos Boredom and Dejection; (8) good advice on how to live when in Rome; (9) authenticated testimony from the district police officer, the parish priest, and the physician of the Anichkov Palace that Zhukovski is alive, that is, that he eats, drinks, sleeps, in

[5] Chapter V, pp. 130–31.

[6] Chapter VI, pp. 138–40.

[7] "There is an unhappy doctor in Grodno, who looked after me in Mikhaylino; in his words, il sert depuis six ans dans la même charactère. Make him change his character: he is a very good German; his teeth have turned black from bad tobacco and from his pipe, which he probably hasn't cleaned for a dozen years." P. A. Vyazemski to A. I. Turgenev, 3 April 1818. *OA*, I, 98.

a word does everything that he has always been accustomed to doing; (10) Batyushkov; (11) your happiness; (12) Zhukovski's virginity; (13) Kozodavlev's eloquence, which flows like oil, that is, sesame-seed oil; (14) and, finally even a spark of my intelligence, which remained on the moon, that is, with you. You see how stupid I am. (*OA*, I, 135; 27 October 1818)

With Arzamasian mock logic Turgenev returned a fourteen-point list of replies but answered Vyazemski's request in a different order and in unexpected ways:

(1) I'll send your rank soon. (2) I don't have Karamzin's "Speech," but I'll tell him your wish. (3) I'll send my brother's book next Wednesday. (4) The rescript to Vyazmitinov is printed in all the newspapers. (5) I'll send the Bible speech next Wednesday. (6) The doctor's reward is in the power of Kavelin, who promises much but produces only children—that is, the recently born Konstantin Dmitriyevich; sorry!—and much good; for this week he collected more than 4,000 rubles and saved five orphans. (7) I let Zhukovski know that a courier is leaving for Warsaw today. He is again under the weather. (8) Batyushkov will not be in Warsaw. (11) My happiness will set off for you tomorrow, that is, Sofya Petrovna; she decided to travel by way of Warsaw and promised me she would see you; watch out, don't sleep through her visit. She is an angel who will light up your Sarmatian dungeon. If you have happened to be a friend in your life, then, if so, but not otherwise, tell her all that I feel upon parting with her. (12) Zhukovski's virginity is at Pushkin's disposal, not mine. (13) I do not have the *Northern Post*. (14) I send you your intelligence in an excerpt from Dmitriyev's letter: "Thank you very, very much for the Warsaw poetry of, I think I can boldly add, Prince Vyazemski. I will sincerely say that the verses are worthy, by their skill, of the talent of Prince Vyazemski."

Have I responded to all fourteen of your points? It seems so, manum de tabula. (*OA, I,* 139; 6 November 1818)

Long lists also serve to organize letters in a paratactic manner. In a letter to Vyazemski describing the daily activities of Zhukovski and Pushkin, A. I. Turgenev continued to list, in no particular order, the pastimes of other Arzamasians.[8] Such lists are a frequent part of their letters, especially when comically concluded with an element from a different level than the previous ones. The last element can undermine the seriousness of the others by its vulgarity or concreteness, as in this closing by Batyushkov: "whatever you say, dear friend, I have little philosophy, little experience, a little mind, a little heart, and a very little purse" (III, 134).

Changing moods accompany this paratactic structuring of the letter, since mood is created not only by the writer's definition of his own emotions but also by the reader's associations with the content of the letter. In keeping with the letter's personal nature, however, the Arzamasians tended to guide their recipients' reaction more directly—by articulating their own feelings and relationship to the events they reported. Dashkov, writing in turn of his own laziness, V. L. Pushkin's translations of Horace, and Batyushkov's mental illness, called attention to his own change of mood through his actions: "farewell. I began the letter with laughter and am ending it almost in tears."[9]

Unusual circumstances might dictate a single mood, just as they sometimes dictated a single compositional principle. More typically, however, the letters change tone. The familiar letter's persona, based on the concept of the *honnête homme,* required the ability to master the emotions, to display the appropriate ones when the occasion required, and not to be dominated by any one of them to the point of comic excess.

[8] Chapter IV, p. 102.
[9] Tsentralni gosudarstvenni arkhiv literatury i iskusstva, Ostafyevski arkhiv, 195/1/1820, sheet 20. Letter to Vyazemski of 10 April 1823.

The Arzamasians often signaled the transition away from serious themes by self-depreciating comments or by such phrases as "this is a long sermon" (Batyushkov, III, 137).[10] Batyushkov, setting off to war, wrote Vyazemski with appropriate solemnity: "If you survive me, get my works from Bludov and do with them as you wish; that is all that I can leave you. Perhaps we shall never see each other! Perhaps a bayonet or bullet will deprive you of the comrade of youth's merry days." However, he quickly added: "but I am writing a letter and not an elegy" and turned to news and greetings for Vyazemski's family (III, 207). Literary self-consciousness, stylistic extravagance, and concrete or vulgar images could also bring the tone of a letter down to humorous, everyday themes.

Movement in the opposite direction, from humorous to serious themes, was often signaled by the phrase "jokes aside." But more clever techniques, witticisms or puns, for example, likewise introduced seriousness. A. I. Turgenev began his theological passage with the pun on Jacobi/Jacobin.[11]

The problem of transitions leads to a final, and very common, principle of organization in the Arzamasian letters: association of ideas. As is well known, associationalist psychology informed many eighteenth-century works.[12] Though only Batyushkov and Karamzin among the Arzamasians seem to have read Locke, associationalist psychology was so much in the air that anyone consciously or unconsciously constructing a mirror of his mind in action would have resorted to chains of association. Pushkin's letter to A. A. Bestuzhev of 30 Novem-

[10] Erasmus used a similar phrase after lecturing a student: "but I am beginning to preach." *Epistles of Erasmus,* I, 110.

[11] Chapter VI, p. 138. Their extensive use of puns distinguishes the Arzamasians from eighteenth-century Russian writers, who used few puns in their writing and rather inept ones at that, to judge from the examples in Ye. P. Khodakova, "Kalambur v russkoy literature XVIII v.," in *Russkaya literaturnaya rech v XVIII veke: Frazeologizmy. Neologizmy. Kalambury,* ed. N. Yu. Shvedova (Moscow, 1968), pp. 201—54.

[12] D. W. Jefferson, "*Tristram Shandy* and the Tradition of Learned Wit," *Essays in Criticism,* I no. 3 (1951), pp. 225–48; Donald J. Greene, "'Logical Structure' in Eighteenth-Century Poetry," *Philological Quarterly* XXXI (1952), 315–36.

167

ber 1825 used this principle more consistently than was usual
in an Arzamasian letter;

I was much gladdened by your letter, my dear fellow—
I was already beginning to think that you were sulking at
me—and I am gladdened by your pursuits. The study of
modern languages must in our time replace Latin and
Greek—such are the spirit and requirements of our age.
You—and, it seems, Vyazemski—are our only littérateurs who are learning; all the others are unlearning. A
pity! The lofty example of Karamzin should have brought
them to their senses. You are going to Moscow—have a
talk with Vyazemski there about a journal. He feels the
necessity of it himself—and it would be a marvelously
good thing. You reproach me for not publishing—I am
sick of publishing—misprints, critiques, defenses, etc. . . .
However, my narrative poems will soon come out. I am
even sick of them; Ruslan is a milksop, the prisoner is a
greenhorn—and alongside the poetry of nature in the
Caucasus, my poetry is Golikov's prose. By the way, who
wrote about mountaineers in *The Bee?* That's poetry!
Wasn't it Yakubovich, the hero of my imagination? When
I talk nonsense with women I assure them that I played
the highwayman with him in the Caucasus, shot it out with
Griboyedov, buried Sheremetev, etc.—indeed, there is
much romanticism in him. It's a pity I didn't meet him in
Kabarda—my poem would have been better. The important thing! I have written a tragedy and am very satisfied with it; but I'm terrified of making it public—our
timid taste will not tolerate true Romanticism. By
Romanticism we mean Lamartine. However much I read
about Romanticism, it's all wrong; even Kyukhelbeker
talks nonsense. What are his *Spirits* like? I haven't read
them yet. I'm waiting for your new novella, but do take
on a whole novel—and write it with all the freedom of
conversation or a letter. Otherwise the style will be
reminiscent of Kotsebull. I greet the planster Ryleyev, as

the deceased Platov used to say—but truly I like poetry without a plan better than a plan without poetry. I wish you, my friends, health and inspiration. (XIII, 244–45; 30 November 1825, to A. A. Bestuzhev)

Pushkin begins his plea for "planless" literature by sharing Bestuzhev's enthusiasm for modern languages, which his mind follows to Vyazemski, who lacked a classical education and whose critical attention focused on modern literature. The next link is Karamzin, whose prose, like Vyazemski's, Pushkin praised highly. Next, remembrance of Vyazemski connects with the idea of publishing a journal in Moscow. Bestuzhev was one of the editors of an annual literary miscellany, *The Polar Star* (*Polyarnaya zvezda*); Vyazemski was instrumental in founding an important journal, *The Moscow Telegraph* (*Moskovski telegraf*), which did much to popularize nascent French Romanticism in Russia.

The publishing projects of Vyazemski and Bestuzhev lead Pushkin to his own plans, then to his own writing and self-criticism by comparison with the clumsy prose of an eighteenth-century Russian historian (Golikov). By 1825 Pushkin was turning to new literary forms—the verse novel (*Eugene Onegin*) and the historical drama (*Boris Godunov*). His Neoclassical comic fantasy, "Ruslan and Lyudmila" ("Ruslan i Lyudmila," 1820) and his Byronic narrative poem, "The Prisoner of the Caucasus" ("Kavkazski plennik," 1821) could not help but seem immature to him as he was reaching creative maturity.

Association links Pushkin's "Prisoner of the Caucasus," the Caucasus, and prose with Yakubovich's article and Romantic adventures in the mountains, which seemed more authentic than the Caucasus viewed largely through Byron's eyes. Romanticism in behavior evokes Romanticism in literature: Pushkin's "Romantic tragedy," *Boris Godunov,* and contemporary Russian opinions on Romanticism, which Pushkin found confusing and inadequate. This in turn calls to his mind a schoolfellow of German descent, Kyukhelbeker, who knew German literature better than other Russian writers of the early nineteenth century.

169

Pushkin's thoughts about his own new work, meanwhile, lead him to remember Kyukhelbeker's. As Pushkin was taking a favorite Shakespearean theme, the struggle for the throne, and developing it against the background of a contrast between medieval Russia and Renaissance Poland, Kyukhelbeker was appropriating Shakespeare to a different Romantic end; Kyukhelbeker's farce, *Shakespeare's Spirits* (*Shekspirovy dukhi,* 1825) uses Oberon, Titania, Puck, Ariel, and Caliban to demonstrate—feebly, alas—the power of poetic inspiration.

In turn, mention of Kyukhelbeker's new work leads Pushkin to inquire about Bestuzhev's latest fiction and to articulate his own new principle of structuring drama and verse novels— Romanticism conceived as freedom from rules and the generic precedents of antiquity.[13] The action of Pushkin's *Boris Godunov* leaps across years and countries to violate creatively the Neoclassical unities; his verse novel, like this letter, makes extensive use of associative rather than narrative-temporal transitions. Hence Pushkin advises Bestuzhev to write with all the freedom of a letter.[14] As an example of contrived, stilted works Pushkin offers the numerous plays of the Sentimentalist Kotzebue. Pushkin made a portmanteau word, "Kotsebull," (*kotsebyatina*) out of his name and *otsebyatina* ("fiction," "invention," "cock and bull"). Pushkin's dislike of obviously planned literature follows, which the Cossack Ataman's pejorative term "planster" (*planshchik*) helps express. One must know Pushkin and his age to see some of these associative links, but many are obvious from the letter itself, and Pushkin's use of "by the way" (*kstati*) calls attention to the process.

Association helped the Arzamasians smooth transitions when lists or the necessity of replying did not otherwise provide them. It rarely organized an entire letter, however, and the Arzamasians, even Pushkin, did not range especially far afield by comparison with the modern stream-of-conscious novelists. In this

[13] For a catalogue of Pushkin's references to Romanticism see John Mersereau, "Pushkin's Concept of Romanticism," *Studies in Romanticism,* III, no. 1, pp. 24–41.

[14] The concluding chapter of this study discusses Pushkin's use of the familiar letter as a model for such "Romantic" freedom.

170

letter, most of Pushkin's associations deal with the literary scene of his time and would be of interest to his recipient, an author and editor. The Arzamasians' frequent use of *kstati, kstati o* (apropos of) and the French *à propos* reveals a certain self-consciousness and restraint in making transitions by association.

In this age of close interaction between salon society and literature, social conventions could easily inform works of literature. Tailoring one's letters to the interests of a recipient is one example that we have already encountered; another is restrained gossip and obscenity. The same awareness of polite social behavior applies to the Arzamasians' manipulation of associative chains. Batyushkov's sense of propriety held his associations under a tight rein. He felt uncomfortable writing about his own works after mentioning those of M. N. Muravyev, whom he revered: "It is permissible to speak of oneself after Muravyev with a friend" (III, 346). After consoling Vyazemski for the loss of a child, he listed Karamzin and Zhukovski among the mourners and was led by association to repeat Zhukovski's wish that he, Batyushkov, publish Vyazemski's poems. He self-consciously justified the chain: "employment and work are the best medicine for grief. This is why I dared to remind you of the editing of your verses during your grief" (III, 491).

Associations of ideas and sounds inspired wit, puns, and analogies. In keeping with the conversational nature of letters, wit and puns were quickly and tersely expressed, and rarely organized a whole letter, as we have seen.

In fact, the reader's sense of a letter's wholeness often depended less upon his awareness of a single organizational principle than upon the letter's conclusion.

171

VIII

The Parts of a Letter: Openings and End Games

> Many lack beginning or ending.
>
> > A puzzled archivist

With an analytic passion that would have delighted a Rabelais or a Sterne, the authors of Latin formularies divided the letter into parts like those of an oration. Erasmus' schemes included *exordium, narratio, propositio, confirmatio, conjuratio,* and (to round it all off) *peroratio.*[1] The Russians simplified the terminology considerably. Both Sokolski and Grech recognized only three parts to a letter—the opening or salutation (*pristup, obrashcheniye*), the materials or content (*materii, soderzhaniye*), and the conclusion (*zaklyucheniye*). A simplified tripartite division encompasses the varied content of a familiar letter better than the more elaborate divisions, which were ultimately guides to the possibilities of a letter rather than lists of obligatory elements for every one. As we have seen in the chapters on organizational principles and epistolary criticism, narrative and persuasive elements have important roles in some letters; many others manage without them. The Arzamasians did not indulge in detailed tripartite analyses themselves, but their statements show that their expectations ran along similar lines. Batyushkov found fault with a letter by Gnedich: "My God, what a letter! Neither end nor beginning, and I shall say nothing about the middle!" (III, 116).

Although they would have agreed with Grech's division of letters into salutation, content, and conclusion, the Arzamasians had little patience with such "well-known formulae" as he recommended. The salutations of their familiar letters did

[1] E. N. S. Thompson, *Literary Bypaths of the Renaissance* (New Haven, 1924), p. 92.

172

"indicate the relationship of the writer to his correspondent"[2] in that they dispensed with formulae because of their friendship with each other or else limited the salutation to the Russian equivalent of "Dear friend," *lyubezneyshi* or *lyubezny drug*. Only Dmitriyev, older and more unbending than the others, adhered to the conventional "My Dear Sir." They were not promiscuous in their use of the friendlier salutation, however, as A. I. Turgenev noted in an edition of Karamzin's letters:

> The difference in years between him and me gave him the right not to call me *friend* in his letters, in spite of his friendship for me. But from the moment I was discharged from my post, all his letters began with the word "friend." This was no simple accident but can be explained only by Karamzin's rare nobility, to which his whole life bears a single uninterrupted testimony.[3]

Turgenev had corresponded with Karamzin for eighteen years before he was discharged.

The Arzamasians reacted to formulaic openings by playing with them, reducing them to a minimum, or omitting them altogether. They rarely opened letters with compliments except when beginning a new correspondence. Typical of their stylistic extravagance is A. I. Turgenev's opening to Vyazemski in the chancellery style: "I have the honor of informing Your Worship that Mr. Nagibin received 600 rubles salary from the Department of Education and that I delivered to him today the 100 rubles that you granted him" (*OA*, I, 85). Vyazemski replied in the same key: "The documents, dispatched by Your Excellency in my name on 4 September, I

---

[2] Appendix II, p. 205. The formulae that Grech suggests are based on the recipient's rank in the military, civil service, or clergy. For superiors, equals, and inferiors he recommends the Russian equivalents of "Dear Sir," "My Dear Sir," and "Sir" (*Milostivi Gosudar, Milostivi Gosudar moy, Gosudar moy*).

[3] Karamzin, "Pisma k A. I. Turgenevu," p. 714. Russian uses three degrees of friendship (*drug, priyatel, znakomets*—"friend," "pal," "acquaintance"), where many Americans use one word, "friend," to express all three degrees.

have had the high and solemn honor of receiving" (*OA*, I, 86). On another occasion Vyazemski sacrilegiously undermined the usual Easter greeting: "Christ is risen, dear Aleksandr Ivanovich! I did not know how to begin my letter and decided to make use of this well-known fairy tale" (*OA*, I, 13).

Professions of friendship proved popular, appropriately enough, for opening familiar letters, as did excuses for not writing and other references to the state of the correspondence. A. I. Turgenev generally acknowledged receipt of a letter by repeating its date, as Grech suggested; other Arzamasians sometimes referred to the received letter with a phrase indicating its place of origin.

On the folder containing the unpublished letters of Vyazemski to Batyushkov, I found that a puzzled archivist had written, "many lack beginning or ending." In fact, most of the letters were intact; the archivist had inadvertently discovered the Arzamasian technique of beginning letters *ex abrupto,* with a word or two of salutation or none at all. The letters in this folder had been sent without envelopes, folded twice with the address on the outside. Omitting the usual formulae proved the best way of filling this limited space with interesting material. Karamzin, like Lomonosov, used the *ex abrupto* opening to achieve striking effect: "Having been at the doors of the tomb, I have remained among the living and am now better";[4] or "I am writing you from the smouldering ruins; three days ago about a half of the magnificent palace here burned down."[5] Read in contrast with his generally phlegmatic openings, Karamzin's use of this device is all the more effective.

Other types of *ex abrupto* beginnings served to lead the recipient quickly into the content of the letter. Batyushkov, A. S. Pushkin, Vyazemski, and Karamzin began a number of letters with verse, more often than not tied to the content of the letter and to the specific situation of the writer and ad-

[4] *Pisma Karamzina k Dmitriyevu,* p. 354. 5 July 1823.
[5] *Ibid.,* p. 287. 14 May 1820.

dressee. Proverbs, literary references, and puns provided similarly arresting openings. A pun begins this characteristically compressed letter by Pushkin, who manages at the same time to involve his recipient in the letter by using a question and brief salutation:

> My dear fellow, how do you translate bévues ["howlers"] into Russian? We should publish a journal *Revue des bévues.* We would include there excerpts from Voyeykov's critiques, Ryleyev's noon-day dawn and his Russian coat of arms on the gates of Byzantium (in the time of Oleg, there was no Russian coat of arms, and the double-headed eagle is the Byzantine coat of arms; it signifies the separation of the Empire into the Western and Eastern parts—with us it has no meaning). Would you believe it, my dear fellow, one cannot read a single article in our journals without finding half a score of these *bévues.* (XIII, 54; to L. S. Pushkin, 1–10 January 1823)[6]

The opening lines of a letter, because they are the first to strike the reader's eye, provide greater emphasis than positions midway through the letter. Vyazemski, who liked to harangue his recipients, reserved the emphatic opening position for extensive reproaches, sarcasm, expressions of indignation, friendly insults, extravagant oaths, and elaborations on Arzamasian nicknames and caricatures. Batyushkov especially enraged him for applauding fellow Arzamasian Dashkov's public attack on the hapless Besedist D. I. Khvostov:

> What do I hear? Et toi aussi Brutus? Even you have surrendered to the stupidity of Petersburg. Even you are on your knees in front of Dashkov; his speech on Khvostov captivates you. That speech is impudence and stupidity. There is no wit in it and much baseness. *Don't hit a man when he's down.* What wisdom is there in chewing

[6] A. S. Pushkin, *Letters of Alexander Pushkin,* p. 106.

out an old man who, although he writes badly, does not deserve the least attention. Let him write! He has no influence on taste; it is not necessary to destroy public opinion on his account, everyone acknowledges that he is a humbug. But such works as the one by Dashkov, whom you apotheosize, can affect your minds, and not for the good. After this you will go through the streets displaying your bare arses to passers-by. What Page Corps tricks! Batyushkov! Batyushkov! What is the matter with you? I can condone Vasili Pushkin's praise of such foolishness and his partiality toward people for reasons he does not know himself, but you should be ashamed of it.[7]

In privacy, it should be added, Vyazemski pilloried Khvostov with no less enthusiasm than his fellow Arzamasian Dashkov did.

Not all the arresting openings of the Arzamasians were clever or successful, of course, but their refusal to be satisfied with such "well-known formulae" as Grech proposed shows the extent of their creative commitment to letter writing.

The conclusion of a letter offers no fewer possibilities for emphasis than its opening. A good conclusion, unless it makes the letter appear too contrived, gives the reader the pleasure of perceiving it as a whole, closed work and supplements the pleasures afforded by the genre's intimacy, liveliness, and literary judgments. While revealing the modern reader's casual attitude toward familiar letters, Barbara Herrnstein Smith raises this essential point:

In informal verbal situations such as chance encounters, letters to friends, or telephone conversations, the eventual obligation to conclude confronts the fact that unstructured discourse offers no handy termination point.

[7] Arkhiv Pushkinskogo Doma, Arkhiv K. N. Batyushkova, fond 19, no. 28, sheet 10.

Since abrupt cutoffs are psychologically unpleasant as well as impolite, we usually make use of some formula of conclusion to signal the approaching termination.[8] Because of the interaction between literature and polite society during the early nineteenth century, concluding a letter well was of literary, as well as psychological or social, importance. Karamzin noted that pleasantness was a quality polite society demanded of literature.[9]

Some conclusion to a letter was expected. Grech suggested that it be tied to the content of the letter,[10] and Lomonosov's letter to Shuvalov demonstrated how this could be done. Nevertheless the possibilities for tight closure in letters are more limited than those in other genres. The epistolarian cannot lean on the novelist's crutches—weddings, deaths, and discoveries of wills or long-lost relatives. Letters lack the formal resources that verse can employ to reinforce closure, such as a sudden shift in metrical and rhyme patterns. Letters rarely feature the tight conclusions of such poetic genres as epigrams. The letter's connection with the events of the moment and its imitation of conversational speech virtually preclude the abstractions, events, actions, and images frought with finality that contemporary poets used to close off such genres as elegies or ballads. The favorite concluding images and themes of Zhukovski's verse—graves, dust, sunsets, night, the beyond, heaven, posterity, God, silence, death, oblivion, and isolation—would have been too solemn for a familiar letter.

The nature of familiar correspondence as an ongoing activity prevented strong closure in any single letter. Questions, requests, and postscripts employed to fill up a page could pry open the ending of a letter, as could the desire to avoid solemn and final themes. The suicides among Russian officers in Warsaw, for example, might have furnished Vyazemski with the material for an entire essay. The Enlighten-

[8] Barbara Herrnstein Smith, *Poetic Closure: A Study of How Poems End* (Chicago, 1968), pp. 186–87.

[9] See Chapter II, p. 44.

[10] Appendix II, p. 206.

ment thought upon which he was raised took issue with the prohibitions of the church and the absolutist state against suicide; the Enlightenment considered the right to dispose of one's own life essential to man's dignity and freedom.[11] Vyazemski wrote to A. I. Turgenev on the subject, but his concern for Turgenev's feelings did not permit him to end the letter on such a solemn theme. Vyazemski chose to change the tone, and he closed on an affirmation of friendship and on a light personal request; since Zhukovski had been mentioned at the beginning of the letter, this request drew a ring around the letter's content and gave it some closure:

How many false concepts are accepted in society as basic truths! For example, is it not mad to consider suicide pusillanimous and criminal? It is very well in one's spare time and at Fortune's bosom to judge the decisive deed of a sufferer, who, after many quarrels with himself, acknowledges that he is the bankrupt debtor of society and, abrogating all his rights to the compassion and help of those close to him, resorts to his final and, in spite of the philosophers' reasoning and the legislators' positions, irrevocable right to dispose of his own life as his property. What good does it do to consider this a crime? Proclaim today to all the people [the Tsar's] most gracious leave to deprive themselves of life; never fear, few will make use of the permission. And before God? But should not a slow suicide, like you for example, who will not follow his doctor's advice and by gluttony hastens his end by some years, be just as guilty? The misfortune is that we measure everything by a common yardstick. We draw God with a beard and represent him as the giver of life or the lender of life. But if one views life as service laid upon us, how can a soldier, having

[11] For an account of Voltaire's opposition to the grotesque punishment of suicides under French law—they were posthumously tried, humiliated, and hanged—see Peter Gay, *Voltaire's Politics: The Poet as Realist* (1959; reprint, New York, 1965), pp. 273–74 and 290. Radishchev, in the "Kresttsy" section of his *Journey from Petersburg to Moscow* (*Puteshestviye iz Peterburga v Moskvu*, 1790) likewise defended a person's right to commit suicide.

sensed his incapacity for service, not leave and yield his place to one more capable? People are so stupid, and I am too! Never fear, however; I preach with words, not deeds. I want to live and love you until I die. Farewell! My letter is mealy mouthed. Do me a favor and, without saying a word, pinch Zhukovski. (*OA*, I, 241; 23 May 1819)

Such loose or arbitrary closure could be tolerated in a literary genre in part because the taste of the age permitted it in other genres as well; verse epistles, comic poems, and satires often share the letter's paratactic construction as well as its minimal closure. Zhukovski even used formulae from prose letters to end some of his verse letters. He ends his "Epistles to Prince Vyazemski and V. L. Pushkin" ("Poslaniya k kn. Vyazemskomu i V. L. Pushkinu," 1814) with a formal epistolary conclusion that he would never have used in a familiar letter: "Dear sirs, I have the honor of being your most humble servant."[12] Pushkin regularly concluded his comic poems with abrupt shifts from the narrative to metapoetic comments, mocking his readers' desire for instructive morals or "serious" purpose. His ribald classic, "Tsar Nikita and His Forty Daughters" ("Tsar Nikita i sorok ego docherey," 1822) ends on just such a light-hearted declaration of poetic independence:

> Some will ask me, eyebrows climbing,
> Why I wrought such fatuous rhyming,
> What the reason for it was?
> Let me answer them: Because.[13]

As we shall see in the afterword to this study, Pushkin even lent an abrupt, epistolary closure to his verse novel, *Eugene Onegin*.

The Arzamasians used a number of devices besides abrupt shifts to give a minimal closure to their letters. It was possible to close by returning to an opening theme, even when the

---

[12] Zhukovski, *Sobraniye sochineni v chetyrekh tomakh*, I, 229.
[13] A. S. Pushkin, *Pushkin Threefold: Narrative, Lyric, Polemic, and Ribald Verse,* trans. Walter Arndt (New York, 1972), p. 58.

writer approached it with such a rush of questions and requests as this:

> Address me right in Riga. Come visit me, Nikolay, for three days and we will go to Petersburg together when my health permits. I would send you money for the journey. It is a fine town. And we could embrace. Well? Think about it and do it! I'm tired of scribbling. Farewell. I expect a reply on a whole quire.
>   Instead of a name: (III, 13; June 1807)

Batyushkov then sketched a portrait of himself on crutches; the letter had begun with a description of his war wound.

Other means of closing included sending regards to or giving news of the members of Arzamas; the membership provided a finite series, which, when exhausted, gave some sense of conclusion. Brief jokes or puns, complete in themselves, ended letters on light-hearted upbeats. Until they outgrew such preciousness, some of the Arzamasians blended Greek mythology and Christian benedictions into endings, such as "may the strength of Apollo and the blessing of the Parnassian maidens be with you!" (Batyushkov, III, 189). Pushkin, like his creature Eugene Onegin, could recall a few Latin tags and sign his letters *vale;* he neatly concluded a letter to Gnedich on censorship problems "Vale, sed delenda est censura" (XIII, 63). Even when they were about to end a letter by exhausting their supply of paper, the Arzamasians made some gesture to justify it, in this case fainting: "it's a pity there is no more room, but I have already written to the point of fainting. Farewell. Oh!" (Batyushkov, III, 426).

Given the thematic importance of friendship to the Arzamasians, it is not surprising to find them concluding their letters by gracefully professing affection and by reaching across the separating distance with warm Russian epistolary gestures. Combined with similarly affectionate openings these closings proved an intimate means of framing a letter's paratactically or associatively organized content.

Conclusion

The Arzamasians' fascination with familiar letters is revealed by their enthusiasm for such foreign epistolarians as Mme de Sévigné, Voltaire, and Galiani; by their impatience with epistolary formulae and dull letters; by the stylistic exuberance that they invested in their own letters; and by the care with which they saved their letters for eventual publication. Arzamas included a few near-professional writers, but they and their fellow members retained enough of the spirit of the gentleman amateur to content themselves with a genre whose radical of presentation required that years elapse before they reached a public larger than their immediate recipients. Writing for friends did not violate their amateur status. When their friends or their heirs published the letters later, they would reach the posterity they may have pretended to scorn in the name of friendship.

Sophisticated, Westward-looking Russian writers of the early nineteenth century willingly accepted familiar letters as a literary genre for a number of reasons. They defined literature broadly anyway, encompassing in it such nonfictional prose genres as history and criticism, which our age has largely relegated to scholarship. Letters expressed their thematic interests, such as friendship, and featured the intimate author-reader relationship that they also cultivated in stories and verse epistles. Letters satisfied their craving for works that could reflect the interests of educated society, give intimate human portraits, provide tasteful judgments, and exploit the stylistic possibilities of Russian prose.

In their letters the Arzamasians attempted to imitate the conversational manner of the salons by a variety of devices: using interrogative, exclamatory, and emphatic intonations; bantering with the imagined interlocutor; recording physical gestures; and employing syntactical organization that seemed conversational against the background of other types of early nineteenth-century prose. The decorum of polite conversation applied to their letters; they tailored the content of the letters to fit their recipients' interests and tried to avoid overly solemn and excessively vulgar themes.

The lexicon of colloquial Russian, which Lomonosov had recommended for familiar letters, proved inadequate for expressing both wide thematic interests and stylistic exuberance. The Arzamasians resorted to Church Slavonicisms, chancellery expressions, and foreign borrowings. They sometimes limited these noncolloquial lexical elements to short phrases, used them terminologically (not as the basis for the language), and colored them with light irony of polite conversation. At other times their sense of stylistic exaggeration spilled out into long stylizations based on these noncolloquial levels of the language. Together with playfully convoluted or disjointed syntax, these stylizations created a desired tension with the devices used to give the illusion of conversational discourse.

Relative to other genres of their time, familiar letters are marked by freedom of content and characterization. The intimacy that readers of familiar letters cherished was conveyed in part by a wealth of concrete detail from everyday life. Unlike the satiric and comic genres of the time, which also featured such detail, letters could employ this domesticity in the description of serious, even tragic, events. The Arzamasians interwove such detail with many comments on literature, verse inserts, and parodies. The practice made such detail literary by contagion; it also suggests that the details could not stand on their own as literature in the minds of the Arzamasians. Batyushkov could not describe the beautiful view from the Island of Ischia or appreciate it in isolation from its associations with his past reading. A sense of propriety and aristocratic fear of ridicule limited the amount of such detail on the writer's life that could enter a letter.

Nevertheless, self-characterization played a large part in the Arzamasian letters and constituted much of their appeal to posterity. The Arzamasians characterized themselves not by

182

intense, subjective self-analysis but by recording their interests, actions, and opinions. They evaluated themselves against a norm consisting of a capacity for friendship, independence, good taste, love of literature, warmth, humor, and harmonious balance of mental and physical activity. They generally found that they measured up to this norm; however, a healthy sense of self-irony distinguishes their letter writing from autohagiography. Their descriptions of others employ the same techniques, but less charitably, and often become entertaining caricatures. The authorial image projected by an Arzamasian letter differs from that of other genres by its freedom to combine elements of all the genres: the melancholy dreaming of an elegy, the ecstatic patriotism of an ode, the righteous indignation of a satire. The familiar letter proved a genre of sufficient length for self-characterization to the Arzamasians because of their indifference to extensive self-analysis and the processes of human change (except by self-will and education).

The Arzamasians found the letter an adequate vehicle for much of their literary criticism as well, since they were not interested in producing works of systematic aesthetics and were content to reveal their tastes or comment on the literary scene. Their letters contain some of their most important criticism, however, because in them they analyzed contemporary works closely. In published articles they feared to arouse squalid controversies by criticizing the works of their opponents too boldly; bonds of friendship generally prevented them from publicly disagreeing with each other. In their letters the Arzamasians frequently showed their disapproval of such targets as odes and saccharine Sentimentalist stories by parody. The criteria that they used in their letters—logic, clarity, verisimilitude, decorum—coincide with those of European Neoclassicism.

Although epistolary tradition offered them many examples of letters on a single topic (narratives, travel letters, wit letters, logical arguments, moral disquisitions), the Arzamasians rarely allowed a single topic, mood, or principle of organization to monopolize their letters. Imitation of the spontaneity of conversation and portrayal of the mind in action led them to paratactic and associative principles of construction. Satires, verse epistles, and essays of the time also featured these principles.

The nature of familiar correspondence as an ongoing activity discouraged strong closure in any single letter, but some conclusion was expected. Such epistolary gestures as embraces; small units complete in themselves, such as epigrams; returning to the themes of the letter's opening; and professions of friendship provided the necessary closure.

Afterword: Beyond the Familiar Letter

The milestones of Russia's transition to the age of Romanticism have been too well charted to warrant extensive attention here. During the 1820s Byron's authorial persona, Sir Walter Scott's fascinating canvasses, the magic world of E. T. A. Hoffmann, and the systematic philosophy of the Germans began to captivate a literature that in preceding decades had slowly adopted the salon phase of Neoclassicism. Haphazard literary judgments, quarrels over style, details from the everyday life of the gentry, the theme of friendship, and joyful Anacreontic verses could no longer satisfy the Russian reading public. Professional editors and critics of non-gentry origin began to flay writers of the older generation for their alleged triviality and mindlessness.

The Arzamasians were men of their own time as well as of the eighteenth century, and they too faced the future. Zhukovski, Vyazemski, and Pushkin greeted Byron enthusiastically (Zhukovski translated "The Prisoner of Chillon"). At the same time as he was imitating Boileau, Vyazemski sent A. I. Turgenev long passages from "Childe Harold's Pilgrimage" in French prose translation. Vyazemski loved its merging of the poet with nature and, under Byron's spell, ecstatically rejected solemn odes, cold narrative poems, the conventional language of verse, and symmetry of words (*OA*, I, 330–32; 17 October 1819).

The letters of the Arzamasians changed with the times. Vyazemski attempted to curb the involved analogies and long sentences of his early letters. Pushkin ceased to insert light verse into his letters. His notes to his wife, among the most popular letters in the language, feature very terse syntax, colloquial lexicon, and abundant social gossip. They lack the persistent literary self-consciousness of his early letters and are best categorized under personal, not familiar, correspondence. As part of his editorial duties in the 1830s Pushkin had to

185

write a number of letters on literary business, but, again, these do not resemble the familiar letters of his youth even when he addressed them to former Arzamasians. Pushkin's last letter, written a few hours before his fatal duel, illustrates the change in his epistolary manner. Although addressed to a fellow writer —the translator and historian Ishimova—it lacks the familiar informality of his earlier letters:

Dear Madam, Aleksandra Osipovna,

I am extremely sorry that it will be impossible for me to appear today at your invitation. Meanwhile, I have the honor of dispatching Barry Cromwell to you. You will find at the end some plays marked with a pencil. Translate them as best you can—I assure you that you will translate them in the best possible way. Today I happened to open your *History in Tales* [a history for children] and could not help becoming engrossed in it. That is how one should write!

With profoundest respect and complete devotion I have the honor of being, Dear Madam,

Your most humble servant.
(XVI, 226; 27 January 1827)

The playful, digressive quality of his familiar letters is gone— but not the dignified persona of an Arzamasian letter. In the face of death Pushkin's graciousness and concern for literature again embody what Zhukovski had called enlightenment: "the art of living, the art of perfecting oneself in that circle in which the Hand of Providence has enclosed you."

Zhukovski continued to write letters on moral and philo-sophical topics, but the other Arzamasians abandoned familiar letter writing as it went out of fashion and as they grew old. The last letters of Severin and Bludov in the state archives are brief and often in French. A series of letters by Bludov to Vyazemski on a monument to Zhukovski illustrates this sorry development: Bludov dictated them to a clerk, and they utterly lack the personal touches and elegiac reflections that the situation formerly would have evoked.

The Arzamasians did not consciously use letters as a "laboratory" for developing new forms, since they did consider familiar correspondence a distinct genre, valuable in its own right. Their more formal works found reflection (if only through parody) in their letters as often as features of their letters helped them create other works. Nevertheless, each new work by an author is in part the product of his total literary experience, and the experience of fragmentary construction, static characterization, and attention to the detail of everyday life proved decisive in the subsequent nonfictional prose of the Arzamasians. As we have seen, they used epistolary form for familiar essays, travel accounts, and literary criticism. A. I. Turgenev wrote a literary chronicle for several journals (1827–45), Zhikharev published his diaries (1853–59), Vyazemski polished his notebooks for the reading public (1826–77), Vigel left posterity a series of witty and malicious sketches in his memoirs (1864–65). The methods of characterization, the style, and the organization of these works reflected the earlier epistolary enthusiasms of their authors.

The brief cult of familiar letters did not, however, spill over into a multitude of epistolary novels, as had been the case in Western literatures. In Russia the Sentimentalist epistolary novel had enjoyed modest success during the late eighteenth century; by the 1820s it was *passé*. Pushkin owned none of the Russian ones.

One may only speculate as to why the Arzamasians did not write epistolary fiction. Their disrespect for early Russian attempts at the novel may explain it in part. Then, too, novels require more sustained creative effort than some Arzamasians cared to expend. Finally, literary self-consciousness marks the letters of the Arzamasians to an extraordinary degree. They would have been forced to surrender much of it to create epistolary novels, in which the actual author's role is that of an editor. Nevertheless, Pushkin started to lend the epistolary novel some

187

of the Arzamasian literary self-consciousness. In.his *Novel in Letters* (*Roman v pismakh,* 1829), the characters discuss literature and Russian literary life. But the draft breaks off after a dozen pages.

The epistolary novel as developed by Richardson and Rousseau did not offer "all the freedom of conversation or a letter" (XIII, 245) that Pushkin thought desirable in the novel. For his "free novel," *Eugene Onegin,* Pushkin creatively drew upon a number of literary traditions. Professor L. N. Stilman, for example, has shown how Pushkin used *Don Juan* and the epistolary novel for the narrator and plot of *Eugene Onegin.*[1] The way in which Pushkin used the tradition of familiar correspondence also merits attention.

Though *Don Juan* offered Pushkin a precedent in verse of the freedom he desired and associated with Romanticism, the freedoms he exercises in his verse novel are those we have encountered in Neoclassical familiar letters: movement between the styles, personae, and moods previously associated with single genres. The variety Pushkin advertises in his dedication recalls the variety Batyushkov attributed to his collected poems, which he separated into genres:[2]

> Unmindful of the proud world's pleasure,
> But friendship's claim alone in view,
> I wish I could have brought a treasure
> Far worthier to pledge to you:
> Fit for a soul of beauty tender,
> By sacred visitations taught
> To blend in rhyme of vivid splendor
> Simplicity and lofty thought;
> Instead—to your kind hands I render
> The motley chapters gathered here,
> At times amusing, often doleful

[1] "Problemy literaturnykh zhanrov i traditsi v 'Evgenii Onegine' Pushkina: k voprosu perekhoda ot romantizma k realizmu," *American Contributions to the Fourth International Congress of Slavists: Moscow, Sept. 1958* ('S-Gravenhage, 1958), pp. 321–65.

[2] See above, chapter II, p. 64.

Blending the rustic and the soulful,
Chance harvest of my pastimes dear,
Of sleepless moods, light inspirations,
Fruit of my green, my withered years,
The mind's dispassionate notations,
The heart's asides, inscribed in tears.[3]

Pushkin set *Eugene Onegin* in the unexotic, everyday world of the Russian gentry: the *grand monde* of St. Petersburg, the more ponderous social rituals of Moscow, the folk heritage and tedious gatherings of the rural landowners. In its setting Pushkin's novel has more in common with his letters than with *Don Juan,* to which it is incessantly compared. Like the letters, *Eugene Onegin* is an encyclopaedia of the Russian and Western literature of its time. The critical judgments of *Eugene Onegin* concern the same issues as the letters: style, decorum, and verisimilitude. Parodies, stylization, literary reminiscences, comments on the creative process, and mockery of literary conventions interrupt the narrative flow of both letters and novel. And, as in the Arzamasian letters, conventions are mocked because they are badly realized, not necessarily because they are conventions. Pushkin's famous epic evocation of the muse provides an illustration of this relationship to conventions. At the end of chapter seven, Pushkin makes fun of evocations—his mocking was in itself, as he well knew, a convention of comic epics. But at the beginning of chapter eight, in some of the most beautiful lines of the novel, he evokes his own muse for a poetic autobiography. The passage blends in with a description of a salon that is conducted by the novel's heroine, Tatiana, who makes the best of social conventions and transfigures the shallow St. Petersburg society described in the first chapter:

The party talk is soon enlivened
By the crude salt of worldly spite;
But, with this hostess, it is light,
Gay nonsense, free of priggish preening,

[3] A. S. Pushkin, *Eugene Onegin* trans. Walter Arndt, p. 1.

189

Or, grave at times, is never brought
To fatuous themes or hallowed thought,
But brims with undidactic meaning;
And its high spirits and good sense
Are powerless to give offense.[4]

Her ability to impose a pleasing order on the otherwise malicious denizens of St. Petersburg parallels the poet's (and letter writer's) ability to create with literary conventions.

As in letters, association with literary topics ("digression") does much to organize *Eugene Onegin,* as much, anyway, as the plot, which has gaps of months and even years. The novel usurps the letter's constant punctuation of plot, characterization, and nature description with these literary associations. The narrator's literary maturation is reflected in the associations. Tatiana, Eugene, and Lensky, the parodistic poet, perceive others and pattern their lives in accordance with literary stereotypes.

The narrator of the novel closely resembles the letter writer in his familiar relationship with the reader; in his self-depreciation, pose of effortless creation, and worldly cynicism; and in his delight in friendship, nature, and literature. The ease with which the poet tosses off his first chapter recalls the Pushkin who lost his collected lyrics in a card game.

I've thought about the hero's label
And on what lines the plot should run;
Meanwhile, it seems, my present fable
Has grown as far as Chapter One.
I have gone over it severely,
And contradictions there are clearly
Galore, but I will let them go,
Pay censorship its due, and throw
Imagination's newborn baby,
My labor's fruit with all its flaws
To the reviewers' greedy jaws;
To the Neva, then, child, and maybe

4 *Ibid.,* p. 206, chapter VIII, stanza 23.

You'll earn me the rewards of fame:
Distorted judgments, noise, and blame![5]

The novel's ending, which leaves Eugene in the midst of an uncomfortable situation, uses devices of epistolary closure. As in a letter, life is presented as something continuing; the narrator leaves his hero abruptly.

Tatyana's husband entered. Here,
At a sore pass in his career,
We leave our hero, reader, brother,
For long . . . forever. Far enough
We trailed his wake through smooth and rough.

The narrator professes friendship for the reader, drops a series of hints that could be fully comprehensible only to friends, and bids farewell, framing the "action" of the novel with a catalogue of its content that echoes his opening dedication:

My reader—friend or not, whichever
You were—now that the story's end
Is here our mingled paths to sever,
I want to leave you as a friend.
Farewell. Whate'er you sought to capture
In my loose rhymes—be it the rapture
Of reminiscence, pause from toil,
Lively tableaux, the piercing foil
Of wit, or bits of faulty grammar—
Please God you found here but a grain
To conjure dreams, to entertain,
To move the heart, to raise a clamor
Of controversy in the press.
Upon this note we part—God bless!
. . . .
But of the trusted band of brothers
To whom the first few quires I read . . .
Some are no more, dispersed the others,
As long before us Sadi said.

[5] *Ibid.*, p. 31, chapter I, stanza 60. Pushkin's letter on his lost verse appears above, chapter IV, pp. 106–7.

Without them was Onegin drafted.
And you, upon whose presence grafted,
Tatyana's form grew animate . . .
Much, oh, so much was snatched by Fate!
Blest he who left in its full glory
The feast of life, who could decline
To drain the brimming cup of wine,
Refused to read life's waning story,
And with abrupt resolve withdrew,
As I from my Onegin do.[6]

Among the genres of his time, only the familiar letter could have given Pushkin so much exercise in this casual, yet subtly ordered, creativity. When Pushkin became a professional writer in the 1820s, he put his accomplishments in correspondence to use in the creation of the larger, more public work, *Eugene Onegin.* Later, as he came to abandon familiar letters, he turned to more rigidly ordered, less fragmentary narratives. Pushkin's *History of the Pugachev Rebellion* (*Istoriya pugachevskogo bunta,* 1834), for example, rejects the epistolary model entirely. Using a terse, formal style it traces the rebellion in a strict chronological order. The account begins by describing the government's harsh economic and administrative treatment of the future rebels—human development is no longer the product of will and education, as it was in the letters, but must be seen against the background of generations of social interaction. And, in fact, the events of Pushkin's narrative proceed from this background situation.

The letters of the early nineteenth century found a less comfortable resting place in Gogol's *oeuvre.* Polite society, which cultivated such genres as the familiar letter, held no positive appeal for Gogol, whose imagination sought the alogical and

[6] *Ibid.,* pp. 220–22, chapter vIII, 48–49 and 51. As Arndt notes, many commentators believe that the "dispersed" friends of the last stanza are Pushkin's friends among the exiled Decembrists, who had tried to impose constitutional rule in Russia and failed in December 1825.

incongruous behind polished façades. It is not surprising that letters in his fiction become a record of human muddle. The note Chichikov receives in *Dead Souls* (chapter VIII) parodies a Sentimentalist love epistle. For it, as Vinogradov has noted,[7] Gogol takes themes from Pushkin's "Gypsies" ("Tsigany," 1824) and Karamzin's "Two Comparisons" ("Dva sravneniya," 1797). The narrator provides ironic commentary on the cliché-ridden note:

> The letter began in very positive terms, precisely as follows: "No, I really must write you!" After that it went on to say that there is such a thing as a secret affinity between souls; this verity was clinched with a number of full stops that took up almost half a line. Then followed a few thoughts quite remarkable for their incontrovertibility, so that we deem it almost indispensable to make an abstract of them: "What is our life? A vale of sorrows. What is society? An insensate human herd." Next the fair writer mentioned that she was bedewing with tears certain lines written by her angelic mother—five-and-twenty years had gone since she had passed from this world; she called on Chichikov to come out into the wilderness, to leave forever the city, where people in stifling enclosures cannot breath the free air; the end of the letter even echoed downright despair and concluded with the following lines:

> > Two turtledoves will show thee
> > Where my cold corpse lies;
> > Their lovelorn cooing tells thee:
> > She died amid tears and sighs.

[7] Vinogradov, *Ocherki po istorii russkogo literaturnogo yazyka*, p. 362. From "The Gypsies" Gogol's epistolarian draws the themes of disillusionment with society and flight from civilization. She adopts the sententiousness of the lines "What is our life . . . herd," from the opening of Karamzin's poem:

> What is our life? A novel.—Who's the Author?
> > > Anonymous.
> We read it haltingly, we laugh, we cry, we sleep.

Karamzin, *Polnoye sobraniye stikhotvoreni,* p. 236.

There wasn't much meter, especially in the last line: this, however, mattered but little—the letter was written in the spirit of that time.[8]

The members of the Romantic generation found other, non-parodic uses for correspondence.[9] Gogol's letters in this case typify their innovations. He returned subjectivity to the letter in a deeper, more complex form than the pleasant expression of sensibility that permeated the letters of Radishchev and the young Karamzin. Gogol's subjective letters contain emotionally heightened self-dramatization, a series of confessions (not always demonstrably reliable), and a far greater gallery of poses than was possible or desirable in an Arzamasian letter. Gogol commenced such analysis in his youth (1827–28). In one of his most complex self-portraits, Gogol begins with conscious posing, but behind the masks stands a person as confused by the reality of his own being as those outsiders who must make sense of his shifting moods and behavior:

When I was home with you I always tried to display absentmindedness, eccentricity, and so forth intentionally, so that you would think that I had little polish and was little oppressed by evil. But can anyone have endured so many expressions of ingratitude, stupid injustices, ludicrous pretensions, cold scorn, and so forth. I endured everything without reproaches without muttering; no one heard my complaints; always I even praised the agents of my grief. In truth, I am considered a riddle for everyone; no one has fathomed me completely. At home they consider me eccentric, some sort of unbearable pedant who thinks that he is more intelligent than everyone else, that he is created

[8] Nicholai V. Gogol, *Dead Souls,* trans. B. G. Guerney (New York, Random House, Modern Library, 1965), pp. 201–2.
[9] In the letters of Bakunin, Herzen, and Ogarev from the 1830s and 1840s L. Ya. Ginzburg finds features similar to those I discuss in Gogol: messianism, a variety of Romantic poses, and sermonizing. *O psikhologicheskoy proze,* pp. 50–56. Readers who do not know Russian will find translated excerpts from interesting letters by Bakunin, Stankevich, and Belinski in E. J. Brown, *Stankevich and his Moscow Circle, 1830–40* (Stanford University Press, 1966).

differently from other people. Would you believe that I
inwardly laughed at myself along with you. Here [at
school] they call me a humble person, the ideal of meek-
ness and patience. In one place I am the most quiet,
modest, respectful; in another I am gloomy, pensive, un-
couth, and so forth; in a third I am garrulous and tiresome
in the extreme. With some I am intelligent; with others,
stupid. . . . Think of me as you will, but only with my real
career will you learn my real character; believe only that
noble sentiments always fill me, that I have never debased
myself in my soul, and that I have fated my whole life to
the Good. You call me a dreamer, precipitate, as if I inwardly didn't laugh at them myself. No, I know people
too well to be a dreamer. The lessons I have received from
them will remain forever ineffaceable, and they are the
true gauge of my happiness. You will see that in time I
shall be in a position to repay all their bad deeds with good
ones, because their evil for me turned to good.[10]

[10] N. V. Gogol, *Polnoye sobraniye sochineni,* 14 vols. (Moscow,
1937–52), x, 123. 1 March 1828, to the author's mother. *The Letters
of Nikolai Gogol,* ed. Carl R. Proffer, trans. Carl R. Proffer in collaboration with Vera Krivoshein (Ann Arbor, 1967), provides excerpts
from Gogol's letters. It is interesting to compare Gogol's solemn sense
of mission with Bakunin's:

The hand of the Lord has etched these holy words on my heart
. . . "He will not live for himself." To sacrifice everything for a
sacred purpose—such is my sole ambition! Don't imagine that I
was mistaken when I told you that every other happiness is closed
to me. Not at all. This is a truth which I feel, which I comprehend,
of which I have become *convinced by the consciousness of my
own being.* The life of man . . . is an eternal striving of the part
toward the Whole. . . . Life is merely a curious journey for those
not possessing a special self-consciousness; for them the external
world is a mass of marvelous things unrelated among themselves
by ideas of perfection and higher necessity, and forming a form-
less conglomeration of curious facts. But for those who really
have a sense of life . . . it is not the separate facts and circumstances that are surprising, but the idea which they express. . . .
And what is this idea? Love for people, love for humanity, and
the striving toward the All, toward perfection. . . . (May 1835, to
Natalie Beyer)

Quoted in Brown, *Stankevich,* pp. 61–62.

This gallery of poses is, of course, as much a haphazard recreation of the Romantic hero as a piece of serious self-analysis. What is important, however, is that it raises questions that the Arzamasians barely recognized about the complexity and inscrutability of the human personality. Unlike the Arzamasians, Gogol was not satisfied with measuring character against the norm of refined society. Wounded by society, not its beneficiary, he entered it to show the inadequacy of its static characterizations. He insisted that he be viewed in relation to a philosophical abstraction ("the Good") and to his own goals.

Gogol's epistolary practice did not differ from the Arzamasians' only in characterization. Writing for his immediate recipients and trusting them to arrange the eventual publication of his letters did not appeal to Gogol. Overcome with messianic fervor, he could not wait for the second coming of his letters. His *Selected Passages from Correspondence with Friends* (*Vybrannye mesta iz perepiski s druzyami,* 1847) assembled and polished the style of his letters to Russia's cultural, political, and religious leaders in an attempt to heal the diseased organs of Russian society. Featuring many rhetorical questions, anaphoric constructions, and polysyndetic sentences, the book is hardly conversational. Although Gogol referred to it as his "letters," he acknowledged its sermonical nature.[11]

Unlike the Arzamasians, Gogol did not view familiar correspondence as an end in itself; the theme of friendship plays almost no role in his letters. He expected his recipients to do research for him and then used their descriptions for his fiction. During his self-imposed exile (1836–48) his letters served as rough drafts for the characterizations and, to a lesser extent, for the plots and imagery of his other writing: "Rome" ("Rim," 1842), *Selected Passages from Correspondence with Friends,* and the second part of *Dead Souls.*[12] In these letters Gogol assumes the poses of the novel's positive characters—social critic, penitent, missionary, and teacher. The Arzamasians had

[11] Gogol, *Polnoye sobraniye sochineni,* XIII, 227. To Vyazemski, 28 February 1847.
[12] For examples see Todd, "Gogol's Epistolary Writing," pp. 72–76.

tailored the content of their letters to the interests of their recipients; Gogol tailored the recipients of these letters to fit his own fictional needs. He transformed them—to their anger and amazement—into the slothful, impious, and sinful creatures of his novel.

It defies common sense and our reading experience to conclude that Russian letter writing died with the Arzamasians. Chekhov's letters, for example, exhibit the conversational manner, acute literary judgments, dignity, and self-irony that distinguished the Arzamasians' correspondence.[13] A letter easily lends itself to the interests and styles of its age. It provides a playground for young authors to explore the possibilities of language, organize their thoughts, and practice reaching a specific audience. I. S. Turgenev, Dostoyevski, L. N. Tolstoy, and Chekhov have left many letters to challenge the scholar and delight the general reader. However, correspondence never again absorbed so much of an age's creative energy after other forms captured the letter's freedoms and offered even more detailed, penetrating treatment of human experience.

[13] Among the many editions of Chekhov's letters available in English translation, *The Letters of Anton Chekhov,* trans. Michael Henry Heim in collaboration with Simon Karlinsky (New York: Harper and Row, 1973) features the best annotations and the most idiomatically accurate translations. By quoting Chekhov's letters in their entirety it shows admirable respect for epistolary art.

APPENDIX I

The Arzamasians

Batyushkov, Konstantin Nikolayevich (1787–1855). Arzamas nickname—Achilles ("Akhill" in Russian, a pun on "Akh, khil"—"ah, I am ill").[1] Nephew of Karamzin's protector, M. N. Muravyev. Educated in St. Petersburg at private pensions. Served in the Ministry of Popular Education, in the army, and as a diplomat in Naples. Wrote tastefully erotic poetry; elegies; imitations of the Greek Anthology, Parny, Tibullus, Tasso, Petrarch, Gresset; literary satires; essays; and criticism of art and literature. Incapacitated by mental illness in 1822.

Bludov, Dmitri Nikolayevich (1785–1864). Cassandra. Privately educated. Served in the College of Foreign Affairs; on missions to Sweden (where he befriended Mme de Staël), England, and Holland; on the court that condemned the Decembrists; in the Ministry of Popular Education; as Minister of Justice and Minister of the Interior. Participated in the reforms of Alexander II. Author of epigrams, maxims, historical studies, and a satire, "Vision in Arzamas" (1815).

Dashkov, Dmitri Vasilyevich (1788–1839). Chu! (an interjection often used in Zhukovski's ballads meaning "hark!"). Studied at the Nobles' Pension at Moscow University. Started his career in the Ministry of Justice under Dmitriyev, served as a diplomat in Turkey, later became Minister of Justice. Wrote articles opposing Shishkov, the "Arzamas Cantata," criticism, and translations from the Greek Anthology.

[1] I give the Russian version of the nickname only when there is a pun involved. The names were taken from Zhukovski's ballads, and they are often used in the letters of the Arzamasians.

Davydov, Denis Vasilyevich (1784–1839). The Armenian. Partisan hero of the war against the French (1812–14). Wrote poetry, hussar songs, essays, and an autobiography.

Kavelin, Dmitri Aleksandrovich (1778–1851). The Hermit. Studied at the Nobles' Pension at Moscow University. Served as a school administrator and Director of St. Petersburg University, where he led a reactionary purge. Together with Dashkov and Aleksandr Turgenev he helped publish the first edition of Zhukovski's poetry.

Muravyev, Nikita Mikhaylovich (1796–1843). Adelstan, Graceful Swan. Cousin of Batyushkov. Studied at Moscow University. Army officer. Exiled to Siberia for participation in the Decembrist Conspiracy. Wrote constitutional projects and a criticism of Karamzin's *History of the Russian State.*

Orlov, Mikhail Fedorovich (1788–1842). Rhine (because of his smoothly flowing speech). Son of an important supporter of Catherine the Great. Cavalry officer, adjutant to Alexander I. Arranged the capitulation of Paris, conducted diplomatic missions on Scandinavian problems, and instituted Lancaster schools for his soldiers. His career was ruined by participation in the early stages of the Decembrist conspiracy. Wrote on economics, education, and history.

Pleshcheyev, Aleksandr Alekseyevich (1775–1827). Black Raven (because of his swarthy complexion). Related by marriage to Zhukovski and to Karamzin. Guardsman, country gentleman. Wrote music, participated in theatrical administration, recited verse and drama.

Poletika, Petr Ivanovich (1778–1849). Enchanted Barque. Diplomat (Stockholm, Naples, Madrid, London, United States) and senator. Wrote memoirs and (in French) on the United States.

Pushkin, Aleksandr Sergeyevich (1799–1837). Cricket. Russia's "national poet," also wrote drama, criticism, historical studies, and prose fiction. Nephew of V. L. Pushkin, entered the Imperial Lycée with the help of A. I. Turgenev, escaped Siberian exile through the efforts of Karamzin and Kapodistrias.

Pushkin, Vasili Lvovich (1770–1830). "Vot," "Votrushka" (there [interjection], Cheese Pie). Guardsman. Squandered away a fortune, traveled in Europe, visited French literary circles. Gallomaniac. Knew French, Latin, English, German, and Italian. Early and passionate opponent of Shishkov. Wrote verse epistles, elegies, fables, and tales. Remembered for his famous nephew and for his scabrous comic poem, "The Dangerous Neighbor" (1811).

Severin, Dmitri Petrovich (1792–1865). Frisky Cat. Studied at the Jesuit Pension in St. Petersburg, served under his father's friend Dmitriyev in the Ministry of Justice, then in the College of Foreign Affairs and on diplomatic missions to Spain, Sweden, and Bavaria. Died in Munich. Translated essays and wrote two fables.

Turgenev, Aleksandr Ivanovich (1784–1845). Aeolian Harp. Son of an influential educator and Freemason. Studied at the Nobles' Pension at Moscow University and in Göttingen. Director of the Department of Foreign Creeds, served on the Law Commission and on the State Council. Career ruined by his brothers' exile and by the rise of Russian Orthodox fanatics to power in 1824. Gathered historical materials and contributed letters on European literature to the journals of A. S. Pushkin and Vyazemski.

Turgenev, Nikolay Ivanovich (1789–1871). Warwick. Brother of A. I. Turgenev, educated at the same institutions. Served on the Law Commission, as Russian commissar at the Allies' council in Germany, on the State

Council, and in the Ministry of Finance. Forced to live in exile for his part in the Decembrist conspiracy. Restored to his former rank years later by Alexander II. Anglomaniac. Author of *An Essay on the Theory of Taxes* (1818) and *La Russie et les russes* (1847).

Uvarov, Sergey Semenovich (1789–1855). The Old Woman. School administrator, diplomat (Vienna, Paris), President of the Academy of Sciences, friend of Mme de Staël, Minister of Popular Education, formulator of the conservative ideology of Nicholas I with its famous slogan "Orthodoxy, Autocracy, Nationality." Author of works on Greek antiquities, on hexameters, and on Goethe. Translated the Greek Anthology together with Batyushkov.

Vigel, Filipp Filippovich (1788–1856). The Crane of Ibycus. Of Estonian descent. Educated privately, in part by the fabulist Krylov. Served in the College of Foreign Affairs, later in the Department of Foreign Creeds. Author of fascinating memoirs, political essays, and denunciations for the police.

Vyazemski, Petr Andreyevich (1792–1878). Asmodeus. Son of a wealthy noble. Brother-in-law of Karamzin. Educated at the Jesuit Pension in St. Petersburg together with Severin. Fought at Borodino, served in Warsaw. Forced to retire because of his liberalism, but later held a boring post in the Ministry of Finance against his wishes. He was forced to leave his final position—head of censorship—for insufficient strictness. Critic, journalist, early Russian admirer of Byron, poet, trenchant satirist, publisher of archival materials, polemicist, and prose stylist. Translated Constant's *Adolphe* and adapted Boileau.

Voyeykov, Aleksandr Fedorovich (1779–1839). Two Giant Hands, Small Smoky Stove. Attended the Nobles' Pension at Moscow University. Married Zhukovski's half-niece. Professor of Russian Literature at Dorpat University, journalist, editor, critic. Translated Virgil, Delille, and Voltaire's historical works. Wrote satires, verse epistles, and denunciations of his fellow professors.

Zhikharev, Stepan Petrovich (1788–1860). Gromoboy. Attended the Nobles' Pension at Moscow University. Friend of Derzhavin and member of the Beseda before joining Arzamas. Served in the College of Foreign Affairs and in the Ministry of Justice, then as a theater administrator, procurator, senator, and bribe-taker. Poet, dramatist, and translator (Voltaire, Crébillon). L. N. Tolstoy used his memoirs for *War and Peace*.

Zhukovski, Vasili Andreyevich (1783–1852). Svetlana. Son of a wealthy landowner and his Turkish prisoner. Attended the Nobles' Pension at Moscow University with Dashkov, Voyeykov, and Aleksandr Turgenev. Served in the militia in 1812 and as tutor to members of the royal family, including the future tsar, Alexander II. Edited *The Herald of Europe* from 1808–1810; wrote prose fiction, criticism, essays, and poetry (especially elegies and ballads). Translated Uhland, Schiller, Bürger, Dryden, Thomson, Gray, Southey, Scott, Thomas Moore, Byron, Homer (*The Odyssey,* from German), La Fontaine, Delille, Parny, and Millevoye. Died in Germany.

Honorary Members

Dmitriyev, Ivan Ivanovich (1760–1837). Educated at home. Served in the guards, then as senator and Minister of Justice. Nephew of Karamzin's step-mother. Wrote songs, verse tales, fables, odes, satires, and memoirs. Translated Pope and Juvenal.

Gagarin, Grigori Ivanovich (1782–1839). Schoolfellow of Aleksandr Turgenev. Diplomat (Rome). Part-time journalist. Translated from French and wrote erotic verse.

Kapodistrias, Ioannis Antonios (1776–1831). Born in Corfu. Greek patriot and republican. Entered the Russian diplomatic service (lower Danube area, Switzerland). Secretary of State (1816–22). He ran the Ministry of Foreign Affairs with Nesselrode, but resigned when Metternich grew influential over Alexander I. Elected Governor of Greece in 1827. Assassinated by members of a rival clan. Spoke and wrote French, but promised Arzamas materials on Europe for their journal. Helped save A. S. Pushkin from Siberian exile in 1820.

Karamzin, Nikolay Mikhaylovich (1766–1826). Educated at home, then in Simbirsk and Moscow. Learned French, German, and English. A friend of Masonic thinkers in Moscow, including the father of Aleksandr Turgenev. Wrote criticism, Sentimentalist poetry, prose fiction, *The Letters of a Russian Traveller* (1791–1801), *The History of the Russian State* (1818), and a *Memoir on Ancient and Modern Russia* (1811). Edited and founded several journals and miscellanies. After 1803 he abandoned imaginative literature and journalism to devote his efforts to historical works. Friend and advisor to Alexander I. Translated Fielding, Shakespeare, Mme de Staël, Gessner, Lessing, and Delille.

Neledinski-Meletski, Juri Aleksandrovich (1752–1828). Studied at the University of Strasbourg. Served in the army, then as an educational administrator and senator. Friend of Karamzin and Dmitriyev. Wrote popular Sentimentalist songs.

Saltykov, Aleksandr Nikolayevich (1775–1837). Served as a State Councilor. Fell into disfavor with Alexander I and retired in 1817.

Saltykov, Mikhail Aleksandrovich (1767–1851). Lover of Catherine the Great. Educational administrator, senator. A liberal aristocrat and admirer of Rousseau. He knew and was interested in Russian literature, unlike many high aristocrats of his time.

N. I. Grech's Essay on Letter Writing

§106. *Letters,* in the exact sense of the word, are conversations or talks with those who are absent. They take the place of oral conversation, but include the part of only one person.[1]

§107. Oral conversation has the characteristics of unprepared, unforced, artless composition—these same characteristics constitute the essential properties of any good letter. There is, however, this difference between them. The action of a letter is more lasting; but conversation receives more expressiveness from the voice in which it is uttered and from the accompanying movements of the body. From this it is evident that in a letter one must be more discriminating in the use and arrangement of words and try for full and clear expression and ordering of thoughts. In composing letters one must follow this rule: write as you would speak in the same situation, but as you would speak correctly, coherently, and pleasantly.

§108. In a letter, as in any other composition, there should be *one* governing feeling by which its dominant *tone* is determined. In this case one must pay attention to the spiritual condition of the person to whom he is writing rather than follow his own; for it can often happen that an object that brings us pleasure arouses quite the opposite feeling in someone else.

§109. The *style* of a letter depends primarily on its content; in this regard it is impossible to prescribe general rules. One must only take pains to avoid grandiloquence and pomposity of expression; simplicity, clarity, and precision are better than any ornament.

§110. The general rules to be observed in composing letters are:

1) Remember *to whom* and *about what* you are writing,

[1] This entire section is taken from N. I. Grech, *Uchebnaya kniga rossiskoy slovesnosti,* I, 52–59.

and conform to this in the style and arrangement of the letter.

2) List all the subjects you wish to write about beforehand in order not to add *postscripta* or additions.

3) Arrange the subjects of a letter in such a way that there be no repetitions and so that it constitute one coherent whole. Place subjects important to the person to whom you are writing at the beginning and those concerning you personally subsequent to them.

4) If you have to prepare the Reader for news you are conveying, then you should pay attention less to the subject itself than to the effect the conveyed news will produce.

§111. In general, letters may be divided into *letters on social subjects* and *Literary letters*. The former, or personal letters, are addressed to those in various conditions of social life who are absent; the latter are narratives, descriptions, or discussions that have only the external form of letters.

I. LETTERS ON SOCIAL SUBJECTS

§112. Letters on social subjects consist of *salutation, content,* and *conclusion.*

§113. The *salutation* indicates how the person who is writing finds himself in relation to the one with whom he is corresponding. Certain well-known formulae are used for this. If you are writing to someone for the first time, at the beginning you can make some apologies and set down the reasons that have compelled you to write. . . .[2]

§114. The *content* of a letter is generally arranged as above in §110. According to their content, which varies infinitely, letters are:

1) *Business,* relating to the chapter on *business documents.*

2) Composed according to the demands of *decorum,* such as *dedicatory, congratulatory, letters of condolence* and *of*

[2] Here follows a page of salutations for people of various ranks and callings.

205

thanks, etc. In such letters there is usually no strong or sincere feeling, and thus it is more difficult to compose them than other letters; meanwhile, one must take pains in them to avoid common, ordinary thoughts and turns of phrase (for example, with news of someone's death listing well-known thoughts about mortality, etc.).

3) *Familiar letters* are easier than the rest, for both the mind and heart take part in them; in these letters one must avoid excessive sensibility, which can easily become saccharine.

4) *Amusing* or joking letters, having the purpose of cheering up the person to whom you are writing, cannot be made subject to rules; but in general you should see to it that the gaiety and wit in them not be pretentious or forced, that feelings and important thoughts not be the subject of your jokes, and that the jokes do not offend the person to whom you are writing.

5) *Didactic* letters have the purpose of instructing the person to whom you are writing in some important or useful manner. In these letters you should avoid pedantry and dryness. These letters usually belong to the category of Literary letters.

§115. Letters are also classified according to the persons to whom one is writing into letters to *superiors, equals,* and *inferiors:* each of these relationships demand special attention: to superiors one must write respectfully but without servility, to equals simply but always decorously, and to inferiors affectionately and without arrogance.

§116. In the *conclusion* to a letter one offers assurances of respect, friendship, etc. This conclusion can be in connection with the ending of the letter's content. Special formulae for this conclusion can be given, but one must take pains to avoid strained and forced expressions. . . .[3]

§117. In letters serving as *replies,* one must observe the following:

[3] Here follows a list of closing formulae for people of various ranks and callings.

206

1) In the opening refer to the letter you are answering and indicate its date.

2) Answer all points that were put to you, if possible in the same order. This rule changes in observing §110:3. Moreover, one should write of important subjects in the beginning and combine the less important ones in a single sentence at the end of the reply, in order that the letter not become too long.

§118. Short letters to friends living in the same city as you are called *notes*. They usually include brief announcements, invitations, questions, etc. No special form is observed in them. Simplicity and naturalness are their chief qualities; but a man of taste can speak intelligently and with feeling even in a brief note.

II. LITERARY LETTERS

§119. *Literary letters,* as was stated above (§111) are a different type of composition, having only the external form of a letter, which is chosen so that the author might have more freedom in arranging and expressing his thoughts.

§120. Subjects of Literary letters can be: narratives about unimportant events, descriptions (mainly travel accounts), critical discussions, communications of the main concepts in certain matters of scholarship of special concern to the heart and imagination, etc. All these subjects are set forth in letters without observation of the strict rules of scholarship, but with ease and simplicity, a letter's necessary qualities.

§121. The style of Literary letters is quite like the style of letters used in society; but since these letters are intended mainly for publication, their language should be more correct than that of the others. They usually borrow their form from familiar letters to persons who are our equals.

§122. *Fonvizin, Karamzin,* and *Muravyev* have written the best letters in the Russian language. The letters of the first have no particular correctness or polish, because they were not intended for publication. *Lomonosov's* letters have all the qualities of good letters; however, their language has become antiquated.

> *Note:* In the letters we offer as examples the difference between letters on social subjects and Literary letters has not been observed because the boundaries between these two types are very ill-defined and because we have very few published examples of the first type. We considered it awkward and unseemly to offer examples we had composed ourselves.

Bibliography

I. PUBLISHED LETTERS

Balzac, Guez de and Voiture, Vincent. *Oeuvres choisies*. Ed. Gabriel Raibaud. Paris: Larousse, 1936.

Batyushkov, K. N. *Sochineniya*. Ed. L. N. Maykov and V. I. Saitov. 3 vols. St. Petersburg: Kotomin, 1885–87.

Chekhov, A. P. *The Letters of Anton Chekhov*. Trans. Michael Henry Heim in collaboration with Simon Karlinsky. New York: Harper and Row, 1973.

Cicero, Marcus Tullius. *Selected Works*. Trans. Michael Grant. Baltimore: Penguin, 1960.

Dashkov, D. V. "Pisma D. V. Dashkova: Vyderzhki iz starykh bumag Ostafyevskogo arkhiva." *Russki arkhiv,* 1866, pp. 491–502.

Dmitriyev, I. I. *Sochineniya*. Ed. A. A. Floridov. 2 vols. St. Petersburg: Yevdokimov, 1895.

Erasmus. *The Epistles of Erasmus: From His Earliest Letters to His Fifty-first Year Arranged in Order of Time*. Trans. Francis Morgan Nichols. 3 vols. 1901–18. Reprint. New York: Russell and Russell, 1962.

Galiani, Ferdinando. *Correspondence avec Madame d'Épinay, Madame Necker, Madame Geoffrin, etc., Diderot, Grimm, d'Alembert, de Sartine, d'Holbach, etc*. Ed. Lucien Perey and Gaston Maugras. 2 vols. Paris: Michel Lévy Frères, 1889–90.

Gogol, N. V. *The Letters of Nikolai Gogol*. Ed. Carl R. Proffer. Trans. Carl R. Proffer in collaboration with Vera Krivoshein. Ann Arbor: University of Michigan Press, 1967.

———. *Polnoye sobraniye sochineni*. 14 vols. Moscow: Nauka, 1937–52.

Fedorov, Boris, ed. *Pamyatnik otechestvennykh muz*. St. Petersburg: 1827.

Kapnist, V. V. *Sobraniye sochineni v dvukh tomakh.* Moscow-Leningrad: Nauka, 1960.

Karamzin, N. M. *Pisma N. M. Karamzina k I. I. Dmitriyevu.* Ed. Ya. Grot and P. Pekarski. St. Petersburg: Imp. Akademiya Nauk, 1866.

———. "Pisma N. M. Karamzina k A. I. Turgenevu." *Russkaya starina,* 1899, nos. 1–4.

———. *Pisma N. M. Karamzina k knyazyu P. A. Vyazemskomu: 1810–1826 (iz ostafyevskogo arkhica).* Ed. N. Barsukov. St. Petersburg: 1897.

Lomonosov, M. V. *Sochineniya.* 8 vols. Moscow-Leningrad: Akademiya Nauk, 1891–1948.

———. *Sochineniya.* Moscow-Leningrad: GIKhL, 1961.

Orlov, M. F. *Kapitulyatsiya Parizha, Politicheskiye sochineniya, Pisma.* Moscow: ANSSSR, 1963.

Pushkin, A. S. *The Letters of Alexander Pushkin.* Trans. J. Thomas Shaw. 1963. Reprint. Madison: University of Wisconsin Press, 1967. For reviews of this edition, see Walter Arndt and Ralph E. Matlaw in the next section of this bibliography.

———. *Pisma.* Ed. B. L. Modzalevski. Vol. I. Moscow-Leningrad: Gosizdat, 1926.

———. *Polnoye sobraniye sochineni.* 17 vols. Moscow-Leningrad: Nauka, 1937–59.

———. "Redchayshaya nakhodka: neizvestnoye pismo Pushkina." *Literaturnaya gazeta,* 9 December 1970, p. 6.

———. *Sobraniye sochineni v desyati tomakh.* Moscow: GIKhL, 1959–62.

Radishchev, A. N. *Polnoye sobraniye sochineni.* 3 vols. Moscow-Leningrad: Nauka, 1938–52.

Turgenev, A. I. "Pisma A. I. Turgeneva k I. I. Dmitriyevu." *Russki arkhiv,* 1867, pp. 639–70.

Turgenev, A. I., Turgenev, S. I., and Turgenev, N. I. *Arkhiv bratyev Turgenevykh.* Ed. Ye. I. Tarasov. St. Petersburg: Akademiya Nauk, 1911–21.

Voltaire, François-Marie Arouet de. *Oeuvres complètes.* Ed. Louis Moland. Paris: Garnier, 1877–85.

Vyazemski, P. A. *Ostafyevski arkhiv knyazey Vyazemskikh.* Ed. V. I. Saitov. 5 vols. St. Petersburg: S. P. Sheremetev, 1899.

———. "Pisma k V. A. Zhukovskomu." *Russki arkhiv,* 1900, pp. 181–208 and pp. 355–90.

Zhukovski, V. A. "Pisma-dnevniki V. A. Zhukovskogo 1814 i 1815 godov." In *Pamyati V. A. Zhukovskogo i N. V. Gogolya,* ed. P. K. Simoni. Vol. I. St. Petersburg: Imp. Akademiya Nauk, 1907. Pp. 143–213.

———. *Sobraniye sochineni v chetyrekh tomakh.* Ed. I. M. Semenko, et al. Moscow-Leningrad: GIKhL, 1959–60.

II. ARCHIVAL COLLECTIONS OF LETTERS

Batyushkov, K. N. Letters to P. A. Vyazemski. Tsentralni gosudarstvenni arkhiv literatury i iskusstva. Ostafyevski arkhiv, 195/1/1416.

Dashkov. D. V. Letters to P. A. Vyazemski. Tsentralni gosudarstvenni arkhiv literatury i iskusstva. Ostafyevski arkhiv, 195/1/1820.

Severin, D. P. Letters to P. A. Vyazemski. Tsentralni gosudarstvenni arkhiv literatury i iskusstva. Ostafyevski arkhiv, 195/1/2727.

Vyazemski, P. A. Letters to K. N. Batyushkov. Arkhiv Pushkinskogo Doma. Arkhiv K. N. Batyushkova, fond 19, no. 28.

———. Letters to V. A. Zhukovski. Arkhiv Pushkinskogo Doma, 27985/ccib44.

III. WORKS ON RUSSIAN LETTER WRITING

Alekseyev, M. P. "Pisma I. S. Turgeneva." Introduction to I. S. Turgenev, *Polnoye sobraniye sochineni i pisem. Pisma.* Vol. I. Moscow-Leningrad: ANSSSR, 1961. Pp. 15–144.

Arndt, Walter. Review of *The Letters of Alexander Pushkin,* trans. J. Thomas Shaw. *Slavic and East European Journal* 9 (1965), 97–101.

Fridlender, G. M. "Pisma Gogolya." In N. V. Gogol, *Sobraniye sochineni v semi tomakh*. Moscow: GIKhl, 1966–67. VII, 5–30.

Fridman, N. V. *Proza Batyushkova*. Moscow: Nauka, 1965.

Grech, N. I. *Uchebnaya kniga rossiskoy slovesnosti ili izbrannye mesta iz ruskikh sochineni i perevodov v stikhakh i proze*. 4 vols. St. Petersburg: Tip. N. I. Grecha, 1819–21.

Grossman, L. P. "Kultura pisem v epokhe Pushkina." *Pisma zhenshchin k Pushkinu*. Moscow: Izd. "Sovremennye problemy," 1928. Pp. 7–23.

Ilyinskaya, I. S. "O yazyke pisem Griboyedova." *Literaturnoye nasledstvo*, 47–48 (1946), pp. 529–34.

Kazanski, B. V. "Pisma Pushkina." *Literaturni kritik*, 1937, no. 2, pp. 90–105.

Levkovich, Ya. L. "Pisma." *Pushkin: Itogi i problemy izucheniya*. Moscow-Leningrad: Nauka, 1966. Pp. 529–34.

Lezhnev, A. Z. *Proza Pushkina*. 1937. Reprint. Moscow: GIKhL, 1966.

Malakhovski, V. A. "Leksika pisem Pushkina." *Uchenye zapiski Kuybyshevskogo Pedagogicheskogo Instituta* 2 (1938), 4–35.

———. "Yazyk pisem Pushkina." *Izvestiya Akademii Nauk SSSR, Otdeleniye Obshchestvennykh Nauk*, 1937, pp. 503–68.

Matlaw, Ralph E. Review of *The Letters of Alexander Pushkin*, trans. J. Thomas Shaw. *Slavic Review* 24 (1965), 344–46.

Maymin, Ye. A. "Druzheskaya perepiska Pushkina s tochki zreniya stilistiki." *Pushkinski sbornik*. Pskov: Izd. Pskovskogo Universiteta, 1962.

Modzalevski, B. L. "Predisloviye." Introduction to A. S. Pushkin, *Pisma*, ed. B. L. Modzalevski. Vol. I. Moscow-Leningrad: Gosizdat, 1926. Pp. iii–xlviii.

Modzalevski, L. B. "Ot sostavitelya." Introduction to M. V. Lomonosov, *Sochineniya*. Moscow-Leningrad: Akademiya Nauk, 1891–1948. VIII, 5–40.

Paperno, I. A. "O dvuyazychnoy perepiske pushkinskoy pory."

Uchenye zapiski Tartuskogo Gosudarstvennogo Universiteta, 358 (1975), *Trudy po russkoy i slavyanskoy filologii,* xxiv, 148–56.

Pushkin, A. S. "Voltaire ('Correspondence inédite de Voltaire avec le président de Brosses, etc.' Paris, 1836)." *Polnoye sobraniye sochineni.* Moscow-Leningrad: Nauka, 1937–59. xii, 75–81.

Semenko, I. M. "Pisma Pushkina." Afterword to A. S. Pushkin, *Sobraniye sochineni v desyati tomakh.* Moscow: GIKhl, 1959–62. ix, 389–407.

Sipovski, V. A. "A. S. Pushkin po ego pismam." In *Pamyati L. N. Maykova,* ed. V. I. Saitov. St. Petersburg: Imp. Akademiya Nauk, 1902. Pp. 455–67.

Sokolski, Ivan. *Kabinetski i kupecheski sekretar ili sobraniye nailuchshikh i upotrebitelnykh pisem.* 2nd ed. Moscow: Reshetnikov, 1795.

Stepanov, N. L. "Druzheskoye pismo nachala XIX v." In *Russkaya proza,* ed. B. Eykhenbaum and Yu. Tynyanov. 1926. Reprint. The Hague: Mouton, 1963. Pp. 74–101. (An abridged version appears in N. L. Stepanov. *Poety i prozaiki.* Moscow: GIKhL, 1966. Pp. 66–91.)

———. "Pisma Pushkina kak literaturni zhanr." *Poety i prozaiki.* Moscow: GIKhl, 1966. Pp. 91–100.

Todd, William Mills, III. "Gogol's Epistolary Writing." In *The Dean's Papers, 1969,* ed. Andrew W. Cordier. Columbia Essays in International Affairs, vol. v. New York: Columbia University Press, 1970. Pp. 51–76.

Tynyanov, Yu. N. *Arkhaisty i novatory.* Leningrad: Priboy, 1929.

Vinokur, G. O. "Pushkin-prozaik." *Kultura yazyka.* Moscow: Federatsiya, 1929. Pp. 286–303.

Vyazemski, P. A. "O novykh pismakh Voltera." *Polnoye sobraniye sochineni.* St. Petersburg: S. D. Sheremetev, 1878–96. i, 65–70.

———. "O pismakh Karamzina." *Torzhestvennoye sobraniye Akademii Nauk 1 dekabrya 1866 goda v pamyat stoletney godovshchiny rozhdeniya N. M. Karamzina.* St. Petersburg: 1867.

213

IV. Miscellaneous

Abrams, M. H. *The Mirror and the Lamp: Romantic Theory and the Critical Tradition*. 1953. Reprint. New York: Norton, 1958.

Akhmatova, Anna. " 'Adolf' Benzhamena Konstana v tvorchestve Pushkina." *Vremennik Pushkinskoy Komissii Akademii Nauk SSSR* I (1936), 91–114.

Aksakov, S. T. "Vospominaniye ob Aleksandre Semenoviche Shishkove." *Sobraniye sochineni v pyati tomakh*. Moscow: Pravda, 1966. II, 258–303.

Anderson, Howard; Daghlian, Philip B.; and Ehrenpreis, Irvin, eds. *The Familiar Letter in the Eighteenth Century*. Lawrence: University of Kansas Press, 1968.

Aronson, M. I. and Reyser, S. A., eds. *Literaturnye kruzhki i salony*. Leningrad: Priboy, 1929.

Auerbach, Erich. *Literary Language and its Public in Late Latin Antiquity and in the Middle Ages*. Trans. Ralph Manheim. New York: Random House, 1965.

Batyushkov, K. N. *Polnoye sobraniye stikhotvoreni*. Ed. N. V. Fridman. Moscow-Leningrad: Sovetski pisatel, 1964.

Berkov, P. N., ed. *Istoriya russkoy literatury XVIII veka: Bibliograficheski ukazatel*. Leningrad: Nauka, 1968.

Borovkova-Maykova, M. S., ed. *"Arzamas" i "arzamasskiye" protokoly*. Introduction by D. Blagoy. Leningrad: Izd. pisateley v Leningrade, 1933.

Brown, E. J. *Stankevich and his Moscow Circle, 1830–40*. Stanford: Stanford University Press, 1966.

Burckhardt, Jacob. *The Civilization of the Renaissance in Italy*. Trans. S. G. C. Middlemore. 2 vols. New York: Harper & Row, Torchbooks, 1958.

Croce, Benedetto. *Aesthetic as Science of Expression and General Linguistic*. Trans. Douglas Ainslie. 2nd ed. London: Macmillan & Co., 1922.

Demetrius. *On Style*. Trans. W. Rhys Roberts. In *Aristotle, The Poetics: "Longinus," On the Sublime: Demetrius, On Style*. Loeb Classical Library. Cambridge: Harvard University Press, 1932.

Derzhavin, G. R. *Stikhotvoreniya.* Ed. G. A. Gukovski. Leningrad: Izd. pisateley v Leningrade, 1933.

Dmitriyev, I. I. *Polnoye sobraniye stikhotvoreni.* Ed. G. P. Makogonenko. Leningrad: Sovetski pisatel, 1967.

Ehrhard, M. *V. A. Joukovski et le préromantisme russe.* Paris: Champion, 1938.

Elliott, Robert C. "The Definition of Satire." *Yearbook of Comparative and General Literature,* vol. XI (1962).

Erlich, Victor. *Russian Formalism: History-Doctrine.* 2nd ed. The Hague: Mouton, 1965.

Foucault, Michel. *The Order of Things: An Archaeology of the Human Sciences.* New York: Random House, 1970.

Frye, Northrop. *Anatomy of Criticism.* Princeton: Princeton University Press, 1957.

Gay, Peter. *Voltaire's Politics: The Poet as Realist.* 1959. Reprint. New York: Vintage, 1965.

Gessen, S. *Knigoizdatel A. S. Pushkin.* Leningrad, Academia, 1930.

Gillelson, M. I. *Molodoy Pushkin i arzamasskoye bratstvo.* Leningrad: Nauka, 1974.

———. *P. A. Vyazemski: Zhizn i tvorchestvo.* Leningrad: Nauka, 1969.

Ginzburg, L. Ya. *O lirike.* 2nd ed. Leningrad: Sovetski pisatel, 1974.

———. *O psikhologicheskoy proze.* Leningrad: Sovetski pisatel, 1971.

Gogol, Nicholai V. *Dead Souls.* Trans. B. G. Guerney. New York: Random House, Modern Library, 1965.

Gorodetski, B. P. "Kotsenke Pushkinym komedii Griboyedova 'Gore ot uma.'" *Russkaya literatura,* 1970, no. 3, pp. 21–36.

Greene, Donald J. " 'Logical Structure' in Eighteenth-Century Poetry." *Philological Quarterly* XXXI (1952), 315–36.

Grits, T., Trenin, V., and Nikitin, M. *Slovesnost i kommertsiya (knizhnaya lavka A. F. Smirdina).* Moscow: Federatsiya, 1929.

Guillén, Claudio. "On the Uses of Literary Genre." *Literature as System: Essays Toward the Theory of Literary History.* Princeton: Princeton University Press, 1971.

Gukovski, G. A. *Russkaya literatura XVIII veka: Uchebnik dlya vysshikh uchebnykh zavedeni.* Moscow: Uchpedgiz, 1939.

Hans, N. A. *History of Russian Educational Policy, 1701–1917.* New York: Russell and Russell, 1964.

Haskins, C. H. *The Renaissance of the Twelfth Century.* Cambridge: Harvard University Press, 1933.

Hornbeck, Katherin Gee. *The Complete Letter Writer in English: 1568–1800.* Smith College Studies in Modern Language, vol. xv, nos. 3–4 (April–July 1934).

Huizinga, Johan. *Homo Ludens: A Study of the Play Element In Culture.* 1950. Reprint. Boston: Beacon Press, 1955.

Irving, W. H. *The Providence of Wit in the English Letter Writers.* Durham: Duke University Press, 1955.

Istrin, V. M. "Druzheskoye literaturnoye obshchestvo." *Zhurnal ministerstva narodnogo prosveshcheniya,* 1910, no. 8, pp. 273–307.

————. "Russkiye studenty v Gettingene v 1802–4 gg." *Zhurnal ministerstva narodnogo prosveshcheniya,* 1910, no. 7, pp. 80–144.

Jefferson, D. W. "*Tristram Shandy* and the Tradition of Learned Wit." *Essays in Criticism,* i (1951), no. 3, pp. 225–48.

Johnson, Samuel. *Johnson's Dictionary: A Modern Selection.* Ed. E. L. McAdam, Jr. and George Milne. New York: Random House, Modern Library, 1965.

Karamzin, N. M. *Izbrannye sochineniya v dvukh tomakh.* Ed. P. Berkov. Moscow-Leningrad: Khudozhestvennaya Literatura, 1964.

————. *Polnoye sobraniye stikhotvoreni.* Ed. Ju. M. Lotman. Moscow-Leningrad: Sovetski pisatel, 1966.

Khodakova, Ye. P. "Kalambur v russkoy literature XVIII v." In *Russkaya literaturnaya rech v XVIII veke: Frazeologizmy. Neologizmy. Kalambury,* ed. N. Yu. Shvedova. Moscow: Nauka, 1968.

Kirpichnikov, A. "Kurganov i yego 'Pismovnik.' " *Istoricheski vestnik,* 1887, no. 9, pp. 473–503.

Kovalevski, Ye. P. *Sobraniye sochineni Ye. P. Kovalevskogo.* Vol. I: *Graf Bludov i yego vremya.* St. Petersburg: Glazunov, 1871.

Kupreyanova, Ye. N. "K voprosu o klassitsizme." *XVIII vek: Sbornik chetverty.* Moscow-Leningrad: Nauka, 1959. Pp. 5–44.

Likhachev, D. S. *Poetika drevnerusskoy literatury.* 2nd ed. Leningrad: Khudozhestvennaya literatura, 1971.

Lotman, Yu. M. "Andrey Sergeyevich Kaysarov i literaturno-obshchestvennaya borba ego vremeni." *Uchenye zapiski Tartuskogo Gosudarstvennogo Universiteta* 63 (1958), 18–76.

———. *Lektsii po strukturalnoy poetike.* Introduction by Thomas G. Winner. Providence: Brown University Press, 1968.

———. "P. A. Vyazemski i dvizheniye Dekabristov." *Uchenye zapiski Tartuskogo Gosudarstvennogo Universiteta* 98 (1960), 24–142.

Maguire, Robert A. *Red Virgin Soil: Soviet Literature in the 1920's.* Princeton: Princeton University Press, 1968.

Makogonenko, G. P. "Byl li karamzinski period v istorii russkoy literatury?" *Russkaya literatura,* 1960, no. 3, pp. 3–32.

Matejka, L. and Pomorska, K., eds. *Readings in Russian Poetics: Formalist and Structuralist Views.* Cambridge: MIT Press, 1971.

Mersereau, John. "Pushkin's Concept of Romanticism." *Studies in Romanticism,* III, no. 1, 24–41.

Meylakh, B. S. "A. S. Shishkov i 'Beseda lyubiteley russkogo slova.' " *Istoriya russkoy literatury.* Vol. V. Moscow-Leningrad: Nauka, 1941.

Meynieux, A. *La Littérature et le métier d'écrivain en Russie avant Pouchkine.* Paris: Librairie des cinq continents, 1966.

———. *Pouchkine homme de lettres et la littérature profes-*

sionnelle en Russie. Paris: Librairie des cinq continents, 1966.

Modzalevski, B. L. *Biblioteka A. S. Pushkina: Bibliografich-eskoye opisaniye.* St. Petersburg: Akademiya Nauk, 1910.

Mordovchenko, N. I. *Russkaya kritika pervoy chetverti XIX veka.* Moscow-Leningrad: Nauka, 1959.

Morozov, A. A. "Parodiya kak literaturni zhanr (k teorii parodii)." *Russkaya literatura,* 1960, no. 1, pp. 48–77.

Muratova, K. D., ed. *Istoriya russkoy literatury XIX veka: Bibliograficheski ukazatel.* Moscow-Leningrad: Nauka, 1962.

Neuhäuser, R. *Towards the Romantic Age: Essays on Sentimental and Preromantic Literature.* The Hague: Martinus Nijhoff, 1974.

Obnorski, S. P. and Barkhudarov, S. G., eds. *Khrestomatiya po istorii russkogo yazyka.* Moscow: Uchpedgiz, 1948–49.

Ocherki po istorii russkoy zhurnalistiki i kritiki. Tom pervi: XVIII vek i pervaya polovina XIX veka. Leningrad: Izd. Leningradskogo Universiteta, 1950.

Panchenko, A. M., ed. *Istoriya zhanrov v russkoy literatury X–XVIIvv.: Trudy otdela drevnerusskoy literatury,* vol. 27 (1972).

Pigarev, K. V. *Russkaya literatura i izobrazitelnoye iskusstvo, XVIII—pervaya chetvert XIX veka: Ocherki.* Moscow: Nauka, 1966.

Pipes, Richard. "The Background and Growth of Karamzin's Political Ideas Down to 1810." *Karamzin's Memoir on Ancient and Modern Russia: A Translation and Analysis.* Cambridge: Harvard University Press, 1959.

"Pochta." *Entsiklopedicheski slovar.* St. Petersburg: F. A. Brokgaus and I. A. Efron, 1890–1907.

Proffer, Carl. *The Critical Prose of Alexander Pushkin with Critical Essays by Four Russian Romantic Poets.* Bloomington: Indiana University Press, 1969.

Pushkin, A. S. *Eugene Onegin: A Novel in Verse.* Trans. Walter Arndt. New York: Dutton, 1963.

———. *Eugene Onegin.* Trans. Vladimir Nabokov. 4 vols.

Rev. ed. Bollingen Series LXXII. Princeton: Princeton University Press, 1975.

————. *Pushkin Threefold: Narrative, Lyric, Polemic, and Ribald Verse*. Trans. Walter Arndt. New York: Dutton, 1972.

Robinson, Howard. *The British Post Office: A History*. Princeton: Princeton University Press, 1948.

Segel, Harold B., ed. *The Literature of Eighteenth-Century Russia*. 2 vols. New York: Dutton, 1967.

Shakhovskoy, A. A. *Komedii, stikhotvoreniya*. Leningrad: Sovetski pisatel, 1961.

Shishkov, A. S. *Zapiski, mneniya i perepiska*. Ed. and pub. N. Kiselev and Yu. Samarin. Berlin: 1870.

Shklarevski, G. I. *Istoriya russkogo literaturnogo yazyka (vtoraya polovina XVIII v.–XIX v.)*. Kharkov: Izd. Kharkovskogo Universiteta, 1967.

Smith, Barbara Herrnstein. *Poetic Closure: A Study of How Poems End*. Chicago: University of Chicago Press, 1968.

Staël, Germaine Necker de. *Madame de Staël on Politics, Literature and National Character*. Ed. and trans. Morroe Berger. New York: Doubleday Anchor, 1965.

Stilman, L. N. "Problemy literaturnykh zhanrov i traditsi v 'Evgenii Onegine' Pushkina: K. voprosu perekhoda ot romantizma k realizmu." *American Contributions to the Fourth International Congress of Slavists: Moscow, September 1958*. 'S-Gravenhage: Mouton, 1958. Pp. 321–65.

Thompson, E. N. S. *Literary Bypaths of the Renaissance*. New Haven: Yale University Press, 1924.

Thraede, Klaus. *Grundzüge griechisch-römischer Brieftopik*. Zetemata: Monographien zur klassischen Altertumswissenschaft, no. 48. Munich: C. H. Bech'sche, 1970.

Timofeyev, L. I., ed. *Kratki slovar literaturovedcheskikh terminov: Posobiye dlya uchashchikhsya sredney shkoly*. 4th ed. Moscow: Uchpedgiz, 1963.

Timofeyev, L. I. and Turayev, S. V., eds. *Slovar literaturovedcheskikh terminov*. Moscow: Prosveshcheniye, 1974.

Tinker, Chauncey Brewster. *The Salon and English Letters:*

Chapters on the Interrelations of Literature and Society in the Age of Johnson. 1915. Reprint. New York: Gordion Press, 1967.

Tomashevski, B. V. *Pushkin.* Vol. I. Moscow-Leningrad: Nauka, 1956.

Venevitinov, D. V. *Polnoye sobraniye sochineni.* Ed. B. V. Smirenski. Moscow-Leningrad: Academia, 1934.

Viëtor, Karl. "Probleme der literarischen Gattungsgeschichte." *Deutsche Vierteljahrchrift für Literaturwissenschaft und Geistesgeschichte* 9 (1931), 425–47.

Vigel, F. F. *Zapiski.* Ed. S. Ya. Shtraykh. 2 vols. Moscow: Krug, 1928.

Vinogradov, V. V. and Shvedova, N. Yu., eds. *Ocherki po istoricheskoy grammatike russkogo yazyka XIX veka.* Moscow: Nauka, 1964.

Vinogradov, V. V. *Ocherki po istorii russkogo literaturnogo yazyka XVII–XIX vv.* 2nd ed. Moscow: Uchpedgiz, 1938.

———. *Yazyk Pushkina: Pushkin i istoriya russkogo literaturnogo yazyka.* Moscow-Leningrad: Academia, 1935.

———. ed. *Slovar yazyka Pushkina.* Moscow: Gos izd. slovarey, 1956–61.

Vyazemski, P. A. *Polnoye sobraniye sochineni.* 12 vols. St. Petersburg: S. D. Sheremetev, 1878–96.

———. *Stikhotvoreniya.* Ed. and intro. L. Ya. Ginzburg. Leningrad: Sovetski pisatel, 1958.

Welch, D. J. *Russian comedy 1765–1823.* 'S-Gravenhage: Mouton, 1966.

Wellek, René. "Genre Theory, the Lyric, and *Erlebnis.*" *Discriminations: Further Concepts of Criticism.* New Haven: Yale University Press, 1970.

Wellek, René and Warren, Austin. *Theory of Literature.* 3rd ed. New York: Harcourt, Brace & World, Harvest Books, 1956.

Wimsatt, William K., Jr. and Brooks, Cleanth. *Literary Criticism: A Short History.* New York: Knopf, 1957.

Wittgenstein, Ludwig. *Philosophical Investigations*. Trans. G. E. M. Anscombe. 3rd ed. New York: Macmillan Co., 1968.

Wolff, Tatiana A., ed. *Pushkin on Literature*. London: Methuen, 1971.

Zeldovich, M. G. and Livshits, L. Ya., eds. *Russkaya literatura XIX v.: Khrestomatiya kriticheskikh materialov*. 3rd ed. Moscow: Izd. "Vysshaya shkola," 1967.

Zhikharev, S. P. *Zapiski sovremennika*. Ed. B. M. Eykhenbaum. Moscow-Leningrad: ANSSSR, 1955.

Zhirmunski, V. M. *Bayron i Pushkin (iz istorii romanticheskoy poemy)*. Leningrad: Academia, 1924.

Zhukhovski, V. A. *Polnoye sobraniye sochineni v dvenadtsati tomakh*. St. Petersburg: Izd. A. F. Marksa, 1902.

Index

Abrams, M. H., 51n
Académie française, 24
Academy of Arts, 46
Academy of Sciences, 27, 74, 201
Akhmatova, Anna, 144n
Aksakov, S. T., 48n
albums, 44
Alembert, Jean le Rond d', 68–69
Alexander I, 38–40, 42, 46, 61, 79, 160ff, 199, 203
Alexander II, 198, 201, 202
allegory, 58ff, 84
amateur theatricals, 48
analogy, 78, 108, 149, 171, 185
Aristotle, 116, 122
Arndt, Walter, 9n
Aronson, M. I., 45n, 57n
Arzamas: amateurs, 3, 50; vs. the Beseda, 49; careers of members, 55; caricature, 109–11, 175; Church Slavonic, 138ff; decline of letters, 186; downfall, 60–62; education, 41, 50, 107; Enlightenment, 3, 53; epistolary persona, 186; and epistolary tradition, 19, 70; foundation, 49; French, 140ff; *galimatias,* 60; on genre, 6, 62; honorary members, 202–3; human development, 107–18, 183; ideal of independence, 68; interests, 49; journalism, 45; letters, 12, 66, 75; libertinism, 137; literary activity of members, 50, 187; literary criticism, 50ff, 58ff, 65, 183; on literature, 78; members in the Beseda, 49; membership, 49–50, 198–202; nonfictional

prose, 187; norm, 69, 97, 103, 108, 196; Neoclassicism, 114; organization, 56; orientation, 3; origins of the name, 57; parody, 57ff; play, 56–67, 62, 63; politics, 60–61, 83; protocols, 58ff, 125–26; religion, 138; self-irony, 98, 100, 103; studies about, 4, 50; style, 135ff
association of ideas, 6, 8, 119
associationalist psychology, 167
associative organization, 7, 72, 156, 166–71, 180, 190
Auerbach, Erich, 20, 22

Bakunin, M. A., 194n, 195n
Balzac, Jean-Louis Guez de, 23, 25
ballads, 56–57, 58ff, 63, 126, 177
Baratynski, E. A., 82
Batyushkov, K. N., 43, 45, 59, 62–63, 167, 198, 199, 201; chains of association, 171; education, 45; elegy, 63; essays, 86; generic variety, 65; letters, 73–74; letters quoted, 77, 82–83, 86–87, 97–98, 107, 109, 137, 138, 144, 150–55, 160–63, 171, 180; literary criticism, 52–53; Lomonosov's letters, 28; "My Penates," 116; on letters, 66–67, 71, 77, 172; on A. S. Pushkin, 107; on V. L. Pushkin, 108; on sincerity, 103; periphrastic style, 145; "The Song of Harold the Bold," 128–29; verse, 81, 188; verse quoted, 64; Voltaire, 54
Belinski, V. G., 194n
Beseda, 48ff, 52, 55–56, 57, 60–

222

223

229